STUDIES IN WELSH HISTORY

Series editors

RALPH A. GRIFFITHS   CHRIS WILLIAMS
ERYN M. WHITE

29

URBAN ASSIMILATION IN POST-CONQUEST WALES

URBAN ASSIMILATION IN POST-CONQUEST WALES

ETHNICITY, GENDER AND ECONOMY IN RUTHIN, 1282–1348

by

MATTHEW FRANK STEVENS

*Published on behalf of the
University of Wales*

CARDIFF
UNIVERSITY OF WALES PRESS
2010

www.uwp.co.uk

British Library Cataloguing-in-Publication Data.
A catalogue record for this book is available from the British Library.

ISBN 978-0-7083-2249-9
e-ISBN 978-0-7083-2250-5

The right of Matthew Frank Stevens to be identified as author of this work has been asserted by him in accordance with Sections 77, 78 and 79 of the Copyright, Designs and Patents Act 1988.

Printed by CPI Antony Rowe, Chippenham, Wiltshire

SERIES EDITORS' FOREWORD

Since the foundation of the series in 1977, the study of Wales's history has attracted growing attention among historians internationally and continues to enjoy a vigorous popularity. Not only are approaches, both traditional and new, to the study of history in general being successfully applied in a Welsh context, but Wales's historical experience is increasingly appreciated by writers on British, European and world history. These advances have been especially marked in the university institutions in Wales itself.

In order to make more widely available the conclusions of original research, much of it of limited accessibility in postgraduate dissertations and theses, in 1977 the History and Law Committee of the Board of Celtic Studies inaugurated this series of monographs, *Studies in Welsh History*. It was anticipated that many of the volumes would originate in research conducted in the University of Wales or under the auspices of the Board of Celtic Studies, and so it proved. Although the Board of Celtic Studies no longer exists, the University of Wales continues to sponsor the series. It seeks to publish significant contributions made by researchers in Wales and elsewhere. Its primary aim is to serve historical scholarship and to encourage the study of Welsh history.

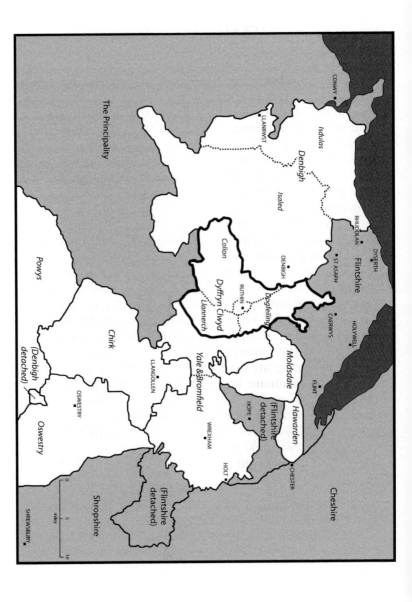

Map 1. The Marcher lordships of north-east Wales in the early fourteenth century

ACKNOWLEDGEMENTS

This book has been a very long time in the making. It began its life as my University of Wales, Aberystwyth, Ph.D. thesis, researched and written between 2001 and 2005 under the supervision of Professor Phillipp R. Schofield, whose encouragement and genuine interest in my research have profoundly shaped my desire to discover the ordinary lives of the peoples of medieval Wales and England. The core of the text presented here remains that of my Ph.D. thesis, and so the acknowledgements included at the front of that document have been reproduced below. Additionally, I must acknowledge the support of those who helped me along the sometimes arduous path which has transformed my thesis, through several rewrites and the addition of much new research, into the book presented here – which nonetheless still bears the hallmarks of a student learning to write history. These include the Economic History Society, without whose generous financial support I would never have got underway, everyone at the University of Oxford who made me feel so welcome during my time there, and the very good friends I have been fortunate to know since moving to the city and University of London, where I have been kindly employed by the Centre for Metropolitan History. In particular, I must thank Mark Merry for his help with the maps, Guy Geltner and Hannes Kleineke for their comments on parts or all of early draft manuscripts and, above all, Ralph Griffiths who so generously offered meticulous and invaluable advice on each draft of this book, and who has done so much to make my prose more intelligible. All remaining mistakes are, of course, my own.

London
March 2009

PH.D. ACKNOWLEDGEMENTS

Where can one begin in acknowledging his debts to all those who have offered support and guidance in a project which has taken years to complete? Most immediate is the huge debt I owe to my supervisor, Professor Phillipp Schofield of the University of Wales, Aberystwyth, who has been both knowledgeable and understanding throughout, having a good sense of humour and a great deal of patience. Similarly patient and helpful has been Sarah Powis, whose efforts to help me resolve countless issues of grammar and spelling have been a blessing to me. More broadly, I need to thank both my American friends (most particularly Warren Love, Matthew Bernosky, Jason Msadoques and Howard Simmerman, whose campaigns and adventures have always inspired me) and my closest British friends (Jamie Tedford, Richard Jones and Richard Cordle, among many others) who have kept me sane and made me feel welcome over the last eight years. Likewise, I have always appreciated the support given to me by Patricia Henninger, who shares my interest in places abroad. Lastly and most importantly, I am grateful for the unflagging love and guidance of my mother and father, the latter of whose advice – 'whatever makes you happy son' – is the most straightforward and valuable I have ever received (and by the way, *this* makes me happy).

Aberystwyth

CONTENTS

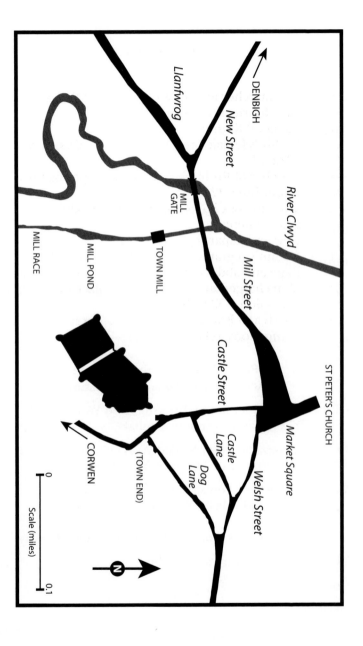

Map 2. Medieval Ruthin

DENBIGH

Llanfwrog

New Street

River Clwyd

MILL GATE

MILL RACE

MILL POND

TOWN MILL

Mill Street

ST PETER'S CHURCH

Castle Street

Market Square

Castle Lane

Dog Lane

Welsh Street

(TOWN END)

CORWEN

0

Scale (miles)

0.1

N

FIGURES

TABLES

ABBREVIATIONS

AC	*Archaeologia Cambrensis*
AHR	*Agricultural History Review*
BBCS	*Bulletin of the Board of Celtic Studies*
Black Book	J. W. Willis-Bund (ed.), *The Black Book of St David's* (London, 1902)
BL	British Library
Caernarvon Court Rolls	G. Jones and H. Owen (eds), *Caernarvon Court Rolls, 1361–1402* (Caernarfon, 1951)
CC	*Continuity and Change*
DHST	*Denbighshire Historical Society Transactions*
*Dyffryn Clwyd Database	R. R. Davies and Ll. B. Smith (eds), machine readable database, *The Dyffryn Clwyd Court Roll Database, 1294–1422* (Aberystwyth, 1995)
EconHR	*The Economic History Review*
HWJ	*History Workshop Journal*
JBS	*Journal of British Studies*
JFH	*Journal of Family History*
JHG	*Journal of Historical Geography*
JIH	*Journal of Interdisciplinary History*
LHR	*Law and History Review*
NLW	National Library of Wales
PP	*Past and Present*
RMS	*Reading Medieval Studies*
THSC	*Transactions of the Honourable Society of Cymmrodorion*
**TNA	The National Archives
TRHS	*Transactions of the Royal Historical Society*
UHist	*Urban History*
UHY	*Urban History Yearbook*
WHR	*Welsh History Review*

*All references to documents calendared in the *Dyffryn Clwyd Database* (that is, great court of Dyffryn Clwyd court rolls, great court of Ruthin court rolls, relief rolls and the commotal court rolls of Llannerch, etc.) and held at TNA, SC2/215/64 – SC2/221/1 1, will be referenced by their database file name, 'GC 1–3', 'Reliefs', 'Llan 1' or 'Roll 1–12', and entry #, followed by the manuscript's TNA reference: for example, 'Reliefs #000, SCO/000/00 m.0'. All references to the 1324 rental of Dyffryn Clwyd, which has been included in the *Dyffryn Clwyd Database*, is held at TNA, WALE 15/8/1, and has also been published by R. I. Jack, 'Records of Denbighshire lordships II – The lordship of Dyffryn Ciwyd in 1324', *DHST*, 17 (1968), shall be made as follows: 'Rental #000, membrane 0, Jack p. 0'. This reference gives the *Dyffryn Clwyd Database* the file name 'Rental' and entry #, the membrane of the original manuscript on which the cited entry may be found, and the appropriate page number of Jack's published edition.

**Records of the borough court of Ruthin from 1312–21, which are held at TNA, SC2/215/64 – SC2/221/11, are the principal foundation of this study, and do not appear in the *Dyffryn Clwyd Database*. All transcriptions/translations from the borough court are the author's. Borough court records are cited by their TNA reference and the consecutive borough court session of the roll on which they are located. For example, 'TNA, SC2/215/75 session 3' would mean the third extant session of the borough court of Ruthin on the roll with TNA reference SC2/215/75. This system has been employed because many of the document membranes in this court roll series have multiple and conflicting membrane numbers stamped or written on one or more corners. References to all other documents held at TNA are given without annotation.

PLACE NAMES AND PERSONAL NAMES

Place names have been modernized, except where used as surnames. Problem place names have been left in inverted commas.

Personal names generally take one of four forms: a Christian name and locational by-name, usually functioning as a surname; a Christian name and descriptive by-name citing a personal quality such as hair colour (for example, black (*Welsh = du*) or red (*Welsh = goch*)), usually functioning as a surname; a Christian name and occupational by-name, most often genuinely reflecting an individual's occupation; and, for Welsh persons, a Christian name and patronymic by-name, indicating their father's (or occasionally their mother's) Christian name, separated by the Welsh word *ap*, meaning 'son of', or *ferch*, meaning 'daughter of'. Patronymic by-names were sometimes extended to include the Christian names of several direct ancestors, for example, 'Ieuan ap Ieuan ap Heilyn'.[1] Two or more of these four forms were sometimes combined, for example, 'Ieuan ap Adda de Ruthin', or used interchangeably, for example, 'Nicholas de Schelton', most commonly known as 'Nicholas *carnifex*' (butcher).[2]

In this book, persons have been identified by their most commonly occurring personal name (of simple or combined form). Christian names have been modernized, including when used as patronymic by-names. Descriptive by-names have been modernized, in English or Welsh respectively. Locational by-names, used as surnames, have been standardized to their most common spelling, but not modernized. Occupational by-names have been retained in their original Latin (and occasionally Welsh) followed in parentheses, where first occurring, by their English equivalent, as above for Nicholas *carnifex* (butcher). In a few instances, where an

---

[1] TNA, SC2/216/3 m.22.
[2] Ibid.

individual's occupational by-name appears in the court record exclusively, or almost exclusively, in English, usually where no obvious Latin equivalent exists, that English by-name has been retained. Problem personal-name elements have been left in inverted commas.

DEFINITIONS

The great famine - the years 1315–22, as defined by William Jordan; this was a period characterized by short and wet summers combined with exceptionally cold and protracted winters, which resulted in a 'long series of catastrophes' unparalleled in later medieval agriculture.[1] Evidence from Ruthin's borough court suggests that the value of wheat in Dyffryn Clwyd probably remained in excess of 7*s.* per quarter, the price horizon above which we can begin to associate scarcity with increased mortality, continuously from 1315 to 1323.[2]

Immigration - long-distance relocation of English men and women to Wales for permanent settlement.

Investment capital - cash, coin or credit to be invested in tools, livestock, land or otherwise in order to increase an individual's prosperity and economic independence.

Migration - localized movement of itinerant labourers and paupers within Wales seeking work, food and shelter, especially during the great famine.

[1] W. C. Jordan, *The Great Famine: Northern Europe in the Early Fourteenth Century* (Princeton, NJ, 1996), pp. 16–19.
[2] TNA, SC2/215/71–SC2/216/3; C. Dyer, *Standards of Living in the Later Middle Ages: Social Change in England, c.1200–1520* (Cambridge, 1989), pp. 264, 267.

INTRODUCTION

This book investigates the role played in the society and economy of post-conquest Wales by Welsh and English townsmen and women, a group of diverse composition, collectively distinct from their neighbours in the countryside. Past writers have, with some justification, tended to see the town as an alien imposition in Wales. The majority of those towns populated by English and Welsh alike in the fourteenth century were indeed Anglo-Norman foundations, directly associated with military initiatives. Any originally Welsh settlements, which may have illustrated urbanizing trends in native society since the late eleventh century, had been overwhelmingly commandeered by Anglo-Norman lords in step with their piecemeal conquest of Wales. Moreover, during the thirteenth and early fourteenth centuries any obvious distinctions between these native settlements and Anglo-Norman foundations had been blurred by the grant of relatively uniform urban privileges by means of borough charters.

The cumulative result of this process of urbanization in Wales was a society proportionately just as urbanized as English society. It has been estimated that around the year 1300 some 46,500 of Wales's 200,000 to 300,000 inhabitants (that is, 16 to 23 per cent) were town dwellers.[1] This corresponds closely to the 15 to 20 per cent of the contemporary English population, numbering about four million, which may be described as urban.[2] Wales boasted a relatively high

[1] I. Soulsby, *The Towns of Medieval Wales: A Study of Their History, Archaeology and Early Topography* (Chichester, 1983), p. 23.

[2] D. Palliser, 'Introduction', in D. Palliser (ed.), *Cambridge Urban History of Britain*, vol. 1, *c.600–c.1540* (Cambridge, 2000), p. 4; J. Russell, *British Medieval Population* (Albuquerque, 1948), pp. 246, 351. Starting with Russell, population estimates for England and Wales have been consistently revised upwards. A good general discussion of medieval Welsh population may be found in K. Williams-Jones (ed.), *The Merioneth Lay Subsidy Roll, 1292–3* (Cardiff, 1976), pp. xxxv–lxvii. For early modern Wales, see L. Owen 'The population of Wales in the sixteenth and seventeenth centuries', *THSC* (1959), 99–113; and N. Powell, 'Urban population in early modern Wales revisited', *WHR*, 23 (2007), 1–43.

number of chartered boroughs in the fourteenth century, approximately one hundred settlements displaying some urban characteristics, as opposed to the 600 boroughs of fourteenth-century England.[3]

These figures represent the apex of urbanization in medieval Wales, but also an unsustainable peak, reflecting the particular social, political and economic conditions of the day. Many small towns founded as military outposts were no longer of strategic importance after the 1282–4 royal conquest of native Wales, and began to decline. Others, originally founded in impractical locations for reasons of security, often high above the surrounding landscape, simply became unattractive to trade and settlement in more peaceful times. The urban network of early fourteenth-century Wales was less mature than its English counterpart, both in its age and especially with regard to the capacity of Welsh towns to endure in response to the changing complexion of Anglo-Welsh politics. The uneven and sometimes rapid urbanization of Wales during the twelfth and thirteenth centuries had been largely the product of military and economic interaction between Welsh and Anglo-Norman societies.

This process of urbanization, and the underlying social changes with which it became entwined, led to the creation of a large number of towns characterized by swift urban reorientation, in which the chief vills of vanquished Welsh lords were transformed into small towns with trading privileges, often of uncertain political or commercial viability. This is to deny neither the relative antiquity of some Welsh towns, nor the long-term political significance of particular boroughs – Carmarthen, for example, had Roman roots and retained an administrative role throughout the medieval period – but rather to assert that by the close of the thirteenth century Wales was functionally overpopulated with small urban centres. As a result, the fourteenth century would see what Ralph Griffiths has characterized as the 'winnowing' and 'reordering' of the urban network as the region embarked on a century of relative peace and political stability unparalleled in

[3]   C. Dyer, 'The consumer and the market in the later Middle Ages', *EconHR*, 42 (1989), 316.

the preceding two hundred years.[4] What dictated the nature of society and commerce in Anglo-Welsh towns during this crucial period, at least for the fifth of all inhabitants of Wales who dwelt in them, were the varying degrees to which urban centres assimilated their Welsh and English inhabitants. Although in the early twelfth century townsmen are thought to have been overwhelmingly Anglo-Norman settlers, it has been estimated that by 1300 more than one in six town dwellers in Wales was Welsh.[5] Over the course of subsequent centuries, those towns which declined to be little more than rural settlements and those which retained urban characteristics into the early modern period would become increasingly Cymricized.

The case study of the seignorial borough of Ruthin presented in this book is first and foremost an attempt to understand the nature and importance of Anglo-Welsh towns in the first half of the fourteenth century. It offers a response to the call for further study issued by Rees Davies as long ago as the late 1970s. At that time Davies postulated that the process of 'cultural assimilation of English and Welsh' in post-conquest Wales, that is from 1282 onwards, needed to be studied 'in depth and with great care' as part of a survey which would 'consider social institutions in the round and assess the measure of conscious decision and unconscious evolution which characterized the process of cultural adjustment'.[6] In reality, that work had already begun to take shape in the 1960s, with the researches of Thomas Jones-Pierce, Ralph Griffiths and a few others.[7] However, Welsh social history has to date failed to develop a historiographical tradition comparable to that established for England by the seminal work of, among others, Rodney Hilton and Michael M. Postan.[8] Nor

---

[4]   R. A. Griffiths, 'Wales and the Marches', in Palliser (ed.), *Cambridge Urban History*, p. 699.

[5]   Soulsby, *The Towns of Medieval Wales*, p. 24.

[6]   R. R. Davies, *Lordship and Society in the March of Wales, 1282–1400* (Oxford, 1978), p. 446.

[7]   See, for example, the two volumes of collected works: T. Jones-Pierce, *Medieval Welsh Society: Selected Essays*, ed. J. B. Smith (Cardiff, 1972); R. A. Griffiths, *Conquerors and Conquered in Medieval Wales* (Stroud, 1994).

[8]   For example, M. M. Postan, *The Medieval Economy and Society: An Economic History of Britain in the Middle Ages* (Harmondsworth, 1975); R. Hilton, *Bond Men Made Free: Medieval Peasant Movements and the English Rising of 1381* (London, 1973).

has there been any detailed study of Welsh society through
the statistical examination of local judicial and administrative
evidence in the way pioneered to slightly differing ends by historians of medieval England like Ambrose Raftis and Zvi Razi.[9]
The most important work of this latter type to use Welsh
sources remains a series of articles arising from the compilation of *The Dyffryn Clwyd Court Roll Database, 1294–1422*,
produced at the University of Wales, Aberystwyth, between
1991 and 1995.[10]

As a result of this historiographical imbalance, this book's
analysis of ethnicity and society in Wales is heavily influenced
by the work of historians studying English sources. The primary concern of the book is to investigate the significance of
ethnicity in Welsh towns through a case study of social interaction in the town of Ruthin, principally by means of an analysis
of the borough's court records. A significant part of it is also
devoted to the status and occupation of the Welsh and English
townswomen of Ruthin and their place in the medieval labour
market. This discussion engages, and takes issue, with the
ideas of Judith Bennett and Jeremy Goldberg, most notably
those regarding the 'place' of medieval women in the public
and the private spheres.[11] Consideration is also given to questions of the institutional development of the borough's
judicial system, the local credit market and of the impact of

---

[9]   J. A. Raftis, 'Social structures in five East Midland villages: a study of possibilities in the use of court roll data', *EconHR*, 18 (1965), 83–100; Z. Razi, *Life, Marriage
and Death in a Medieval Parish: Economy, Society and Demography in Halesowen, 1270–
1400* (Cambridge, 1980).
[10]   Compiled under the direction of R. R. Davies and Ll. B. Smith (eds), *The
Dyffryn Clwyd Court Roll Database, 1294–1422* (available from the Economic and
Social Research Council on request, award number R000232548), was designed to
make the court rolls of the Welsh marcher lordship of Dyffryn Clwyd
(Denbighshire) accessible in machine-readable format, in order to facilitate
research by both specialists and non-specialists. A description of this project and
some of its early findings, as well as a list of articles arising from it, appears as A.
Barrell, R. R. Davies, O. J. Padel and Ll. B. Smith, 'The Dyffryn Clwyd court roll
project, 1340–1352 and 1389–1399: a methodology and some preliminary findings',
in Z. Razi and R. Smith (eds), *Medieval Society and the Manor Court* (Oxford, 1996),
pp. 260–98.
[11]   J. Bennett, *Women in the Medieval English Countryside: Gender and Household in
Brigstock Before the Plague* (Oxford, 1987); P. J. P. Goldberg, *Women, Work, and Life
Cycle in a Medieval Economy: Women in York and Yorkshire, c.1300–1520* (Oxford,
1992).

the great famine of 1315–22 on Ruthin's economy and society.

In terms of their wider historiographical context, the key issues of ethnicity and society are approached from a framework of two superficially incongruous views of later medieval Wales. On the one hand, the relationship between English and Welsh has been characterized by chronologically or geographically wide-ranging research as an English 'occupation' equating to an early form of 'internal colonialism'.[12] Concerned primarily with administrative elites, Rhys Jones has asserted that 'the English would have viewed the land as a resource base for their political ambitions and nothing else'.[13] Similarly, Rees Davies described Reginald de Grey, the first English lord of Ruthin (and the surrounding marcher lordship of Dyffryn Clwyd) as a 'high handed and tyrannical official' who aimed to 'bully native society into submission'.[14]

On the other hand, research at the local level, specifically concerned with Welsh towns, has suggested that post-conquest Wales was in many ways a tolerant society. Most influentially, Glyn Roberts argued that the importation of English boroughs and burgesses into Wales introduced 'potentialities of racial feud and hatred', but that these potentialities were overshadowed by a 'tendency to compromise with the new system' which by the fourteenth century amounted to 'a pattern of co-operation'.[15] The work of Ian Jack on medieval Dyffryn Clwyd consistently depicts the lordship as a cooperative community.[16] Jack argued that although various regional and racial restrictions concerning Welshmen were in place, the borough at Ruthin appears to have assimilated all elements, 'not without tension but without excess

[12] M. Hechter, *Internal Colonialism, the Celtic Fringe in British National Development, 1536–1966* (London, 1975); R. R. Davies, 'Colonial Wales', *PP*, 65 (1974), 3–23.

[13] R. Jones, 'Changing ideologies of medieval state formation: the growing exploitation of land in Gwynedd, *c.*1100–*c.*1400', *JHG*, 26 (2000), 512.

[14] R. R. Davies, *The Age of Conquest: Wales, 1063–1415* (Oxford, 1987), p. 348.

[15] G. Roberts, 'Wales and England, antipathy and sympathy, 1282–1485', *WHR*, 1 (1963), 383, 386.

[16] R. I. Jack, 'The cloth industry in medieval Ruthin', *DHST*, 12 (1963), 10–25; 'Records of Denbighshire lordships II. – The lordship of Dyffryn Clwyd in 1324', *DHST*, 17 (1968), 3–18; 'Welsh and English in the medieval lordship of Ruthin', *DHST*, 18 (1969), 23–49 ; 'The medieval charters of Ruthin borough', *DHST*, 18 (1969), 16–22.

tension'.[17] Likewise, Ralph Griffiths found of medieval Cardigan that as early as the 1260s Welsh and English burgesses seem to have lived together in relative harmony.[18] While Cardigan experienced a period of ethnic exclusion and disharmony during the final Edwardian conquest of north Wales in the late thirteenth century, the town's Welsh and English seem inevitably to have gravitated back towards coexistence and power-sharing.[19]

These two views are not mutually exclusive. The fourteenth century would see the distinction between Welsh and English more clearly defined in formal and institutional terms than ever before or since.[20] In most areas of Wales each group held land by a different form of tenure, paid different seignorial dues, resolved disputes by means of different legal processes, in accordance with either Welsh or English law, and, particularly in south Wales, often lived in geographically distinct Welshries and Englishries.[21] Yet, to quote Rees Davies, 'behind the façade of an institutionalized racial distinction, Welshmen and Englishmen within Wales were reaching accommodation with each other, as indeed they had done for generations'.[22]

This book explores the driving force behind this cultural assimilation, which took place despite an atmosphere of 'racial' inequality, in terms of the pursuit of shared socioeconomic interests that transcended ethnic divides. It demonstrates that Ruthin's court rolls and related administrative documentation indicate that in the early fourteenth century borough status and prosperity were more closely related to access to capital than to ethnicity or race. It is concluded that the principal force behind Anglo-Welsh assimilation was unity of action in the pursuit of common social and economic goals, with the urban arena providing a venue whereby this process could happen more readily than in the surrounding countryside.

[17] Jack, 'Welsh and English', 47.
[18] Griffiths, *Conquerors and Conquered*, pp. 287–8.
[19] Ibid., p. 293.
[20] Davies, *The Age of Conquest*, p. 419.
[21] Ibid., pp. 419–20.
[22] Ibid., p. 421.

RUTHIN IN CONTEXT: THE ORIGINS
OF THE ANGLO-WELSH TOWN

Conquest and town foundation

The general and widely accepted view of urbanization in Wales is a largely militarist one, focusing on Anglo-Norman conquest as a historical determinant. Although this view must be tempered by an awareness of native town initiatives and strong economic motives for urbanization (which will be returned to later), any internally generated social or economic impetus for town foundation and growth has to be understood in terms of a response to conquest and interaction with Anglo-Norman society.[23] The density and distribution of urban settlements in early fourteenth-century Wales and the chronology of their foundation undeniably relate closely to the advance of Anglo-Norman power.[24] At the time of the Norman conquest of England, Wales was politically and geographically divided into a number of small kingdoms. The most significant of these Welsh kingdoms were Gwynedd in north Wales, Powys in mid-Wales, Dyfed-Deheubarth in the south-west and Morgannwg (or 'Glamorgan') in south-east Wales.[25] Shortly after establishing control over England, between 1067 and 1071, William the Conqueror created three border earldoms facing these Welsh kingdoms, focused on Chester, Shrewsbury and Hereford, in an attempt to secure the western reaches of his new realm.

Given free rein to push Norman conquests west and effectively to hold what lands they might annex there as their own lordships, rather than as a further extension of William's England, the new earls in these border districts, or march, soon set about expanding their holdings.[26] By the early twelfth

[23] For recent overviews, see N. Edwards, 'Landscape and settlement in medieval Wales: an introduction', in N. Edwards (ed.), *Landscape and Settlement in Medieval Wales* (Oxford, 1997), pp. 8–9; and Griffiths, 'Wales and the Marches', p. 685.

[24] This chronology has been detailed with considerable skill by both Soulsby and Griffiths, and hence much of what follows necessarily draws on their work: Soulsby, *The Towns of Medieval Wales*; Griffiths, 'Wales and the Marches'.

[25] For a full account of the changing fortunes of these and the other dynastic houses of Wales in this period, see Davies, *The Age of Conquest* (especially p. 59).

[26] Welsh lands acquired by English lords were often the product of private military initiative and so did not become part of the realm; they instead remained jurisdictionally outside of the normal administrative control of the crown. English

century a pattern of morselization had evolved along the
Welsh border (by sea and land), in which private territorial
gains were secured by the construction of fortified strong-
holds and the plantation of attached boroughs for their
military and economic support.[27] The first wave of Norman
conquest and settlement in Wales, between 1066 and the mid-
twelfth century, established at least twenty-six towns along the
march, stretching from Haverfordwest to Chepstow along the
south Wales coast and as far as Rhuddlan in the north-east.[28]
This initial period of Anglo-Welsh conflict and colonization
accounts for around one-quarter of all town foundations in
medieval Wales, and established a territorial status quo. Most
intense was the urbanization of south Wales, where the old
Welsh kingdom of Morgannwg all but melted away in the face
of Norman aggression and the kingdom of Deheubarth was
reduced after being weakened by a change of dynasty in
1093.[29]

With the tumultuous reign of King Stephen (1135–54) the
rapid advance of conquest-driven town foundation faltered,
and the surviving Welsh dynasties of Gwynedd, Powys and
Deheubarth consolidated their holdings. Despite numerous
royal, Welsh and English campaigns, the Anglo-Welsh frontier
would remain largely unchanged until the reign of King
Edward I (1272–1307). Instead of notable territorial gains, as
in the late 1070s to 1120s, there prevailed in the 1130s to
1260s very modest advances of English lordship, which were
likewise secured through castle and borough foundation.

'lords marcher' ruled their Welsh lands with the absolute powers which they had
assumed from their vanquished Welsh predecessors. Hence, the king's writ did not
run in privately held marcher lordships such as Dyffryn Clwyd (in which Ruthin was
located), Oswestry, Radnor, Brecon, or Glamorgan, to name but a few of the more
notable.
[27] The term 'plantation borough' is, in this book, used to denote boroughs
founded on typically 'green-field sites' by Norman or English conquerors. Although
only patchily enforced, new borough regulations often initially disallowed
Welshmen from owning property or residing in, or freely trading *outside*, these
boroughs.
[28] Soulsby has identified these as (anticlockwise from mid-Cardigan Bay):
Cardigan, Fishguard, St David's, Wiston, Haverfordwest, Pembroke, Tenby,
Carmarthen, Kidwelly, Swansea, Neath, Kenfig, Bridgend, Cardiff, Newport,
Caerleon, Chepstow, Usk, Monmouth, Abergavenny, Brecon, Hay on Wye,
Presteigne, Prestatyn, Rhuddlan and Caernarfon. *The Towns of Medieval Wales*, p. 8.
[29] Davies, *The Age of Conquest*, pp. 28–39.

Among the better documented of the quarter or more of all medieval Welsh towns founded throughout the March during this period are Llandovery (1185), Llanelli (1190), Builth (1217), Montgomery (1223–7), Painscastle (1231), Deganwy, Dyserth, New Radnor (all three, 1245–8) and Caerphilly (1268).[30]

Only with the emergence of Gwynedd as the pre-eminent Welsh polity, from the mid-thirteenth century, and with the rise of personal and political discord between the Crown and the prince of Gwynedd, Llywelyn ap Gruffydd (d. 1282), did the territorial status quo of the March change radically. Exerting hegemony over all of native-ruled Wales, Llywelyn styled himself 'prince of Wales' from 1258. Politically, the Welsh principality evolved, from the 1250s to the 1270s, into the most centralized native Welsh state of the Middle Ages, and was formally recognized by a domestically embattled Henry III in 1267.[31] However, following the accession of Edward I in 1272, Anglo-Welsh relations deteriorated rapidly, one point of friction between Edward and Llywelyn being royal indifference to disputed marcher foundations such as Caerphilly castle. In November 1276, after several years of increasing strain and Llywelyn's refusal to do homage to the new king, Edward declared Llywelyn a rebel. In November 1277, Llywelyn was forced to concede military defeat and come to terms with Edward.

As a result of this campaign Llywelyn's principality was much reduced and, in order to consolidate this change in Anglo-Welsh relations, Edward sponsored castle-boroughs at Flint in the north-east and Aberystwyth (as distinct from neighbouring Llanbadarn) on the west coast. Meanwhile, other frontier settlements brought firmly under English control during the 1276–7 campaign, such as Rhuddlan, Builth, Hope and Ruthin, received new or additional fortifications. Significantly, not all of these sites remained in English hands. Ruthin, perhaps the foundation most intrusive to Llywelyn's patrimony, together with the nascent settlement of Hope, given by the Crown to Llywelyn's estranged brother Dafydd ap

[30] Ibid., pp. 46–52; Soulsby, *The Towns of medieval Wales*, pp. 11–12, 92, 185, 218; M. Beresford, *New Towns of the Middle Ages* (London, 1967), pp. 343–4.
[31] Davies, *The Age of Conquest*, p. 317.

Gruffydd in 1277. But shortly thereafter these localities reverted to English lordship after Dafydd broke out into open rebellion in March 1282.

In December 1282, Llywelyn himself died while leading an uprising described by Rees Davies as 'a massive act of protest against English rule'.[32] Following the subsequent defeat of the dynasty of Gwynedd, and the allied princely line of Deheubarth, some thirty towns were founded *de novo*, and evidence suggests that a similar number experienced significant expansion.[33] Among the most important, work began on the impressively fortified new castle-towns of Harlech, Caernarfon and Conwy, displacing whatever degree of Welsh settlement may already have been present on those sites.[34] Lastly, Edward quelled at least two significant revolts by force, in 1287 and 1294, re-securing the country with further castle-borough foundations, including Dryslwyn (Carmarthenshire) and Beaumaris.[35]

The final quarter of the thirteenth century thus saw the most intensive process of conquest and urbanization in Wales since the Norman advances of the late eleventh and early twelfth centuries, and it resulted in around one-third of all town foundations in medieval Wales. Two centuries of conflict for seignorial control along the eastern and southern fringes of native-ruled west, mid- and north Wales had resulted in an unusually high degree of urbanization focused on the crescent of southern coastal plains and fertile eastern border regions first encroached upon by Norman invaders in the eleventh century. Setting the number of towns in each of the pre-1974 counties of England and Wales against the area of each county, Maurice Beresford calculated that by the fourteenth century the towns of seven of Wales's thirteen counties would have had catchment areas of eighty square miles or less, while only eleven of England's thirty-nine counties were as densely urbanized.[36]

[32] Davies, *The Age of Conquest*, p. 349.
[33] Soulsby, *The Towns of Medieval Wales*, p. 13.
[34] It is notable that in July 1283 twenty men were paid for five days' work in clearing away the timbers of the demolished houses of a Welsh settlement to make way for construction of Caernarfon's new town. K. Williams-Jones, 'Caernarvon', in R. Griffiths (ed.), *Boroughs of Medieval Wales* (Cardiff, 1978), p. 75.
[35] Soulsby, *The Towns of Medieval Wales*, pp. 133–4, 78–90.
[36] Beresford, *New Towns of the Middle Ages*, pp. 284–5, 346: Pembrokeshire 49 sq.

This narrative provides a context for the case study of Ruthin and also conveys Ruthin's unexceptional character. By the thirteenth century, Welsh and English living anywhere along the crescent of the marcher frontier which lined south and east Wales would have understood towns within a framework of continuity, in the sense that most towns, once founded, continued in some form irrespective of the ethnicity or political leanings of the local lord at any given time. In contrast, local lordship would have been understood within a framework of changeability for many years following a new town's foundation, due to the often short-term dominance of localities by individual Welsh or English lords who were dependant on prevailing military realities.

The decades prior to Ruthin's incorporation as a borough in 1282 witnessed, in north-east Wales, a territorial tug-of-war between Welsh and English lords for lands less than a day's ride (twenty to thirty miles) west and south of the Anglo-Welsh frontier, while relative stability prevailed in the growing towns immediately east and north of that same frontier – juxtaposing lordly instability and urban stability in a manner which had been mirrored throughout the March during the preceding two centuries. The Welsh *cantref* or district of Dyffryn Clwyd, in which Ruthin was situated, had passed from Welsh to royal control after Henry III's campaign of 1245–7. In 1254 Dyffryn Clwyd had been granted to the king's heir, the Lord Edward (later Edward I), who was present there in July and August 1256, but who had lost control of the district to Prince Llywelyn ap Gruffydd by early 1257. In 1277 Dyffryn Clwyd was again captured by the Crown, only to be returned directly to native rule until its reconquest and grant in 1282 to the royal favourite Reginald de Grey, who almost immediately thereafter provided Ruthin with a borough charter. Meanwhile, in addition to the royal centre of Chester about twenty-two miles to the east, the small borough of Dyserth persisted throughout this period barely fifteen miles north of Ruthin on the River Clwyd, while a similar distance to the north-east the market and mining settlement of Holywell

m, Carmarthenshire 45 sq. m, Glamorgan 47 sq. m, Monmouthshire 34 sq. m, Radnorshire 50 sq. m, Montgomeryshire 64 sq. m, and Flintshire 27 sq. m.

developed. Hence, although Ruthin was a late foundation, the circumstances of its creation make it likely that the process of Anglo-Welsh cultural adjustment and assimilation which took place following the borough's inception provide a valuable window onto the history of earlier settlements.

Of course, very different customs were adopted by the various lords of Wales's many new towns. At one end of the spectrum was private seignorial policy, as was followed at Ruthin and which did not distinguish between English and Welsh burgesses in the early fourteenth century. At the other end was Edward I's policy of segregation, banning Welsh burgesses from his new boroughs of north Wales. However, it is likely that the principles which underlay urban assimilation in relatively liberal environments, such as Ruthin, were not too dissimilar from those at work in the most heavily segregated of communities. Welsh tenants bought, sold and eventually integrated in all settlements in spite of seignorial restrictions, inexorably associating the prosperity of towns with local Anglo-Welsh relations. This reality could not have been lost on even the most inflexible of English settlers and, in circumstances of fluctuating Welsh and English lordship, moderated the readiness of new town dwellers to chastise their urban or rural neighbours.

Chronologically, Ruthin's history begins with the last chapter of town foundation in Wales. As Griffiths has rightly observed, for many towns 'by the time phases of subjugation and conquest had ended ... original *raisons d'être* had already begun to disappear', but this reality would have been far from clear to most contemporary townsmen and women.[37] Moreover, the reluctance of local lords to revoke urban privileges and retreat from the level of urbanization which had developed by 1300, both in Dyffryn Clwyd and throughout Wales, was based on more than fear of Welsh rebellion. The continued regional importance, if not prosperity, of Ruthin and many other towns beyond the 'age of conquest' is indicative of an underlying socio-economic transformation as profound and lasting as the political subjugation of Wales.

[37]   Griffiths, 'Wales and the Marches', p. 685.

Economic development and native towns

The chronology of military advance necessarily forms the skeletal framework of town foundation in Wales, but a strictly 'barracks view' underestimates the role of the market and fails to explain fully the continuation of town life and borough foundation after periods of conquest.[38] Roughly one-third of Welsh boroughs are likely to have been native foundations which came about in a context of increased trade and the growth of a money economy introduced in Wales by Anglo-Norman conquerors.[39] The role of towns as vital points of exchange in the money economy, once established, served to perpetuate their importance throughout the later Middle Ages. As William Rees asserted in the opening of his social and agrarian study *South Wales and the March*, 'it may be established as a general rule, that economic expediency rather than political passion is the guiding principle in conquest'.[40]

The topography of Wales is divided into upland districts penetrated by, and focused on, fertile lowland valleys. This landscape was conducive to the creation of simple, largely self-contained, economic units by native and alien powers alike. Prior to the Norman arrival, these economic units comprised two principal elements, the local native lord with his retinue on the one side, and the wider community of the district on the other. As a largely non-monetary, subsistent society of warriors and peasants, seignorial surpluses were relatively small and quickly expended on conspicuous consumption, gift-giving or military exploits.[41]

These small economic units proved very attractive to encroaching Norman lords, who often had access to relatively limited resources themselves. However, given the often absentee character of alien lordship and the more demanding military-economic needs of Norman warfare, coupled with an expanding population and the transformation of the peasant economy, conquest resulted in economic reorganization. From the eleventh century, the main alteration to the pattern

[38] Beresford, *New Towns of the Middle Ages*, pp. 181, 528.
[39] Ibid., p. 16; R. Griffiths, 'Wales and the Marches', p. 705.
[40] W. Rees, *South Wales and the March, 1284–1415: A Social and Agrarian Study* (Oxford, 1924), p. 1.
[41] Davies, *The Age of Conquest*, pp. 157–8.

of Welsh administration was the addition of a town or fixed market, as a third element in local economic units. Most borderland or coastal lordships would come to contain, in Rees's terminology, the castle, representing the lord and his administrators; the manor, representing the peasant community at large; and the borough, representing the lordship in its trading capacity.[42] The emergent town or borough was intimately linked with its role as a point of exchange for the conversion of agricultural surpluses into coin, and the acquisition of key goods and services by lord and peasant, Welsh and English.

By the early thirteenth century at the latest, powerful undercurrents of demographic, agricultural and economic change were apparent throughout Wales. It is generally held that the population of Wales and England increased rapidly in the 250 years after 1066, perhaps trebling in some rural areas.[43] Throughout these centuries the majority of Welsh people lived in the lowlands and practised mixed agriculture, rearing upland flocks and sowing lowland crops. But, as the population grew, the average size of holdings shrank, leaving an increasing number of peasants unable to satisfy their subsistence needs without recourse to a market.[44] The high grain prices connected with population growth encouraged native Welsh lords and Anglo-Norman conquerors alike to promote the expansion of arable agriculture on their demesne lands, in a distinct shift towards an 'economy of profiteering'.[45] Finally, these centuries witnessed a significant monetization, or commutation of the traditional renders and services of the tenantry into cash payments, especially among free tenantry, initially in south Wales and by the thirteenth century also in the north.[46]

The introduction of market towns in Welsh localities helped to satisfy the needs of a growing population by allowing them

[42] Rees, *South Wales and the March*, pp. 28–9.
[43] Davies, *The Age of Conquest*, pp. 157–8; see note 2.
[44] Davies, *The Age of Conquest*, pp. 148–9; for a brief account of the interaction of peasant landholding and the 'market', see P. R. Schofield, *Peasant Community in Medieval England, 1200–1500* (Basingstoke, 2003), pp. 131–7.
[45] Davies, *The Age of Conquest*, p. 157.
[46] Rees, *South Wales and the March*, pp. 173–83, 222–3; T. Jones-Pierce, 'The growth of commutation in Gwynedd during the thirteenth century', in J. B. Smith (ed.) *Medieval Welsh Society* (Cardiff, 1972), pp. 103–26.

the exchange mechanism necessary to sell their produce and meet seignorial commitments in coin rather than kind, more readily to acquire consumables and durables (for example, shoes, leather goods, crockery and metal items) and to access a place in which to sell their services as labourers and domestic servants. Town and borough markets also formed natural points of departure for extra-lordship exchange, especially in areas of relative isolation where boroughs were also convenient ports, such as at Cardigan or Bangor. In this manner urban expansion and rural economic transformation were recipro-cally beneficial.[47] Equally, a marcher lord might make use of the market as a consumer or employer, he often retained rights of purveyance similar to those enjoyed by the king and, in some instances, he could summon burgesses to arms as their feudal lord, for example, under the provisions of Swansea's twelfth-century charter.[48] In addition, the construction of the castle itself stimulated the borough economy through the wages paid to masons, smiths, carpenters and other craftsmen. One signifi-cant example is the castle built at Ruthin; other examples include the similarly sized royal castles of Flint and Ruddlan on which some £6,000 and £9,000 respectively were spent on con-struction and maintenance between 1277 and 1330.[49]

The importance of towns as points of intersection between lord and peasant, irrespective of their Englishness or Welshness, cannot be overstated. As the central element of the economic unit formed by a lordship or a locality, each new town was typically granted a monopoly of trade within a speci-fied market district, encompassing a generous hinterland, if not the bulk of a marcher lordship then at least the locality in which the town was situated.[50] Demonstrating the promotion

[47] Points in this paragraph are drawn, in general, from Beresford, *New Towns of the Middle Ages*, especially pp. 58, 60, 75.

[48] W. Robinson, 'Swansea' in R. A. Griffiths (ed.), *Boroughs of Medieval Wales*, pp. 264–5.

[49] A. Taylor, *The King's Works in Wales, 1277–1330* (London, 1974), pp. 327–9, 1029.

[50] Lewis provides a detailed discussion of the economic privileges of the Crown's boroughs of north-west Wales, E. A. Lewis, *The Medieval Boroughs of Snowdonia* (London, 1912), pp. 166–218. While similar in function, the size of bor-ough 'market districts' varied widely. For example, Edward I ordained that the men of three Anglesey commotes adjoining his new borough of Beaumaris were to trade there and there alone (ibid., p. 175). By comparison, from 1280 the burgesses of

of urban foci at its most extreme, in the post-conquest shires of Anglesey, Caernarfon and Merioneth it was ordained that no markets or fairs for the trading of goods other than 'small articles of food such as butter, milk and cheese, should be held elsewhere than the boroughs of Conway, Beaumaris, Newborough, Caernarvon, Cricieth, Harlech and Bala'.[51] While the policing of novel market controls in the midst of a rural Welsh population used to the unrestricted sale of such goods must have been difficult, amercements for trading outside borough markets or market hours are nevertheless common in borough court records.[52] Hence, Lewis described such ordinances as 'transitional links between the old and the new economy', between a system of diffuse and unregulated exchange, on the one hand, and a system of centralized and controlled exchange, on the other.[53]

However, this transition from a diffuse, native economy in kind to a centralized, Anglo-Norman economy in coin did not always take place as a result of conquest alone. At least two major caveats must be observed in relation to this account of socio-economic reorganization at the hands of the invaders. First, the progressive promotion of commutation by increasingly cash-hungry native Welsh princes can be tied, from at least the mid-thirteenth century, to their own encouragement of embryonic towns. In particular, attempts by Llywelyn ab Iorwerth (d.1240) and Llywelyn ap Gruffydd (d.1282) to create a strong feudal state in north Wales fuelled moves towards economic centralization. In thirteenth-century Gwynedd, efforts were made to delineate territorial districts of administration more clearly. The large, regional economic unit of the *cantref* was superseded by one or more commotes (smaller units corresponding roughly to English hundreds), while the chief princely residence of a more favourably situated commote showed a tendency to develop along commercial lines.[54]

Carmarthen enjoyed a monopoly of organized trading within a five-league (15-mile) radius of the borough (R. A. Griffiths, 'Carmarthen', in Griffiths (ed.), *Boroughs of Medieval Wales*, p. 147).

[51] Lewis, *The Medieval Boroughs*, p. 175.

[52] Ibid., p. 176; Williams-Jones, 'Caernarvon', p. 98; G. Jones and H. Owen (eds), *Caernarvon Court Rolls, 1361–1402* (Caernarvon, 1951), pp. 113, 136–7.

[53] Lewis, *The Medieval Boroughs*, p. 175.

[54] There has been some disagreement as to the nature of subdivisions within a

Aware of the revenue-generating and strategic potential of the towns of their English rivals, Welsh lords fostered in some commotes what Jones-Pierce termed 'manorial boroughs', as distinct from English plantation boroughs.[55]

Commutation and economic centralization were largely interdependent and, in the absence of planned towns, regions in which princely policy and economic exigencies combined to inspire town growth, notably in Anglesey and the Llŷn peninsula, developed a greater capacity for commutation and a higher degree of centralization.[56] Hence we can trace the appearance of fledgling towns such as Pwllheli, Tywyn, Barmouth, Nefyn and Llanfaes, and identify towns in north-east Wales which were appropriated and chartered by Anglo-Norman conquerors, such as Ruthin and Caerwys.[57] Lastly, those few Welsh lords who survived the conquest of 1282, primarily of the princely line of Powys in mid-Wales, formalized the privileged status of certain nucleated settlements so as to promote urban development of a non-military nature. The unfortified boroughs of Machynlleth and Llanfyllin in Powys and Lampeter in Dyfed are examples of this final phase of non-conflict urban foundation driven mainly by economic change.[58] The presence of such diverse settlements within and beyond Gwynedd modifies the common correlation between alien lordship, urban implantation and the development of economic centralization.[59] But, as Davies cautions, the administrative changes effected in the governance of native Wales 'were at best tentative and inchoate ... first hesitant steps in exploiting the resources of native kingdoms'.[60]

---

commote. R. Jones, 'Problems with medieval Welsh local administration – the case of the *Maenor* and the *Maenol*', *JHG*, 24 (1998), 135–46; Lewis, *The Medieval Boroughs*, p. 7; Rees, *South Wales and the March*, pp. 7–19; Davies, *The Age of Conquest*, pp. 264–5.

[55]   Jones-Pierce, *Medieval Welsh Society*, p. 128.

[56]   D. Stephenson, *The Governance of Gwynedd* (Cardiff, 1984), pp. 68–9; Jones-Pierce, *Medieval Welsh Society*, p. 123.

[57]   Griffiths, 'Wales and the marches', p. 685; Soulsby, *The Towns of Medieval Wales*, pp. 94, 232.

[58]   Soulsby, *The Towns of Medieval Wales*, pp. 157, 180, 167.

[59]   It is possible that the positioning of some south Wales plantation boroughs is also associated with embryonic native towns, but the early date of conquest there makes this less likely or more difficult to discern.

[60]   Davies, *The Age of Conquest*, p. 265.

The second caveat to the story of economic centralization through conquest turns on the existence of clerical lords. The most notable of them in Wales were the episcopal lords of the cathedral towns of Bangor, St David's and St Asaph (no significant settlement seems to have grown around Llandaff, the site of Wales's fourth cathedral) whose temporalities were, as one might expect, often subject to the vicissitudes of Anglo-Welsh politics.[61] However, cathedral sites, as well as monastic institutions, sometimes gave rise to essentially native towns which persisted throughout the Middle Ages in parallel with plantation boroughs and princely manorial towns. Examples include the episcopal settlement of Bangor and the monastic town of 'Old Carmarthen' (as distinct from the Norman foundation of 'New Carmarthen') each of which periodically received princely or English patronage, but nevertheless remained subject to autonomous clerical control.[62]

For ecclesiastical lords who did not struggle for territorial hegemony, the incentive to seek an economic reorientation of Welsh society was muted. For native lords, the pull towards change grew stronger throughout the twelfth and thirteenth centuries. But, constrained by the strength of immutable custom, the commutation of food renders and the promotion of centralized commercial exchange were an arduous process. The resistance faced by Welsh lords is amply demonstrated by the long list of *gravamina* of the community of Gwynedd against the revenue-raising expedients of Llywelyn ap Gruffydd, as expressed by Welsh freemen before royal officials only months after the final conquest of 1282.[63] Only for non-Welsh, Norman or English lords did the clean break of conquest pave the way for a reordering of social institutions and customs in a manner more consistent with their economic needs.[64]

[61]   Davies, *The Age of Conquest*, pp. 188–94.
[62]   Lewis, *The Medieval Boroughs*, pp. 179–80. The priors of Old Carmarthen resisted both the pressures of local officials and attempts by the Black Prince 'to make Old Carmarthen a suburb of the New'. Griffiths, 'Carmarthen', pp. 140, 153–4.
[63]   Ll. B. Smith, 'The *Gravamina* of the community of Gwynedd against Llywelyn ap Gruffydd', *BBCS*, 31 (1984), 158–76.
[64]   See J. Given, 'The economic consequences of the English conquest of Gwynedd' , *Speculum*, 64 (1989), 11–45. Owen has likewise suggested that some Welsh rulers attempted economic change at times of reconquest, introducing the native landholding and administrative unit of the *gwely* following twelfth-century

The early history of Ruthin is part of this story of socio-economic transformation. The Welsh *cantref* of Dyffryn Clwyd, encompassing the lowland vale of Clwyd and flanked by the uplands of the Clwydian range, typified the self-contained economic unit characteristic of medieval Wales. As the native *caput* of Dyffryn Clwyd, Ruthin was the focus of a princely administration whose novel and unpopular revenue-raising tactics paralleled those cited in the *gravamina* of 1282. At the very least, by the 1280s the *cantref* had been partitioned into the three administrative commotes by which it would be governed for the remainder of the Middle Ages, namely, Colion, Llannerch and Dogfeiling. As a sizeable native township, Ruthin was apparently fortified during the thirteenth century by the Welsh princes, who also promoted proto-urban settlement at the site.[65] And, by the beginning of the fourteenth century, the lowland vale of Clwyd was dedicated overwhelmingly to the production of wheat and other marketable cereals (the upland areas necessarily retaining their pastoral character).[66]

In short, when finally placed in permanent English lordship in 1282, the old Welsh *cantref* of Dyffryn Clwyd had already undergone much of the economic transformation that accompanied conquest in many other Welsh localities. When Ruthin was granted a borough charter and trading privileges in the new lordship of Dyffryn Clwyd, prosperity quickly followed. The creation of the borough brought economic opportunity to both Welsh tenants, who continued to hold their town property, and to the new wave of English settlers who arrived soon afterwards.

Dyffryn Clwyd's high degree of pre-conquest development, and its re-creation as a marcher lordship without widespread, wholesale displacement, are the key to understanding Ruthin's early history and form the basis of the case study presented in

Welsh reconquests in north-east Wales. D. H. Owen, 'The Middle Ages', in D. H. Owen (ed.), *Settlement and Society in Wales* (Cardiff, 1989), p. 203.

[65] Soulsby, *The Towns of Medieval Wales*, p. 232.

[66] Evidence of Ruthin's native character is discussed in chapter I below. Evidence of the division of agriculture is indirect but ample. For example, following the introduction of the recording of murrains, from October 1341 to October 1343 the only murrains reported by the upland vill of Penbedw, in the north of Dyffryn Clwyd, affected fifteen sheep; while those of lowland Colion, in the south-east, featured twelve cows/plough beasts. TNA, SC2/17/7–SC2/17/10.

this book. Some marcher lords radically transformed the social and economic order of their newly conquered lands by going so far as to divide them into lowland 'Englishries' and upland 'Welshries', thereby creating functionally English and Welsh administrative districts as a starting-point for the socio-economic development of the lordship. Economically revolutionary breaks in continuity, like the formation of ethnically distinct Englishries and Welshries through escheat and compulsory exchange, could facilitate the importation of a more profitable English manorial economy in lowland districts. Employed extensively by Henry de Lacy in the aftermath of his foundation of the town and surrounding Englishry of Denbigh in 1282, just 8 miles from Ruthin, these tactics brought long-term commercial change but spawned equally enduring hatred among the disfranchised and implied an initial period of economic dislocation.[67] Perhaps not wishing to cause undue disruption to an already centralizing local economy, the new lord of Dyffryn Clwyd elected not to adopt such draconian methods. Economic reorientation in Dyffryn Clwyd did not, therefore, come on the back of sweeping segregation or disfranchisement. Instead, Ruthin quickly emerged as a thriving, mixed community at the lordship's commercial centre, in a manner more akin to Aberystwyth in west Wales, or Knighton in mid-Wales.[68]

METHODOLOGY AND STRUCTURE

Over the years, virtually all the towns of medieval Wales moved, at different speeds, in the direction of Anglo-Welsh urban assimilation. A lack of documentation makes it impossible to gauge the rate of integration in all but a few of the later foundations, but it is evident that within a century of establishment even the inhabitants of a legally segregated town, such as Edward I's castellated borough of Caernarfon, were regularly working together, living together and even intermarrying.[69] The advantage of a case study that focuses on a town which

---

[67]   D. H. Owen, 'Denbigh', in Griffiths (ed.), *Boroughs of Medieval Wales*, pp. 165–7.
[68]   J. Sanders, 'The boroughs of Aberystwyth and Cardigan in the early fourteenth century', *BBCS*, 15 (1954), 282–93; TNA, E179/242/57.
[69]   Williams-Jones, 'Caernarvon', pp. 94–5.

lacked the institutionalized affectations of cultural or ethnic supremacy that went hand in hand with urbanization in some parts of Wales is its capacity to illustrate the workings and pace of this process of assimilation. One town where this process began almost immediately, as English burghal life was imposed on an existing Welsh settlement, was Ruthin.

When the first English marcher lord of Ruthin, Reginald de Grey, issued a borough charter within four weeks of acquiring the Clwyd valley in 1282, he opened the lordship and borough to English immigration and initiated a period of low-level urbanization.[70] In the following decades, the community reached a pre-plague population peak of between 500 and 600 persons. Ruthin's charter set out market liberties and trading privileges for the burgesses, differentiating them from the men and women of the surrounding countryside, but not distinguishing between English and Welsh, and thus avoided the impediment of segregation which formally excluded Welsh burgesses from other post-conquest plantation boroughs.[71] In common with many Welsh localities, Ruthin had experienced conquest, reconquest and economic transformation over the preceding century, and yet even in the light of its thirteenth-century charter it was as much a Welsh town as an English one. Furthermore, Ruthin's size and function as a centre for local governance and trade made it typical of the small towns which came to populate the March of Wales as crucibles of ethnic, social and economic assimilation.

Of more immediate advantage to the historian, Ruthin is unique in Wales as a borough for which relatively complete and plentiful court records survive.[72] A case study of Ruthin offers, therefore, a particularly valuable model for the interpretation of the sparser evidence from other Anglo-Welsh

---

[70] NLW, Chirk Castle MS F.8355; Jack, 'The medieval charters of Ruthin', 16–21.

[71] Jack, 'The medieval charters of Ruthin', 18.

[72] Records of court sessions pertaining to the borough appear interspersed with those of the commotal courts of the lordship of Dyffryn Clwyd. Excluding only a few small fragments held in the National Library of Wales, these court rolls are stored in TNA, SC2/215/65–SC2/226/6, and cover the years 1294–1610. Around 50 to 60 per cent of the court records survive, gaps being numerous but small, typically no more than two or three consecutive court sessions (at three- to four-week intervals).

towns. In addition, supplementary to Ruthin's charter and court record, there exists a rental of the town from 1324 detailing each burgess, his or her property, and how much he or she paid in rents per annum.[73] This latter document allows a much fuller reconstruction of the borough's society than would otherwise be possible, and provides an important backdrop against which patterns of property-holding in other towns can be viewed.

The following chapters seek to present data drawn from the records of Ruthin before contextualizing their interpretation with information from other Welsh towns, and finally they relate that collective body of evidence to the situation in similar English communities. Every attempt has been made to create a comprehensive snapshot of Ruthin's community in and around the years 1312–21 as a springboard for broader investigation. Where it has been advantageous to do so the book has also called on evidence, from Ruthin and elsewhere, relative to those decades immediately preceding and following 1312–21 in order to establish longer-term trends. This study therefore ranges from 1296, the first year for which Ruthin's court rolls survive, to 1348, just prior to the Black Death. However, while developmental aspects of society, such as changes to the economy and labour market in response to the great famine of 1315–22, are central to this book, no attempt has been made to track demographic change by calculating aggregate court appearances or property transactions.

This case study of medieval Ruthin is subdivided into three parts, two major and one minor. The first major part (part 1) reconstructs the community through an analysis of the distribution of propertied wealth as indicated by the borough rental of 1324 and supported by court roll evidence; and by building an image of social status through evidence of male office-holding. The activities of borough jurors are given special attention. Finally, the borough's credit network is briefly examined, in order to explore an alternative, comparative, determinant of wealth and status.

The second major part of the study (part 2) builds on the conclusion of the first, namely, that access to capital and status

---

[73] TNA, WALE 15/8; Jack, 'Records of Denbighshire lordships II'.

was more important than ethnicity in dictating a person's socio-economic role in the borough, testing this theory against a dedicated study of Ruthin's townswomen. Three groups of borough townswomen, those with access to high, moderate and low levels of investment capital, are examined. In these analyses, issues of ethnicity have been given special attention only where they bear directly on an understanding of the court roll evidence. Thus, an attempt is made to create a flexible model of the way in which specific social and economic factors, and particularly personal capital, shaped the borough's wealth and status structures irrespective of Welshness or Englishness.

The third and final part of the study (part 3) is concerned with the town's known ethnic inequalities; it seeks to explain them against the backdrop of the general model of equality by wealth-level laid out in parts 1 and 2. Male occupation is examined in relation to access to capital, and consideration is given as to whether the dominance or scarcity of Englishmen vis-à-vis Welshmen earning their livelihood in any particular manner was an issue of accommodation, or one of discrimination. This part concludes by considering the broad range of shared experiences endured by the poorest and least skilled of male labourers in Anglo-Welsh towns, and suggests ways in which these experiences may have inured poor townsmen and males on the margins of society to their common plight.

The findings of these three sections are drawn together in the book's Conclusion. It is argued that there was a primacy of access to capital and associated levels of prosperity in determining the interests and actions of particular groups of urban dwellers, and the relevance of Ruthin's socio-economic workings to an assessment of the fortunes of Welsh towns and townspeople during the fourteenth century is demonstrated. The exploration of Ruthin's society against the backdrop of the experience of other communities provides valuable clues to the mechanisms which underlay urban assimilation in post-conquest Wales.

Part 1

MEN AS PROPERTY HOLDERS
AND THE SOCIAL ELITES

Chapters I and II lay out in turn the distribution of wealth and status in Ruthin. Ruthin's residents would each have been members of a number of 'overlapping communities' defined in different ways, including ethnicity, status, neighbourhood and economic interest.[1] By examining the differing levels of prosperity experienced by Ruthin's English and Welsh towns-people (chapter I), and assessing whether those differences were reflected in the social status and interactions of persons within the borough's judicial system and credit network (chapter II), we can reach an understanding of some of the town's collective values.

---

[1] Davies, *Lordship and Society in the March of Wales, 1282–1400* (Oxford, 1978), p. 460.

I

POPULATION, PROPERTY AND WEALTH

Population

Population, while invariably difficult to gauge, is a natural starting point for the exploration of any community. Two principal documents aid us in establishing Ruthin's population. Most helpful is a rental of the lordship of Dyffryn Clwyd which survives from 1324. This document served as an administrative stocktaking of every Dyffryn Clwyd tenant-in-chief, how much land he or she held and what annual rent was paid to the lord for those lands.[2] In addition, thirteen 'relief rolls', reports typically compiled twice annually to record relief and entry payments within the lordship, survive for the period 1299 to 1318.[3] Supplemented by some data from the records of the great court of Dyffryn Clwyd, the great court of Ruthin and the borough court of Ruthin, these documents allow insight into the inseparable issues of population and wealth within the community.[4] They also help to indicate the ethnic composition of Ruthin.

[2] TNA, WALE 15/8/1. The edited version of this rental is R. I. Jack, 'Records of Denbighshire lordships II', *DHST*, 17(1968), 7–53. The rental was also put into machine-readable form as part of R. R. Davies and Ll. B. Smith (eds), *The Dyffryn Clwyd Court Roll Database, 1294–1422* (Aberystwyth, 1995), available from the Economic and Social Research Council on request, award number R000232548. Hereafter, all references to the 1324 rental shall be as follows 'Rental #000, membrane 0, Jack p. 0'. This reference gives the *Dyffryn Clwyd Database* file name 'Rental' and entry #, the membrane of the original manuscript on which the cited entry may be found, and the appropriate page number of Jack's published edition.

[3] A 'relief' in Dyffryn Clwyd was the death duty payable upon the inheritance of land. Due to changes in administrative practice, relief rolls were not compiled for Dyffryn Clwyd after 1318. Beginning in 1319, land transfers were typically noted on the court roll of whichever administrative region, or commote, of the lordship the land in question lay. Hereafter, all references to entries appearing in the lordship's relief rolls or those court rolls that are also covered by the *Dyffryn Clwyd Database* (that is, great court of Dyffryn Clwyd court rolls, great court of Ruthin court rolls and the manorial court rolls of Llannerch) will be referenced by their database file name, 'Reliefs', 'GC1', 'Llan1' or 'Roll1–12', and entry #, followed by the manuscript's TNA reference: for example, 'Reliefs #000, SC0/000/00 m.0'.

[4] Fourteenth-century poll tax data do not exist for Dyffryn Clwyd.

That portion of the 1324 rental which pertains to the borough indicates that the town contained almost exactly one hundred burgages, thereby placing Ruthin at the centre of Wales's contemporary urban hierarchy, in which a middling third of about one hundred Welsh towns contained between fifty and 150 burgages.[5] If the rental is taken at face value as complete,[6] those burgages were held by seventy-one individuals of different familial or trade names. Following the methodology used by Soulsby in his survey, *The Towns of Medieval Wales*, this information may be used to calculate the population of Ruthin by multiplying the number of town burgesses by an estimated, mean household size.[7] Historians have disagreed about the size of the typical medieval household. Principal reasons for doubt revolve around medieval fertility rates, incidence of illegitimacy, age of marriage, the number of extended family members who typically lived together and the extent to which these aspects of family life may have altered over time given varying degrees of mortality, industrialization and urbanization.[8] However, using the same

[5]   Jack, 'Welsh and English in medieval Ruthin', *DHST*, 12 (1969), 23–49. Welsh burgage totals have been derived from Soulsby (I. Soulsby, *The Towns of Medieval Wales: A Study of Their History, Archaeology and Early Topography* (Chichester, 1983), especially pp. 19–24), and Griffiths (R. A. Griffiths, *Boroughs of Medieval Wales* (Cardiff, 1978)), supplemented by J. W. Willis-Bund (ed.), *The Black Book of St David's* (London, 1902 (*Black Book*)); B. Howells, T. A. James, D. Miles, J. Howells and R. F. Walker, 'The boroughs of medieval Pembrokeshire', in R. F. Walker (ed.), *Pembrokeshire County History*, vol. 2: *Medieval Pembrokeshire* (Haverfordwest, 2002), pp. 426–79; and Ll. B. Smith, 'Towns and trade', in J. B. Smith and Ll. B. Smith (eds), *History of Merioneth*, vol. 2: *The Middle Ages* (Cardiff, 2001), pp. 225–53.
[6]   The rental seems to contain numerous mistakes. Several persons are listed without any record of what property they held or the rent on that property. Also, some properties and their possessors seem to have been excluded. For example, one of Robert *faber*'s burgages is described as being 'beside the burgage of John de Helpston' (Jack, 'Records of Denbighshire lordships II', 16), but John de Helpston is not otherwise recorded as a burgage holder. This points to an underestimation of the number of burgages listed in the rental.
[7]   Soulsby, *The Towns of Medieval Wales*, pp. 19–24.
[8]   See L. Poos, Z. Razi and R. Smith, 'The population history of medieval English villages: a debate on the use of manor court records', in Z. Razi and R. Smith (eds), *Medieval Society and the Manor Court* (Oxford, 1996), pp. 298–368, but the debate is a much older one. Some of the more important contributors to this debate on the household multiplier are J. Russell, *British Medieval Population* (Albuquerque, 1948), multiplier 3.5; J. Krause, 'The medieval household: large or small?', *EconHR*, 9 (1957), 420–32, multiplier 4.3–5.2; J. Titow, *English Rural Society, 1200–1350* (London, 1969), multiplier 4.5–5; P. Laslett, *Household and Family in Past Time* (Cambridge, 1972), multiplier 4.75; Z. Razi, *Life, Marriage and Death in a*

rough household multiplier of five employed by Soulsby as well as by Hilton in his comparable study of the English borough of Thornbury, Ruthin's population can be estimated at 355.[9] If we do not apply the household multiplier to the personal names (and households) of five unmarried daughters, two widows and three other apparently single women unlikely have represented entire families, a slightly lower estimated population of 315 borough residents results. This method of deriving population, based on probable non-single tenants-in-chief, produces a figure that can be taken confidently as a minimum community size. However, there are strong reasons why Soulsby's conservative methodology, based solely on tenants-in-chief, is likely to produce a significant underestimate.

First, contemporary population density per household may have been higher in Ruthin and other newly founded Welsh towns, some of which saw their population double within fifty years of foundation, than in older, more demographically stable medieval communities.[10] In the case of Ruthin, the surviving rental's date of composition (1324) was only forty-two years after Dyffryn Clwyd's final change of possession into the hands of the Grey family, and the founding of the borough. In what survives of the record for the interim (1282–1324), Jack has counted just over four hundred persons mentioned as

Medival Parish: Economy, Society and Demography in Halesowen, 1270–1400 (Cambridge, 1980), multiplier/mean family size 5.8.

[9] The multiplier of 5 seems a moderate estimate. Soulsby, *The Towns of Medieval Wales*, pp. 19–24; R. Hilton, 'Low-level urbanization: the seignorial borough of Thornbury in the Middle Ages', in Z. Razi and R. Smith (eds), *Medieval Society and the Manor Court* (Oxford, 1996), p. 490.

[10] It is likely that Ruthin doubled in size with the arrival of English immigrants: an exclusively Welsh community under native rule in 1282 grew to be one in which approximately half of burgesses were English in 1324, an implied population increase of 100 per cent. Over a similar period at Llandovery, where borough growth was encouraged from 1276, the number of burgages rose from thirty-seven in 1299 to eighty-one in 1317, an implied growth of about 120 per cent (Soulsby, *The Towns of Medieval Wales*, p. 162). By comparison, at Pembroke, where a town had existed since the reign of Henry I, contemporary growth was much more modest, the number of burgage plots rising from 200 in 1246 to 220 in 1324, implying a population increase of just 10 per cent (Howells, James, Miles, Howells and Walker, 'The boroughs of medieval Pembrokeshire', p. 471). Likewise in England, Poos and Smith, working with data generated by Z. Razi, have estimated for the agrarian community of Halesowen, Worcestershire, an overall population fluctuation of no more than 11 per cent during 1293–1321 (Poos, Razi and Smith, 'Population history of medieval English villages', p. 317).

holders of town property at one time or another, including forty-six wives holding jointly or widows enjoying dower. Taken as a whole, this group was about one-third Welsh and two-thirds English. Similarly, excluding the small minority of wives and dowagers, as well as a few individuals in transactions not specifying the sale of a burgage or part-burgage, the ethnic ratio of persons we know to have held burgage property at some point between 1282 and 1324 was around one part Welsh (about 110 persons) to two parts English (about 200 persons).[11] By contrast, the ethnic ratio of those men and women listed in the rental of 1324 is almost exactly half and half: thirty-six Welsh, thirty-five English and one individual called Hugh Scot.[12]

These data represent a pattern of rapid turnover among arriving and departing English burgesses, likely to have been fed by immigration, and roughly twice that of their Welsh counterparts. Thus there probably existed in Ruthin a fairly stable, established Welsh community alongside a fluctuating English immigrant population. A similar conclusion was reached by Jack, who estimated that English immigration, 'while on a fairly massive scale, was very unstable'.[13] In such an environment it is likely that the number of families resident in the town would have outstripped the total number of burgesses. An unsettled and rapidly increasing population would have struggled to build dwellings at a pace in keeping with its own expansion, and the more economically feasible solution to immigrant housing needs would have been the subdivision of pre-existing properties, resulting in a greater population density per burgage. This notion is reinforced by the presence of no less than seventeen independently held half-burgages or small parts of burgages appearing in the 1324 rental.[14] It is important to note that the margin by which the

[11]   Jack, 'Welsh and English', 38–9.
[12]   This count has been given careful consideration as Jack identified 'around forty' Welsh from the same record (ibid., 39), perhaps choosing differently how to handle such names as 'Martin Goch'. Martin was an unusual name among the Welsh but 'Goch', meaning red (probably referring to hair colour), was a common descriptive qualifier. Also, in one instance the rental describes an article of borough property as being held jointly by two Welsh brothers. Here, they have been counted separately, but in table 1.1 below they have been counted as one because it is impossible to know how much of the recorded rent each brother paid.
[13]   Jack, 'Welsh and English', 39.
[14]   See below, this chapter, for further discussion of partial burgages.

number of households in any Welsh town may have outstripped the number of recorded burgesses would, in the long term, have varied according to local levels of migration, immigration and economic growth or decline.[15] But certainly during the initial years of expansion which followed the foundation of most boroughs, not all persons moving to new Welsh towns necessarily bought, or had the opportunity to buy, a part of the limited volume of burgage property made available by seignorial officials.[16]

Ruthin's population is also likely to have exceeded the total calculable from the number of property holders in 1324 (that is, 315 residents) due to burgage accumulation. The scope for entrepreneurial property speculation in a community subject to a steady inflow of outsiders, inevitably seeking short- and long-term shelter, would have been considerable. In 1324 the number of burgage plots in Ruthin (approximately one hundred) exceeded the number of burgesses (seventy-one) by 29 per cent. Of the one hundred or so burgage plots identifiable in the 1324 rental, fifty-four and one-half were held by twenty-four accumulators; that is to say, about half of Ruthin's burgages were held by only one-third (34 per cent) of property owners. Moreover, at the top of the scale, six men, four of whom were English and two Welsh (together 9 per cent of property owners), held twenty-one and one-half of the town's 100 burgages.[17]

Such speculation in property was not uncommon in medieval England and Wales, where in some boroughs accumulation had started in the thirteenth century and possibly even in the twelfth. At Cambridge, for example, where burgesses enjoyed liberties from at least the mid-1100s, there were already about twice as many houses as there were

[15] 'Migration' and 'immigration' are employed here as in the Definitions page above.

[16] Following town foundation, an initial surge of immigration seems often to have been followed by a period of borough boundary readjustment. For example, at Llawhaden, in Pembrokeshire, burgage plots were added to meet demand. A 1326 extent of this 1280s foundation shows a core community of about forty Welsh and English burgesses holding fixed-rent burgage plots, supplemented by some 130 higher-rent burgage plots with attached acreage held almost exclusively by English immigrants (*Black Book*, pp. 139–51).

[17] Four Englishmen: Richard *forestarius*, Hugh the son of Stephen *janitor*, Hugh *parcarius* and Hugh *faber*. Two Welshmen: Dafydd ap Bleddyn and William *saer*.

burgesses when the hundred rolls were compiled – a trend which in most towns accelerated over the course of the fourteenth and fifteenth centuries.[18] In Wales, the growing borough of Carmarthen in 1268 already featured 26 per cent more burgage plots on which homes were built than it did burgesses, while at the bishop of St David's new town of Llawhaden, founded only a few years before Ruthin, the number of occupied burgage plots in 1326 exceeded the number of burgesses by about 27 per cent.[19] In the decades on either side of 1300, when medieval urban population was at its peak density, a steady flow of immigrants from outside lordships such as Dyffryn Clwyd and migrants from within them would have presented an ongoing opportunity for motivated property holders to increase their wealth by letting town accommodation.[20] However, burgage accumulation by burgesses (burgage tenants-in-chief) and subtenancy by non-property-owning townspersons has inevitably resulted in the documentary illusion that fewer households – only those represented by burgesses – were present in any community than were actually resident at the time of the compilation of any medieval rental.

Lastly, consideration must be given to the presence of a numerically incalculable body of 'marginals' or poor, unestablished migrants. These people, the destitute, prostitutes, unskilled workers and other groups unlikely to hold property, were common in small market towns.[21] It has been shown by a case study of St Ives, for example, that in the period between 1270 and 1320, though being poor did not necessarily entail destitution, between 2 and 4 per cent of the population comprised 'paupers' at any given time.[22] Accordingly, incidents concerning paupers and other habitually present

[18]   M. DeWolf Hemmon, *Burgage Tenure in Medieval England* (London, 1914), pp. 149–50. For Cambridge, see F. W. Maitland, *Township and Borough* (Cambridge, 1898), pp. 66–9.
[19]   Griffiths, 'Carmarthen' in Griffiths (ed.), *Boroughs of Medieval Wales*, p. 149; *Black Book*, pp. 139–51.
[20]   R. Holt and G. Rosser (eds), *The English Town in The Middle Ages* (London, 1990), p. 16.
[21]   R. Hilton, *English and French Towns in Feudal Society* (Cambridge, 1992), p. 61.
[22]   E. Wedemeyre Moore, 'Aspects of poverty in a small medieval town', in E. DeWindt (ed.), *The Salt of Common Life: Individuality and Choice in Medieval Town, Countryside and Church* (Kalamazoo, 1995), pp. 123, 143.

marginals were fairly regular occurrences in Ruthin. For example, a few women are identified by occupation in the borough court of Ruthin records as 'public' or 'common' prostitutes (usually described as *meretrix*).[23] Other women were sometimes defamed as such. A typical court record is that describing a brawl between two women, Lleucu the daughter of Ieuan Felyn ('Velhyn') and Gwerful Llwyd, in July 1313. The borough court roll of this month states that Lleucu was amerced for having verbally abused and beaten Gwerful 'within a margin of bloodshed' in response to Gwerful's having called her a 'thief, whore and other enormities'.[24]

Unestablished local migrants, forming a certain transient quotient of the resident population, were also regularly cited in the town's courts, and notably so during the great famine of 1315–22.[25] Alice 'le Blowestere' (the boaster?), for example, was fined in the great court of Ruthin in April 1317 for habitually entertaining strangers,[26] and in the same session Nicholas, son of the established immigrant Geoffrey de Shirland (Derbyshire, a Grey family holding), was amerced 12*d.* for beating a certain outsider (*extraneus*) in the house of Adam Moton.[27] These unnamed persons were themselves unlikely to have remained in the borough long enough, or to have had the wherewithal, to initiate legal actions; Nicholas's victim, for instance, never sought compensation. But the continuous presence of immigrants, migrants and marginals in Ruthin and similar towns added a distinct flavour to the social and curial life of urban environments which were kept intimately familiar with persons on the fringes of the community.

In the light of these considerations – a population density heightened by immigration and migration, burgage accumulation and the regular presence of social marginals – Ruthin would have contained a significantly larger population than can be calculated by employing Soulsby's methodology of multiplying a total number of burgesses by a mean household size. A more accurate estimate of Ruthin's population, and

---

[23] *Dyffryn Clwyd Database*, Forties #426, SC2/217/9 m.11; and Forties #1968, SC2/217/14 m.33d.

[24] TNA, SC2/215/72 session 3.

[25] See chapter III for famine-period migration.

[26] *Dyffryn Clwyd Database*, GCl #1271, SC2/215/76 m.14d.

[27] Ibid., GCl #1264, SC2/215/76 m.14d.

the population of other small towns during periods of growth, is better attained by multiplying the known number of burgages, rather than the total number of burgesses, by a household multiplier.[28] If calculated in this manner, again using a household multiplier of five, the town's population would equate to approximately five hundred persons rather than the minimum of 315 (as above). While it is impossible to know the borough's population with complete certainty, collaborative court roll evidence of rapid immigration and the presence of non-property-owning marginals suggests that at the time of the rental's compilation Ruthin's population stood at the high end, if not beyond, this range of 315 to 500 souls.

PROPERTY HOLDING AND RENT[29]

Patterns of property holding

Patterns of property holding in Ruthin are illustrated in table 1.1, which has been compiled by totalling the various rents paid by persons known from the 1324 rental to have held some property in the borough. If an individual is indicated in the rental as having held property outside the borough as well as within it, then the value of the properties both outside and inside the borough have been totalled in order to place such persons within the appropriate band of rent payers in table 1.1. Thus the table reflects the relative wealth of persons who held property in Ruthin, not just their relative wealth in burgage property. In a few cases, where the rental has listed a burgess's holdings but not his rents, individual rent values have been estimated by reference to other holdings of the same size in the same location. Also, in a small number of instances Welsh naming practice has made an exact determin-ation of an individual's total holdings impossible to ascertain. But these anomalies, and those instances where the size of a person's holding is entirely unknown, represent less than

---

[28]   Contrast Soulsby, *The Towns of Medieval Wales*, pp. 20–4.
[29]   Part of the research presented in this section has been published in M. Stevens, 'Wealth, status and "race" in the Ruthin of Edward II', *UHist*, 32 (2005), 17–32.

10 per cent of land holders identifiable in that part of the rental which pertains to Ruthin town.

Based on this methodology, the figures in table 1.1 contrast with what is generally concluded in the historiography of post-conquest boroughs in Wales, whose very existence is claimed to have 'crystallized the feelings of Welshmen that they were an underprivileged race'.[30] In early fourteenth-century Ruthin, Welsh property holders had a strong foothold. They represented a majority of the borough's poorest tenants, but they also represented a majority of those middling burgesses paying 13*d.*–36*d.* per annum in rents. While Welshmen were in the minority among those holding enough property to justify paying over 70*d.* per annum in rents, they were not totally absent from the wealthiest groups of property holders. And this division of wealth was not unique to Ruthin. Direct comparison can be made with other mixed communities, such as the similarly sized Radnorshire town of Knighton, where in 1292–3 all town dwellers possessing moveable goods worth 15*s.* or more paid a royal tax, or lay subsidy, of one-fifteenth of the value of their goods (that is to say, 1*s.* in tax for every 15*s.* worth of goods possessed). Records of those assessed show that in Knighton, like Ruthin, about 60 per cent of the middling bulk of tax payers, in this case those taxed more than 1*s.* and no more than 3*s.*, were Welsh; while among the top quarter of tax payers, who were required to pay in excess of 3*s.* to the royal purse, Welshmen formed a significant 35 per cent minority of those assessed.[31]

Ruthin's particular ethnic grouping by rent level expressed in table 1.1, which is also paralleled in other communities, can be explained in two ways. First, a few persons, such as the Ruthin burgess Almary de Marreys, seem to have received their lands in bulk from the lord. Far and away the wealthiest individual to maintain a burgage in Ruthin, Almary had close connections with the Greys, appearing as a witness to their

---

[30]   R. R. Davies, 'Race relations in post conquest Wales, confrontation and compromise', *THSC* (1974–5), 49.

[31]   TNA, E179/242/57. There were seventy-one Knighton tax payers in 1292–3, their names suggesting thirty-seven Welsh and thirty-five English: seventeen paid more than 3*s.*, six Welsh and eleven English; forty-six paid 1*s.* 1*d* – 3*s.*, twenty-nine Welsh and seventeen English; nine paid 1*s.*, two Welsh and seven English.

Table 1.1. Ruthin property owners as in the 1324 rental, by rent paid*

	1 Rent	2 Total persons	3 % of total	4 % Welsh	5 % English	6 Holding property on Welsh St.†	7 Women	8 Office holders / Tradesmen	9 PILOB**
A	2d.–12.5d.	20	30%	70% (14)	30% (6)	9 Welsh 1 English	4 Welsh 4 English	–/6	–
B	13d.–36d.	18	25%	24% (6)	76% (12)	2 Welsh 1 English	2 Welsh 2 English	2/3	–
C	37d.–70d.	15	20%	60% (9)	40% (6)	7 Welsh 1 English	1 Welsh	3/4	1 Welsh
D	71d.–200d.	13	18%	38% (5)	62% (8)	3 Welsh	–	3/5	4 Welsh 1 English
E	201d. & up	3	4%	33% (1)	66% (2)	1 Welsh 1 English	–	1/–	1 Welsh 1 English
Unknown		2	3%	–	100% (2)	NA	–	NA	NA
Totals		71	100%	49% (35)	51% (36)†	22 Welsh 4 English	7 Welsh‡ 5 English	9/18	5 Welsh 2 English

Source: Dyffryn Clwyd Database, 'Rental'; TNA, WALE 15/8/1; Jack, 'Records of Denbighshire lordships II'.

* The Welsh brothers Ieuan ap William *saer* (carpenter) and Ieuan Du have been counted in 4C as one because they are listed as holding together in the rental and it is impossible to know what portion each paid of the total rent due. *Dyffryn Clwyd Database,* Rental #106 & 107, membrane 7r, Jack p. 17. There is also some circumstantial evidence to suggest that they were still in their minority.

** This column is for landholders whose Primary Interest Lay Outside the Borough, that is, they possessed property of greater value outside the borough than within.

† Hugh Scot was counted among the English as he is a likely post-conquest immigrant.

‡ One of whom is a co-holder listed with a husband.

acts in the time of the first two Grey lords between 1282 and 1320.[32] He even received a charter from the lord which specified the special terms and extent of his land tenure, though it no longer survives.[33] Nevertheless, only a minority of persons closely affiliated with the lord, like Almary de Marreys, owed their extensive holdings and wealth to that connection. Secondly, for most of Ruthin's burgesses, the accumulation of property, and the wealth which accompanied it, probably took place over an extended period of time as the availability of capital permitted. But, critically, while both Welshmen and Englishmen demonstrated a capacity to invest in trade and property, and to profit from their investments, access to significant levels of investment capital was not equally enjoyed by both ethnic groups, a point which warrants exploration.

For the very fortunate, the eventual acquisition of properties for subletting provided a potentially lucrative source of additional revenue. The Welsh carpenter William *saer*, for example, was by 1324 one of Ruthin's top burgage accumulators, holding four full burgages. He can be tracked in the borough's records as having acquired one burgage in April 1314, another half-burgage in 1314–15, an eighth of a burgage sometime after Easter 1317, and as entering into one other full burgage after Easter 1318.[34] Records of the additional one and three-eighths burgages held by William in 1324 are now lost, but that property also was probably acquired piecemeal. The entry fees on the transactions recounted here amount to almost 9*s.*, but the actual cost to William for these properties would have been much greater.

With regard to the last full burgage mentioned here, which was entered after Easter 1318, William had begun arrangements to obtain the property some months before, during the last weeks of 1317 or at the beginning of 1318. At that time the bondman Hwfa *carnifex* (butcher) had paid the lord 20*s.* for a licence to grant the reversion of the burgage to William and his wife Tangwystl upon the death of the burgage's current

[32]   A. Barrell and M. Brown, 'A settler community in post-conquest rural Wales: the English of Dyffryn Clwyd, 1294–1399', *WHR*, 17 (1995), 337.

[33]   Ibid.; specifically mentioned in *Dyffryn Clwyd Database*, Llann1 #1470, 1486; SC2/216/5 m.22d, 23.

[34]   In order, ibid., Reliefs #198, 242, 335, 362; SC2/215/73 m.1, SC2/215/74 m.1d, SC2/216/1 m.1, SC2/216/1 m.2.

occupant, Madog Cuyt, presumably a man to whom Hwfa was destined to be heir.[35] This transfer from Madog to William then came to pass as planned at the time of Madog's death early in 1318. As the making of this arrangement had cost Hwfa 20s., presumably William repaid to Hwfa at least this amount and likely something more to make the entire exchange equitable for Hwfa. If one imagines that the total outlay to acquire a single burgage may have been in excess of 27s., including the additional 7s. 8d. which William paid to the lord in entry fines for this particular property, the large amount of coin, kind, or credit necessary to afford as many as three or four full burgages would indeed have had to be spread over many years.

It follows from this that a socially stable environment existed at Ruthin, in which long-term property accumulation could be carried out by Welsh and Englishmen alike. This is in contrast to most of those Crown boroughs founded by Edward I in other parts of the conquered Welsh principality, such as Harlech and Caernarfon, which had been established exclusively 'for the habitation of Englishmen'.[36] But, for Ruthin, many other marcher foundations and even some of the Crown's new castellated boroughs, such as Aberystwyth, pretence of segregation was either never articulated in local law or quickly gave way to the economic expediency of Anglo-Welsh assimilation following the cessation of widespread hostilities.[37] From the dawn of the fourteenth century, only the most vehemently monopolistic of trading communities, such as the Edwardian boroughs of Harlech, Caernarfon and Conwy, or those steeped in their own long histories as front-line English military outposts, such as Brecon, failed to assimilate Welshmen as townsmen. In this latter minority of Anglo-Welsh communities, Welshmen generally failed to become shop owners or office holders until the late fifteenth century, if at all, due to their English burgesses' fears of losing commercial or military dominance. But Welsh persons were

---

[35] *Dyffryn Clwyd Database*, Reliefs #345, SC2/216/1 m.1d.
[36] R. R. Davies, *The Age of Conquest: Wales, 1063–1415* (Oxford, 1987), pp. 372–3.
[37] R. A. Griffiths, 'Aberystwyth', in *Boroughs of Medieval Wales* (Cardiff, 1978), p. 33.

present in even these towns as buyers and sellers of goods, servants and no doubt non-property-owning subtenants.

Evidence from Ruthin suggests strongly that there were no ethnic restrictions in place concerning the market for burgage property. There survive one hundred or so unrestricted trans-actions involving the purchase and sale of burgage property by Welsh men and women prior to 1324. Similarly, in the one surviving account of a Welsh heir paying relief for entry into his father's burgages at Ruthin, Bleddyn ap Dafydd is allowed to enter into the two burgages which his father, Dafydd Llŷn ('Leen'), had held, for 'services due and accustomed'.[38] This being the standard phrase employed in most relief entries, and there being no mention of other co-heirs, it is probable that here too no special restrictions were in place concerning the transferral of burgage property between generations of Welshmen. Such would have made Ruthin and similar towns legal islands, within the boundaries of which Welshmen could pass their inheritances to their children in the English fashion of primogeniture. This privilege may have allowed Welsh burgesses to avoid the posthumous fragmentation of their holdings between all co-heirs within a three-generational kin group in accordance with Welsh law, a custom increasingly viewed with ambivalence among prominent Welsh families in the surrounding countryside where native law and practice prevailed.[39] Hence, there is no evidence to support the sugges-tion that the Welsh of Ruthin were legally underprivileged with regard to the acquisition and accumulation of burgage property.

Instead, most Welshmen were simply lacking the available capital necessary to invest in such property on a scale similar to that of their English neighbours. Of the thirty-six Welsh burgesses listed in the 1324 rental, twenty held some property on Welsh Street, and in the majority of cases fractions of a burgage. Equally, of Ruthin's thirty-five English burgesses, only four held property on Welsh Street, those four holding between one and four full burgages each. These were probably

---

[38]   *Dyffryn Clwyd Database*, Reliefs #204, SC2/15/73 m.1.
[39]   For an excellent example of the accumulation and subsequent fragmentation of the holdings of prominent Welsh families in Dyffryn Clwyd, see M. Brown, 'Kinship, land, and law in fourteenth-century Wales: the kindred of Iorwerth ap Cadwgan', *WHR*, 17 (1995), 493–517.

sublet properties, rather than personal residences, as their holders were property accumulators. Similarly, of the five Welshmen whose primary landed interests can be shown to have lain outside the borough, three owned most of their Ruthin property on Welsh Street and, of the two who did not, one was Dafydd ap Ieuan de Mold whose origin-specific name marks him out as a probable migrant. Cumulatively, these data suggest the continuation of a small, focused Welsh community located there in pre-conquest times. We may also surmise that this native settlement included investment properties held by wealthier landholders based outside the community. That Welsh community must then, by 1324, have been numerically matched or slightly surpassed by new English immigrants. Contemporary tenant and taxpayer lists from similar Anglo-Welsh towns, at Knighton and Llawhaden, for instance, reinforce this view, suggesting that it was not uncommon for an existing Welsh community to be subsumed into an English borough foundation.[40]

Unfortunately, for want of pre-conquest records, such a conjecture cannot be directly verified, but the circumstantial evidence is compelling. It is probable that the lesser but parallel distribution of wealth among Welsh property holders alongside their English neighbours, as illustrated by table 1.1, offers an image of a relatively complex and stratified native Welsh community which has been swallowed up by a more affluent English one. The overall lesser wealth of Welsh property holders can be drawn from table 1.1, visible as the rough equivalence of those groups in boxes 4A and 5B, 4B and 5C, and 4C and 5D. This 'leap-frogging' of Welsh and English groups in terms of prosperity can be best regarded as evidence that the Welsh community's wealth, though less significant, was similarly distributed in a hierarchical fashion. A loose parallel can again be drawn between Ruthin and Knighton where, though Welsh and English displayed a range of wealth levels, about twice as many English as Welsh were among the richest 25 per cent of townsmen required to pay more than 3s. in royal taxation in 1292–3.[41] A parallel can also be drawn

---

[40]   Knighton, TNA, E179/242/57; Llawhaden, *Black Book*, pp. 139–51.
[41]   TNA, E179/242/57; see note 31 above for a breakdown of Knighton taxpayers by rate of taxation.

between Ruthin and the predominantly Welsh Cardiganshire borough of Adpar, where a 1326 list of burgesses indicates that none of the 20 per cent English minority of burgesses (nineteen of ninety-five burgesses being English by name) was among the five individuals holding less than a full burgage, while four of the six burgesses holding seven or more burgage plots were English.[42]

The result of such a relative step up the rent/wealth scale by English burgesses is probably a reflection, at least in part, of the greater amounts of ready capital in the hands of English immigrants in comparison with their long-settled Welsh neighbours. Englishmen are likely to have brought capital into the community with which to establish themselves in Dyffryn Clwyd or elsewhere, and to have perpetuated that wealth through various entrepreneurial endeavours. A study of surnames tracking the origins of Ruthin's population in the fourteenth century has shown that a disproportionate number of the borough's traceable English settler families – at least 44 per cent of those involved in land transactions between 1300 and 1352 – originated from locations over 80 miles from Ruthin.[43] These settlers were typically men recruited from other estates of the Grey lords of Ruthin, and were doubtless allowed to relocate to the town as individuals who could be trusted to make a contribution to the life of the borough.[44] Such was certainly the tenor of a 1282 royal commission given to the king's military commander in west Wales, Gilbert de Clare, earl of Gloucester and Hertford and lord of Glamorgan, that he should 'receive burgesses and others willing to come' and settle at Aberystwyth, some of whom similarly bore locative surnames from places as distant as Lichfield, Staffordshire, 120 miles away.[45] It is unlikely that persons deliberately invited or compelled to relocate over great distances would have been men possessing little or no capital with which to spur on the development of the market town.

[42]   *Black Book*, pp. 219–27.
[43]   E. H. B. Rees, 'A study of urban populations in fourteenth-century Wales: a case study of Ruthin' (unpublished MA thesis, University of Wales, Aberystwyth, 1999), 74.
[44]   Ibid., 72.
[45]   Griffiths, 'Aberystwyth', p. 32; I. J. Sanders, 'The boroughs of Aberystwyth and Cardigan in the early fourteenth century', *BBCS*, 15 (1954), 287; TNA SC12/17/72.

Among Ruthin men is John *cissor* (tailor), whose name first appears in the records of the lordship from October 1313, when he served as a surety.[46] By the following spring John had successfully established himself as a tradesman, appearing in a March 1314 borough court case concerning the sale of a tunic, and buying his first half-burgage in Ruthin shortly after Easter 1314. [47] John thereafter remained active in the community for another decade, appearing in a court roll entry of 1320 which records a suit of unjust detention against Peter *faber* (smith) for back rent of 3*s*. 8*d*. due on a house which John must have acquired and sublet in the intervening six years.[48] Similarly, Adam *carectarius* (carter), a member of a relatively low-status occupation, first appears in Ruthin's written record from June 1317 when he entered into a half-burgage.[49] Adam thereafter appears in the borough court record about once a year. Indeed, if we search out those burgesses likely to have had access to capital after settling, skilled English tradesmen such as John *cissor* were surpassed only by English office holders.

Supporting evidence for this assertion can be drawn from an assessment of the rents paid by Ruthin's burgesses in 1324. But before we analyse the community in this way, an exception must be dealt with: the Englishman Almary de Marreys paid a grossly disproportionate £3 7*s*. 8*d*. in annual rents, a sum several times that paid by any other burgess.[50] As mentioned earlier, Almary was unique in that he had been personally endowed by the lord with extensive lands outside the borough, a privilege he had probably received as part of Ruthin's conquering retinue.[51] Thus, while Almary was active in the borough, and some of the capital generated by his rural estate undoubtedly found its way into the town, he and the rents he paid may be excluded from the discussion in order to grasp what the situation was like generally for the borough's later English settlers.

[46]   TNA, SC2/215/72 session 4.
[47]   TNA, SC2/215/73 session 5; *Dyffryn Clwyd Database*, Reliefs #215, SC2/215/73 m.1d.
[48]   TNA, SC2/216/3 session 1.
[49]   *Dyffryn Clwyd Database*, Reliefs #316, SC2/215/76 m.1d.
[50]   Ibid., Rental #50, 546, 547, 579; membranes 5d, 7d; Jack pp. 15, 36, 38.
[51]   Almary held these lands by charter. Ibid., Llann1 #1470, SC2/216/5 m.22d.

If, then, one deconstructs the community along lines of ethnicity, the representative wealth gap between the sum total of annual rents paid by Welsh as opposed to English burgesses was about 16 per cent (614*d.*) in favour of English burgesses.[52] This gap is more than accounted for by the high rents of just four English office holders and tradesmen. The combined rents paid in 1324 by Ruthin's most prominent parker and forester, seemingly the borough's two most lucrative offices, together with those paid by the town's two wealthiest smiths, equated to 25 per cent (913*d.*) of all rents paid by Ruthin burgesses (excluding Almary de Marreys).[53] Furthermore, all but one of Ruthin's burgess-foresters, -parkers and -smiths were English during the 1312–21 period. To put it another way, if we leave aside the rents of Englishmen doing jobs for which Welsh participation is rarely evident, both ethnic groups possessed near equal wealth.

This is not to say that Welshmen did not hold office or engage in trade, since the rental of 1324 names two Welshmen who served as bailiff, an ale taster, carpenters, cobblers and tailors.[54] Likewise, one Welsh smith, Tudur *faber*, is mentioned in connection with the borough during the thirty years between 1294 (the year of the earliest surviving borough court rolls) and 1324. But, poignantly, Tudur, first named in a court roll of 1296 and perhaps a pre-conquest resident of Ruthin, is recorded in a relief roll entry of 1317 as selling his forge (*toralle*) to a certain Englishman named Richard, almost certainly the same Richard *ferrator* or *forbisour* (smith or furbisher/armourer) who would thereafter rise to prominence in Ruthin

---

[52]   If one adds up the entire amount of rents, known or estimated on similarly sized holdings in the same location, and paid to the lord in 1324 by Ruthin burgesses, the rough sum would equal £18 15*s.* 6*d.* (or 4506*d.*). If we subtract from that the £3 7*s.* 8*d.* (812*d.*) of Almary de Marreys, who held his property by special gift of the lord and whose singular wealth was disproportionate, that total comes down to £14 17*s.* 10*d.* (3694*d.*). Of the remaining rents paid by Ruthin burgesses, 58 per cent (2154*d.*) was paid by English tenants and 42 per cent (1540*d.*) by Welsh tenants. The wealth gap between the two communities was around 16 per cent (614*d.*).

[53]   Hugh *parcarius* – *Dyffryn Clwyd Database*, Rental #77, 78, 790, 791; membranes 7r., 2r.; Jack pp. 16, 47. Richard *forestarius* – Rental #3, 4, 5, 6, 7, 8, 9; membrane 7d.; Jack p. 13. Robert *faber* – Rental #89, 90, 91, 92, 285, 795; membranes 2r., 5r., 7r.; Jack pp. 16, 26, 47. Peter *faber* – Rental #53, 54; membrane 7r.; Jack p. 15.

[54]   See table 6.3 and table 6.4 for the range of occupations engaged in by Welsh office holders and tradesmen.

by the early 1320s.[55] Tudur, then, also sold his modest half-burgage in Ruthin to Ieuan Du in 1318 and was afterwards inactive, perhaps due to old age.[56] Moreover, Welshmen rarely acted as parkers or foresters within the borough's jurisdictional area (though it was not uncommon to have Welsh foresters in the lordship's rural commotes).

Crucially, however, Ruthin's strongest associations between wealth and occupation were demonstrated by the town's typically English parkers, foresters and smiths, all but one of whom paid at least 10s. (120d.) in annual rents.[57] A lack of equally full documentation from other Welsh towns, for which few or no court records survive to supplement our knowledge of the occupations of those named in tenant or taxpayer lists, makes it difficult to gauge how typical Ruthin was in this respect. Nevertheless, the impression given by other ethnically mixed towns like Knighton and Aberystwyth is that office holders and certain groups of tradesmen, in particular metal workers, tended to be both English and more prosperous than their neighbours. At Knighton, for example, in 1292–3 two smiths, both English, were among the ten men most heavily taxed.[58] At Aberystwyth, a list of burgesses from the first decade of the fourteenth century includes one smith, the lead worker at royal castles in west Wales, the castle's current constable and the widow of the former constable, all of whom were English and ranked among the top 29 per cent of burgesses who held more than one full burgage.[59]

Investment from within: the accumulation of wealth and property
How did those with access to relatively large quantities of capital put their gains to use? The way of reinvesting capital most visible in borough records has already been touched on – property accumulation. Just as those tradesmen and office holders who had acquired, and were paying rents for, multiple properties by 1324 must have had a substantial income in

---

[55]   *Dyffryn Clwyd Database*, GC1 #29, SC2/215/66 m.1; Reliefs #297, SC2/215/76 m.1.

[56]   Ibid., Reliefs #363, SC2/216/1 m.2.

[57]   See below, chapter V.

[58]   TNA, E179/242/57.

[59]   Sanders, 'The boroughs of Aberystwyth and Cardigan', 287–9; TNA, SC12/17/72.

order to maintain their holdings, they must also have been reinvesting a significant portion of their revenues in the property market in order to have built up those holdings in the first place. The potential result of this cycle of acquisition and reinvestment was an overall increase in wealth which favoured those persons who had the most capital to reinvest.

The seignorial rent level of burgage plots in Ruthin was typically 1s. per annum, a sum small enough to have created ample opportunity for accumulators to profit from renting burgages to multiple occupants. The degree of success of burgesses in such profiteering would have been dependent on at least two factors. The first of these is the portion of a burgage plot which typically comprised a residence. The second is the amount of rent a burgess could raise from each of these residences.

Burgage plots in larger English towns such as Liverpool contained divisions as minute as one-forty-eighth of a plot.[60] In response to such extreme fragmentation, minimum property holding restrictions were set in place in order to limit the acquisition of burgage rights in some locations. Cardiff's charter, for example, contained a clause which limited the extension of burgage privileges to those possessing half or more of a burgage.[61] The charter of Ruthin did not explicitly contain a similar restriction, but such small fractions of a burgage were nonetheless rare, one-half being the most common division found in the 1324 rental (see table 1.2). While three Ruthin burgesses did possess as little as one-sixth of a burgage, each of these men also held additional property within or outside the borough and so probably did not maintain these small fractional holdings as dwellings, though the possibility that these holdings were let to poor subtenants can not be ruled out.[62]

---

[60] DeWolf Hemmon, *Burgage Tenure in Medieval England*, p. 108. Such minute divisions probably represent little more than administrative loopholes through which otherwise unpropertied individuals accessed borough liberties.

[61] Ibid., p. 109.

[62] Those parts as small as 1/6 are: Madog ap Madog Fychan – *Dyffryn Clwyd Database*, Rental #101, 616; membrane 7r., 9r.; Jack pp. 17, 39. Dafydd ap Ieuan de Mold – Rental #51, membrane 7d.; Jack p. 15; and probably Rental #923 or #230, membrane 10r. or 4d.; Jack p. 52 or p. 24. Hywel *saer* – Rental #98, 99; membrane 7r.; Jack p. 17.

Table 1.2. Ruthin's common burgage divisions in 1324

Burgage division	Frequency of division
⅙	3
¼	4
⅛	3
½	29
⅔	2
¾	3
Whole	73

Source: as for table 1.1 (not a comprehensive account of all mentioned burgages).

It is probable that the smallest division of a burgage representing a residence in Ruthin was one-quarter. In three of the four instances where a quarter-burgage is listed in the rental, it was the holder's sole possession in Dyffryn Clwyd. One of these quarters was the possession of Angharad the widow of Bleddyn Bustak,[63] another was held by Iorwerth *clericus* (clerk),[64] and a third by Dafydd ap Madog Fychan[65] who was perhaps the less wealthy brother of Madog ap Madog Fychan.[66] Of these three, the widow Angharad especially was likely to have maintained her quarter-burgage as a sole residence.

In addition to full and partial burgages, persons in the 1324 rental are associated with items of less clear measure described as tenements, cottages, places and particles (*particula*). Setting aside whatever size of residences these terms imply, if a half-burgage is assumed to have been the minimum space required to fit a building and maintain a household, the possible rent-earning potential of persons holding multiple burgages grows considerably.[67] For example, Hugh *faber*, who had accumulated

[63] Ibid., Rental #26.; membrane 7d.; Jack p. 14.
[64] Ibid., Rental #87.; membrane 7r.; Jack p. 16.
[65] Ibid., Rental #102.; membrane 7r.; Jack p.17.
[66] Ibid., Rental #101, 616; membrane 7r., 9r.; Jack pp. 17, 39.
[67] This also holds implications for the estimated population of the borough. If, for example, working from the figures above, around 50 per cent of Ruthin's burgages were held by around 33 per cent of Ruthin property owners, this leaves a surplus of around 17 per cent, or roughly seventeen burgages which could be offered as accommodation or commercial premises. If each of these burgages were divided conservatively into halves, this would be thirty-four halves, raising the total

three full burgages by 1324, may have occupied only one-half of a plot and sublet his remaining five half-burgages separately. Thus Hugh's properties could have had more than twice the profit potential offered if an entire burgage were to have been necessary to maintain a residence for hire or occupation. As one possible measure of how invested capital could profit a burgess such as Hugh, the following calculations depict the amount of rent which each of these half-burgages could have generated through subletting.

Though not often expressly described as such, entries occasionally appear in the borough court rolls concerning a tenant's payment of rent to a burgess for a sublet property. In March 1316, for example, Philip Passavant brought a case of unjust detention against Robert de Muninton. Robert had stood surety for Cecily de Chester concerning 3s. 4d. for Philip's house (*domus*) in Ruthin, and Cecily had failed to pay the sum.[68] Although the entry does not clearly say so, a couple of factors strongly suggest that the amount sought was a sum of overdue rent for a sublet property. It was said by Philip that Cecily should have paid him the 3s. 4d. in question at Christmas and Michaelmas, and that Cecily had been responsible for the maintenance of the house. In this latter obligation she had failed, occasioning damages of 5s.

While 3s. 4d. was not an insignificant amount, it would have been a small sum compared to the cost of acquiring a burgage from the lord. Common figures of how much the lord charged for entry into a burgage property ranged from 10s. for one vacant acre under burgage tenure within Ruthin,[69] to 20s. for a burgage in Llanfwrog on the outskirts of the community.[70] It is unlikely, then, that Cecily could have acquired a house and the land on which it stood for as little as 3s. 4d. It is also unlikely that the outright purchase of a property would have obligated Cecily to certain conditions of maintenance.[71]

number of residences for family units in Ruthin by seventeen and increasing the potential population (using the multiplier of five) by about eighty-five.

[68]   TNA, SC2/215/75 session 1.

[69]   *Dyffryn Clwyd Database*, GC1 #2239, SC2/216/10 m.28.

[70]   Ibid., GC1 #2839, SC2/216/5 m.31.

[71]   The sellers of burgages occasionally retained a life interest in properties they had held, demanding of the new holder a token rent and thus maintaining a right

If, instead, Cecily were subletting a house from Philip and should have paid him monies at Michaelmas, and again three months later at Christmas, and was finally brought before the court after another three months in March (just before the feast of the Annunciation of the Blessed Virgin Mary), it is probable that she been obligated to pay quarterly. In this case, if 3s. 4d. was the total of those two quarters for which she was in arrears, the sublet rent value of her property would have been 1s. 8d. per quarter, or 6s. 8d. per year (being exactly one half-mark, a likely amount). If it is postulated that the house occupied all of a single burgage plot to the exclusion of any other profit-making features (for example, a cellar or garden which might be let separately), the income value of the property would have been over six and a half times the seignorial burgage rent of 1s. per annum shown in the 1324 rental. Additionally, as we know was the case between Philip and Cecily, if the occupier was obligated to maintain the property, all moneys received by a burgess above and beyond his own rent to the lord would have been clear profit.

This profit margin may have been reduced if, as is possible, 1s. per annum was the rent charged in Ruthin for burgages as a measure of land, with additional rents added pro rata for burgage plots containing particularly large, well-placed or valuable tenements. This was the practice in some other small, chartered boroughs in the March, such as Llandovery, Oswestry and Denbigh.[72] But rents at Ruthin were generally consistent with a flat rate of 1s. for a whole burgage. Ruthin's charter is unhelpful on this point, stating rather vaguely that free burgages were to be held 'for a certain rent to be paid at established terms each year', and the 1324 rental is not specific enough to allow us to comment effectively on deviations from the norm of 1s. per full burgage.[73]

Nevertheless, even if we allow for a 50 per cent margin of error and assume that Cecily was subletting an entire burgage, the relationship between Philip and Cecily could have provided a clear profit of at least 2s. 4d. per annum (that is, 3s.

of escheat, but no direct evidence of such exists in Ruthin. See DeWolf Hemmon, *Burgage Tenure in Medieval England*, p. 80.

[72]   Ibid., p. 71.

[73]   Jack, 'The medieval charters', 18.

4*d*. minus 1*s*. rent to the lord). Alternatively, were a single burgage plot to contain two houses, or households, and the 6*s*. 8*d*. rate of rent per annum prove to be accurate, the profit income generated by a single burgage could have been something in the region of 12*s*. 4*d*. per annum (that is, 13*s*. 4*d*., or one mark, minus 12*d*. rent to the lord). With this in mind, it is worth reiterating the earlier comment on Ruthin's population: six men, four of whom were English and two of whom were Welsh (9 per cent of property owners), held twenty-one and one-half of the town's 100 burgages.[74] Acknowledging the potentially disproportionate amount of capital which these persons' burgages could produce, in relation to the annual rents they rendered to the lord, is important when considering their relative wealth and influence in the community. The eventual fruits of such influence can be seen in the more mature borough of Cardigan, founded in the twelfth century, where by 1301–2 the Blakeney family controlled seventeen and one-quarter burgages, or approximately one-seventh of the town, and had recently provided a constable of the castle.[75]

If we look more broadly for those likely to have had capital to invest in Ruthin, the 1324 rental records seventy-one burgesses paying forty-eight different rents to the lord. The total amount of rent paid per annum by Ruthin's property holders ranged from the substantial £3 7s. 8*d*. paid by Almary de Marreys for his burgage and approximately one hundred and thirty acres in rural estates, to 2*d*. paid by the holders of one-sixth parts of burgages. If these different rents are ranked, £3 7s. 8*d*. being first and 2*d*. being forty-eighth (as has been applied in table 1.3), some accumulators, such as Hugh *faber* and Hugh the son of Stephen *janitor* (castle porter), rank quite low. It is likely, however, that as property accumulators their expendable income in relation to that of their neighbours allowed a standard of living and influence within the community more akin to those of men like Hugh *parcarius* whom the rental records as more conspicuously wealthy. For these men, again less commonly Welsh than English, capital

[74] See note 17.
[75] Sanders, 'The boroughs of Aberystwyth and Cardigan', 284–5; TNA, SC11/771.

Table 1.3. Wealth ranking of most significant property accumulators in 1324

Person	Number of burgages held	Wealth ranking by rents paid
Richard *forestarius* (forester)	4½	4th
Hugh *parcarius* (parker)	4	2nd
William *saer** (carpenter)	4	21st
Dafydd ap Bleddyn	3	3rd
Hugh *faber* (smith)	3	20th
Hugh the son of Stephen *janitor* (castle porter)	3	29th

Source: as for table 1.1.
* Recently deceased.

spent on property may have been the key to enhancing their prosperity.

As in explaining the proportionally greater wealth of Ruthin's English community in comparison with that of the borough's Welsh property holders in table 1.2, why particular persons in table 1.3 happen to have been property accumulators is most likely to be explicable in terms of expendable income; and large quantities of expendable income tended to be more consistently available to Englishmen. Richard *forestarius* (forester) and Hugh *parcarius* (parker) held offices, as their names suggest, which were typically occupied by English burgesses and through which they would have been able to access a steady in-flow of capital 'by farming (that is, renting) these offices from the lord, or by receiving a fixed stipend which may or may not have been supplemented by fees from various office-related sources'.[76] There is no evidence that Hugh, the son of Stephen *janitor*, inherited his father's position as porter of the castle of Ruthin, but after the death of Stephen *janitor* sometime between March 1321 and September 1323 Hugh had inherited his father's accumulated

[76] A. Berry, 'The parks and forests of the lordship of Dyffryn Clwyd', *DHST*, 42 (1993), 10–11. For a good general account of how lucrative the practice of farming a lordship's offices was, see Ll.B. Smith, 'Seignorial income in the fourteenth century: the Arundels of Chirk', *BBCS*, 28 (1978–80), 443–57.

property, which was likely to have been purchased with the income of a borough office.[77]

Unfortunately, evidence concerning the specific details of the payment of Ruthin's officials is limited. From at least as early as 1306 the bailiffs of Ruthin maintained the farm of stallage in Ruthin's market, in addition to their stipend or farm of the bailiffry.[78] In 1332 the office of Welsh bailiff, or *rhingyll*, of Llannerch was farmed for 45*s.* per annum (the 'farm' allowed the *rhingyll* to retain all monies annually collected in excess of that amount), implying that at least this value of money or goods, and probably more, passed through the officer's hands.[79] The comparative affluence of at least some officers and the way they discharged their duties (backed by the authority of the court) were also a cause of occasional resentment in the community. John *forestarius*, for example, was a forester of Llannerch throughout 1312–21 as well as holder of the farm of the mill of Garthgynan; the latter was a valuable farm, for in 1311 he was awarded 5*s.* in compensation for the withdrawal of suit of mill by just one man.[80] John was similarly not averse to the persistent use of the court in demanding goods which had been bailed to him, and in 1312 was even publicly accused by Dafydd Llwyd, chaplain of Llanfair, who said 'before good and grave men ... (that his actions) ... harmed the whole country and the church'.[81] Consequently, by the time of the 1324 rental, John had managed to accumulate over one hundred acres of land in Llannerch.[82]

Among Ruthin's non-office-holding property accumulators, Hugh *faber* was a wealthy tradesman with a forge and curtilage on Mill Street, which probably adjoined two of his burgages.[83]

---

[77] Stephen *janitor* seems to have died between March 1321, when he last appeared in the court of Ruthin, and September 1323 when a William *janitor* appeared in the great court of Ruthin. Stephen *janitor* was regularly referred to as '*janitor* of the castle of Ruthin', for example, in *Dyffryn Clwyd Database*, Reliefs #310, SC2/215/71 m.1; Stephen also seems to have resided in the castle, as he was assaulted in his bedchamber there in 1320. Ibid., GC1 #1554, SC2/216/3 m.19.

[78] Ibid., Llan1 #74, SC2/215/69 m.13.

[79] Ibid., Llan1 #2211, SC2/216/13 m.16.

[80] Ibid., Llan1 #204, SC2/215/71 m.9

[81] Ibid., Llan1 #339, SC2/215/72 m.10 (demanding goods bailed); Llan1 #235, SC2/215/71 m.9d.

[82] Ibid., Rental #525.; membrane 5d.; Jack p. 36.

[83] Ibid., Rental #19.; membrane 7d.; Jack p. 14

His wealth ranking was quite low, Hugh paying only 64d. in rents annually, but it is curious to see that the other two persons appearing in the 1324 rental with the trade name *faber* – the same Robert *faber*[84] and Peter *faber*[85] mentioned earlier – are ranked sixth and ninth on the basis of their respective rents of 129d. and 120d. per annum. Smiths, or men so named, were far and away the most consistently wealthy tradesmen in Ruthin, and they seem to have been consistently English.[86] The combined rent paid by the three smiths mentioned in the 1324 rental was over twice the total of rents paid annually by tradesmen identifiable as working in any other single craft. So, with regard to Hugh *faber*, as undoubtedly to his fellow smiths, the ability to accumulate wealth and property was likely to be a product of access to capital, in this case attained by practising a lucrative trade rather than collecting an office holder's income, and probably perpetuated through investment. Furthermore, the obvious wealth of Hugh's fellow smiths, whose total rents were driven up at least partly by their possession of acreage outside the borough, is a compelling argument for the possibility that low and relatively standardized burgage rents to the lord of 12d. per annum underestimate the actual moveable wealth of burgage accumulators.

The only other tradesman to be a significant borough property accumulator was Welsh, and the town's most wealthy carpenter, William *saer*. Ranking just below Hugh *faber* in his rents paid, William illustrates two points. First, tradesmen other than smiths appear to have prospered by holding, and investing in, Ruthin's burgage property. Secondly, Welsh tradesmen as well as English accumulated and reinvested capital.[87] It must be stressed, however, that William appears to have been unique as a Welsh tradesman who accumulated property.

[84]   *Dyffryn Clwyd Database*, Rental #89 –92.; membrane 7r.; Jack p. 16.
[85]   Ibid., Rental #53, 54.; membrane 7r.; Jack, p. 15.
[86]   See below, chapter V.
[87]   William was recently deceased in 1324 and the rents paid by his sons on burgage property have been used in estimating his wealth. If the rents paid by his widow are added to those of his sons, his rents would have slightly exceeded those of Hugh *faber*.

Lastly, appearing in table 1.3 is Dafydd ap Bleddyn, the only other, and non-artisan, Welshman identifiable as a significant accumulator of burgage property in Ruthin. Dafydd too was exceptional, in so far as he was the only accumulator whose primary landed interest was outside Ruthin. In addition to his burgages and 'two places, one acre' at Town End, the rental lists him as holding 2 acres, one messuage and one carrucate (between 80 and 120 acres) in Colion, Dyffryn Clwyd's western commote.[88] Given his sizeable holding, there is no great mystery as to how Dafydd came by the wealth necessary to purchase his burgages. Why he chose to invest in burgage property, however, is not immediately obvious, unless it was a personal initiative to invest capital in burgage acquisition. It may be that Dafydd recognized the potential for property speculation to increase his personal wealth in a period of agricultural crisis caused by the great famine of 1315–22.[89]

The flow of capital into and out of the community
Dafydd ap Bleddyn's particular situation raises the wider issue of capital generated outside the community and invested in the borough. Leaving aside burgage accumulation, Dafydd was one of a small group of persons in table 1.1 who possessed property within and outside the borough of Ruthin, but whose primary landed interest lay outside the town. This group of five Welshmen and two Englishmen represented only 10 per cent of property owners in Ruthin but all paid at least 3 7d. (table 1.1, rows C–E) in annual rents and six of the seven paid at least 71d. (table 1.1, row D–E). Among these, Dafydd ap Bleddyn was the wealthiest Welshman, paying 300d., or £1 5s. (table 1.1, row E), in annual rents.

It is among this group, rather than as an accumulator, that Dafydd was most significant, as the wealthiest among a body of landed Welshmen who were both well established in the countryside and willing to invest in the growing borough by the

---

[88] *Dyffryn Clwyd Database*, Rental #66–68, 657, 806; membranes 7r, 1d, 2r; Jack pp. 15, 41, 47; A Dafydd ap Bleddyn is listed among the Welsh of Llannerch as holding an unrecorded amount of property with 'his brother'. Rental #486; membrane 8d.; Jack p. 34.

[89] Cattle murrains affected the region concurrently with harvest failures during the great famine of 1315–22. See below, chapter V.

1320s. Just as office holders and tradesmen based in Ruthin were eager to invest in the borough, so too were persons from outside willing to invest there. And it is not surprising that the majority of these latter were Welsh, given that a numerically superior group of moderately wealthy Welshmen existed in the surrounding countryside. It has been shown, for example, that in 1316 Dafydd ap Bleddyn had no fewer than twenty-seven living, male kinsmen in rural Dyffryn Clwyd.[90] At similarly mixed boroughs, such as Aberystwyth, a limited number of Welsh families came to dominate the affairs of the town during the fourteenth century, some of whom were rural landowners of substance.[91] By comparison, even in the 1320s, the rural English immigrant population was still a recently settled minority in Ruthin amidst a large and potentially hostile native population.[92] The only two Englishmen to hold property in Ruthin and yet maintain a majority of their holdings outside the town were Almary de Marreys and Hugh *parcarius*. Almary, as mentioned earlier, received his extensive holdings as a gift from Reginald de Grey, and was certainly a man of rural estate. Hugh, by contrast, quite possibly received more of his income from his office and from the subletting of the four burgages he had accumulated in Ruthin than from the messuage and 30 acres he held in Colion.[93]

Thus, Hugh may be representative of something else. In addition to those seven persons whose primary landed interest lay outside Ruthin (and excluding Hugh), there were six whose most valuable holdings were within Ruthin, yet who owned some lands outside the borough. Of these latter, four Welshmen and two Englishmen, Robert *faber* owned the greatest amount of property outside the borough that can be identified with certainty, 12½ acres in Dogfeiling.[94] The second greatest amount was held by Henry le Messager, 7½ acres in Colion.[95] Both men were minor accumulators, holding two and one-half burgages each in Ruthin. They were members of two groups

[90]   M. Brown, 'Kinship, land and law', 'kin' here recognized as the Welsh *gwely*, or four-generational agnatic kin group.

[91]   Griffiths, 'Aberystwyth', p. 39.

[92]   Barrell and Brown, 'A settler community', 340.

[93]   *Dyffryn Clwyd Database*, Rental #790; membrane 2r.; Jack p. 47.

[94]   Ibid., Rental #285; membrane 5r.; Jack p. 26.

[95]   Ibid., Rental #794; membrane 2r.; Jack p. 47.

that were wealthy and likely to have had capital to invest, one a smith and the other an office holder. And, like Hugh *parcarius*, they were probably settled within the borough and had decided to invest some of their wealth in land outside the town. However, while English burghal families in the first half of the fourteenth century were not unwilling to make rural investments, they were cautious buyers at best. For example, the Wynter family of Abergwili, Carmarthenshire, had by 1326 accumulated twenty and one-half burgage plots, or about 40 per cent of the town's property.[96] Additionally, in neighbouring Carmarthen, persons with the same family name paid to enjoy burgess status and held one garden.[97] But, outside Abergwili and Carmarthen, the Wynter family held a comparatively insignificant 30 acres of land and a parcel of marsh 'beyond the river Towy'.[98]

It is more difficult to qualify the only Welshman to hold a minority of his property outside the borough. Ieuan ap Heilyn held a variety of small parcels outside Ruthin as well as two and one-half burgages within the borough, after the fashion of his English counterparts.[99] Neither an office holder nor associable with a particular trade, Ieuan nevertheless ranked at the eleventh highest rent level among persons owning property in Ruthin, paying about 113d. per annum in rents. Given this wealth, and at least some borough property accumulation, it is likely that he was a town dweller engaged in some limited speculation in the countryside. It is impossible to know with certainty, but again property investments outside the borough may have been funded in part by the capital acquired as a multiple burgage owner. As a result, it is possible to say that both wealthy Welsh and English burgesses invested,

96 *Black Book*, pp. 247–9.
97 TNA, SC12/20/32.
98 *Black Book*, 247–9.
99 *Dyffryn Clwyd Database*, Rental #152, 207 & 208, 705 & 706, 755; membranes (respectively) 4r, 4d, 1r, 1r; Jack pp. 19, 23, 43, 45. The other Welsh burgesses with property outside the town do not fit the pattern. For one, Ieuan ap William, the rental lists his name in connection with property outside Ruthin but neither the quantity nor the rent. For another, Dafydd ap Iorwerth, the one messuage and 4 acres he held in Dogfeiling are specified in the rental as 'from free inheritance' and so would not seem to have been investment property. Lastly, for one additional Welshman, his common name, Madog ap Dafydd, makes identifying him with specific extra-burghal properties difficult.

however tentatively, not only in property within, but also outside the borough.

On the whole, those with capital to invest were probably afforded opportunities to increase their total wealth. This applied to both rural dwellers investing within the community as well as established burgesses investing within and beyond the borough's boundaries. Most prominent among this latter group are certain office holders and tradesmen. By comparison, those burgesses not obviously associated with sources of what may be termed start-up and maintenance capital do not feature in the record as noticeably wealthy men.

Conclusion

At least two main themes are evident in the distribution of wealth in the borough of Ruthin. The first is ethnicity; the second concerns the availability of capital. Despite the borough's obvious material inequalities, there are some inconspicuous equalities. Four truisms regarding the community's material inequalities are these: the majority of Ruthin's poorest burgesses were Welsh; the majority of Ruthin's richest burgesses were English; the majority of those holding the smallest fractions of burgages in Ruthin were Welsh; and the majority of the community's burgage accumulators were English. However, institutionalized inequality is less clearly noticed. The disproportionately greater wealth of Ruthin's English burgesses was probably the result of a pre-existing Welsh community being subsumed into a wealthier English immigrant community. There is no evidence of any ethnic restrictions involving the purchase, sale, or free demise of burgage property in Ruthin; and, leaving aside the holding of some borough offices, Welshmen were not obviously denied wealth-producing opportunities, such as burgage accumulation within Ruthin, or land speculation outside the borough.

Only in the particularly lucrative trade of smithery were Welsh burgesses lacking; it is possible that this is simply due to Welsh naming practice taking precedence over the use of trade names among Welshmen. As an example, it is possible that Ieuan ap Heilyn was a smith by trade. He was certainly a man of similar wealth and property to those identified in the

1324 rental as *faber*. But it is unlikely; there is nothing to indicate that he was a tradesman, and some Welshmen such as William *saer* did indeed take trade names. A more reasonable explanation is that for certain practical or social reasons Welsh burgesses did not elect to engage in this particular trade.[100] Likewise, only from a few lucrative posts, such as those of parker and forester, were Welshmen excluded from borough office holding. It is entirely possible that a Welshman became a borough forester or parker but did not appear in what survives of the written record; Welsh foresters were certainly active in the rural commotes of Dyffryn Clwyd.[101] Once again, the extant evidence suggests that it is simply unlikely.

Hence, inequality within the borough may have been present only in a couple of limited, but potent, circumstances. It appears probable that Welsh burgesses could not or did not engage in one particular area of trade work, and they are unlikely to have held at least two town offices. Conversely, ethnic equality was generally current in Ruthin in relation to generating, investing and perpetuating wealth. While it could be argued that institutionalized ethnic discrimination was a contributing factor in the distribution of wealth in the borough, it is doubtful that ethnic discrimination was the prime determinant. As exemplified by William *saer*, those Welshmen with capital were just as capable of perpetuating and increasing their wealth as were their English neighbours.

Ultimately, access to capital within the community seems to have been more important than ethnicity. The adage 'it takes money to make money' may be applied to town life in early fourteenth-century Ruthin. English immigrants are likely to have brought capital with which to establish themselves in the borough. The ethnic inequality illustrated in columns 4 and 5 of table 1.1, the quick trade establishment and betterment of many English immigrants and the higher level of property accumulation achieved by English burgesses hint at an ongoing concentration of wealth among English burgesses living cheek by jowl with long-established and consistently poorer Welsh neighbours.

[100] See below, chapter VI.
[101] See table 6.3 and ensuing discussion.

That Welshmen, by 1321, took part in neither the most lucrative of manorial offices nor the metalworking trades perpetuated their lack of access to at least some of those ready supplies of capital which were afforded the community's Englishmen for entrepreneurial reinvestment. Consequently, a significantly lower number of Welsh than English engaged in such activities as burgage accumulation in the town and investment in land beyond its boundaries. This was necessarily a long-term and perennial problem harmful to the potential of the Welsh community to prosper through reinvestment for profit within the town. It may be in this light, rather than the result of legal inequality, that circumstances in the borough of Ruthin could have 'crystallized the feelings of Welshmen that they were an underprivileged race'.[102] It was Ruthin after all which was subject to Owain Glyn Dŵr's first raid in 1400, not one of the plantation boroughs in the Crown lands where legal restrictions on trade and burgess status were sometimes strictly applied to the exclusion of Welshmen.[103] Additionally, the practice of partible inheritance among Welsh land holders outside the borough would have significantly reduced the number of Welshmen who possessed the expendable capital necessary to invest in the borough itself.[104]

The overall impression of Ruthin in 1324 is that of a developing community in which there were different standards of wealth among Welsh and English inhabitants, but one in which those standards were not unilaterally restrictive. Social or even 'class' mobility is unlikely to have been overtly hindered by anything except the availability of capital. Certain tradesmen, such as smiths and manorial office holders, were at the top of a resident social hierarchy, neither exclusively Welsh nor English, which looked within and outside the borough for property investment opportunities. Occasionally, even wealthier and probably non-resident men of substance

---

[102]   Davies, 'Race relations in post conquest Wales', 49.

[103]   This could have been a local motivation additional to Glyn Dŵr's dispute with the lord of Dyffryn Clwyd, Reginald de Grey, rather than the sole reason why Ruthin was struck first.

[104]   Brown, 'Kinship, land and law'. This article offers a well-documented and detailed example of the way in which, generation after generation, members of the kindred of Iorwerth ap Cadwgan faced the compulsory break-up of a lifetime's accumulation of land by the practice of partible inheritance.

settled on large rural estates, such as Almary de Marreys and Dafydd ap Bleddyn, took an interest in the borough as an opportunity for investment, and were representative of as many as 10 per cent of Ruthin's property holders. Finally, to this mix can be added a steady inflow of capital from English immigrants, fuelling trade in goods and housing as well as spurring on undercurrents of low-level cosmopolitan urbanization, complete with relatively ultra-wealthy elites and an amorphous body of impoverished marginals at the other end of the wealth spectrum.

II

STATUS AND DOMINANCE

INSTITUTIONAL DEVELOPMENT:
COURT JURORS AND SURETIES[1]

The environment, evolution and significance of a great court of Ruthin jury

Status, like wealth, can only be measured indirectly and by a limited number of indices. These status indicators include records of frequent litigation, property accumulation, ecclesiastical vocation and office holding.[2] The most accessible and well defined of these indicators available for Ruthin derive from the records of the borough's curial administration. Five extant lists of the great court of Ruthin presentment jurors, from 1319 to 1323, are analysed here with reference to personal activities in the borough court of Ruthin during 1312–21.[3]

Ruthin's court rolls survive in a relatively unbroken, if not always fully intact, series from 1294 to the seventeenth century. Most importantly, Ruthin stands alone as a borough of medieval Wales for which the community's curial apparatus can be observed during the period of its early development and formalization from the 1290s to the 1320s. An examination of these early court rolls allows us to see the evolution of jurisdiction between borough courts and the emergent significance of court jurors who, by the late 1320s, were extremely influential men in Ruthin whose rise to prominence had paralleled that of court jurors in other boroughs. By comparison, other early to

---

[1] Elements of the research presented in this section and section III, appear in M. Stevens, 'Wealth, status and "race" in the Ruthin of Edward II', *UHist*, 32 (2005), 17–32.

[2] For property accumulation, see chapter I. For other indices, see below, especially table 2.6, with accompanying text, and chapter VI.

[3] Broadly speaking, this is the approach employed by the 'Toronto School' of historians, including J. Raftis, E. Clark, S. Olson and others. See below, this chapter. Jury lists: *Dyffryn Clwyd Database*, GC1 #1421, 1692, 1723, 1969, 1996; SC2/216/2 m.6, SC2/216/3 m.23, SC2/216/3 m.22, SC2/216/4 m.30, SC2/216/4 m.31.

mid-fourteenth-century court rolls for Wales are limited to a smattering of town court rolls from Caernarfon, dating from 1361–1402; two regional Wrexham bailiwick court rolls of 1339–40 and 1344–5 covering the *villa mercatoria* of Wrexham (further rolls survive from the 1380s onwards), together with a 1391 list of Wrexham extracts dating from as early as 1329; and a relatively small number of individual court roll extracts and fragments from other parts of Wales.[4] These latter sources offer points of comparison with Ruthin's courts, but due to their relatively late date they reveal only fully formed curial systems in which the roles of officers and participants are already well defined.

As an independent marcher lordship, the legal system of Dyffryn Clwyd was a self-contained, independent hierarchy. It adjudicated all of what we would today term 'civil' and 'criminal' cases involving its tenants, free from royal sanction. In addition to what might now be compared to 'misdemeanours', its remit included both felonies and debt cases in excess of 40*s.* (business which would have fallen under royal jurisdiction in England).[5]

At the apex of the lordship's legal hierarchy was the biannual great court of Dyffryn Clwyd, dealing with civil and criminal cases originating from all parts of the lordship. Below the great court of Dyffryn Clwyd were three monthly courts, typically dealing with less serious legal infractions and interpersonal litigation from the lordship's three rural regions or commotes. Also beneath the great court of Dyffryn Clwyd, and coexisting with the lordship's three commotal courts, were the courts of Ruthin borough. A microcosm of the wider lordship, the borough was subject to its own biannual great court

---

[4]   G. Jones and H. Owen (eds), *Caernarvon Court Rolls, 1361–1402* (Caernarvon, 1951); the Wrexham bailiwick extracts, or 'precedents', appear at the end of a 1391 survey. BL, Add. MS 10013. Other select cases may be found in NLW, Peniarth MS 404D. Early Wrexham bailiwick court rolls are TNA, SC2/226/17 and TNA, SC2/226/18. Notable among early fourteenth-century fragments is a 1343–4 Radnor court roll catalogued as NLW, 'Miscellaneous Documents, co. Radnor', and a 1301–2 Aberystwyth hundred roll, TNA, SC2/215/20.

[5]   From the early 1290s, debts exceeding 40*s.* were typically reserved for royal adjudication in England. P. Brand, 'Aspects of the law of debt, 1189–1307', in P. R. Schofield and N. Mayhew (eds), *Credit and Debt in Medieval England, c.1180–c.1350* (Oxford, 2002), p. 25.

of Ruthin (*magna curia de Ruthin*) as well as its own monthly borough court of Ruthin. The jury lists which form the body of evidence upon which this chapter is based were generated by the great court of Ruthin, which was usually held between mid-April and mid-May in the spring, and again in autumn during October. It was presided over by the lordship's constable and attended by the town's principal property holders, or suitors.[6]

The great court of Ruthin's suitors made judgments on, and set questions of, legal custom whenever they arose, acting as the collective memory of the community.[7] Since the beginning of Dyffryn Clwyd's surviving records, the suitors and the presiding constable together comprised the basic apparatus of Ruthin's courts, hearing complaints brought by individual litigants and manorial officials. By the 1320s there were also some innovations in the great court of Ruthin; most prominently there appeared juries of inquest and juries of presentment. These two appendages to the judicial system worked in different ways, but both effectively focused the powers of the court and its suitors in fewer hands.

Juries of inquest were small groups of men appointed by the court to determine the details surrounding a piece of litigation and to present those findings to the court, their findings typically indicating the guilt or innocence of all parties involved. Their power was limited in scope to matters concerning parties involved with the particular case they were formed to investigate, and the inquest jury's duration did not exceed the duration of that case. Extant records from Dyffryn Clwyd indicate that this form of jury was already being employed in the lordship in 1295, and quite possibly could have been known in Ruthin before that time.[8] Later court rolls of Caernarfon borough and Wrexham bailiwick confirm

---

[6]   Suit of court was a customary obligation associated with property holding, generally requiring male tenants in chief to attend all sessions of the manorial court. About fifty of Ruthin's seventy-one burgesses are specifically noted in the 1324 rental as owing suit of court, but it may be that this number should be greater given a minority of instances in which the rental does not record the terms by which certain properties were held.

[7]   J. Beckerman, 'Procedural innovation and institutional change in medieval English manorial courts', *LHR*, 10 (1992), 201.

[8]   *Dyffryn Clwyd Database*, Llann1 #31, SC2/215/64 m.3.

that inquest juries were, by the mid-fourteenth century, common throughout Wales.[9]

The second kind of jury found in Ruthin's courts – that with which we are most concerned in this chapter – was the presentment jury, for which there survive lists of members, or 'jury lists'. More comprehensively empowered, the presentment jury was not subject to the limitations of an inquest jury. It was a standing jury of twelve men appointed for the six months from one of the great court of Ruthin's two annual sessions to the next (roughly Easter to Michaelmas or Michaelmas to Easter) and, by the focus period of this study, 1312–21, presentment juries were virtually unrestricted with regard to the variety of crimes that they could report. As early as 1307 indictments had been presented in the great court of Ruthin concerning crimes as serious as theft and bloodshed.[10]

This tradition of the great court of Ruthin presentment juries in the early fourteenth century developed out of an older institution of the late thirteenth century, when two distinct groups of six assessors (*taxatores*) existed. One of these groups was simply referred to as the 'assessors of the great court' and the other as the 'assessors of court for indictment (*taxatores curie de dytamento*) concerning the assize of bread and ale'.[11] Together they probably formed what was referred to in a great court of Ruthin record of 1296 as 'the twelve of Ruthin', a body which had the power to regulate at least some market prices within the borough.[12] This group subsequently evolved into the grand jury, or presentment jury, of the great court of Ruthin and was referred to by name as early as 1312, when John Trigomed was fined for non-attendance as a member of the 'grand jury' of the great court of Ruthin.[13]

Practice varied in medieval England concerning whether presentment jurors responded to the articles presented to them at the same court at which they were appointed or whether they returned their verdict at the following court

---

[9] *Caernarvon Court Rolls*, pp. 4–8; D. Pratt, 'Medieval Bromfield and Yale: the machinery of justice', *DHST*, 53 (2004), 43–6.

[10] *Dyffryn Clwyd Database*, GC1 #214, 213; SC2/215/70 m.5.

[11] Ibid., GC1 #27, 28; SC2/215/66 m.1.

[12] Ibid., GC1 #24, SC2/215/65 m.4.

[13] Ibid., GC1 #380, SC2/215/72 m.1.

session, but there is evidence that in the great court of Dyffryn Clwyd and the great court of Ruthin jurors presented at the court following their appointment.[14] For example, on 16 October 1307 William Ross was fined for 'not coming with his colleagues to terminate articles of indictment' at the great court of Dyffryn Clwyd.[15] Presumably these men could not have been expected to appear at court for that purpose unless they had been previously appointed.[16] In the neighbouring marcher lordship of Bromfield and Yale, where jurors also presented at the court session following their appointment, presentment jurors were cautioned that if they learnt of persons guilty of felonies they should inform the steward but otherwise keep the criminals' names secret until the court's next sitting lest the felons flee.[17] The difference between these two procedures is significant. If jurors were obliged to be present on the day of their appointment concerning matters spanning the previous six months, it is unlikely that they would have been able to adjudicate concerning any but the most memorable of past events and whatever should have come to their attention on the day of court. Alternatively, appointment at one great court and presentment at the next would lend itself to a policing role in the community, where conscientious appointees would be on the look-out for offences to report on their forthcoming day as presentment jurors. This second scenario would potentially offer jurors a greater degree of social sway and control.

Into the hands of this one group, then, were gathered the powers of regulation and indictment within the community. In theory, during the second decade of the fourteenth century the court's suitors, either collectively or as represented by a twelve-man jury of suitors, still decided on questions of custom and dictated the guilt or innocence of litigants when those litigants appealed to 'the country' for judgment. But, procedurally, their authority was being undermined by the new institution of the presentment jury. By the fourteenth century, to put a case to the country for judgment in any of Dyffryn Clwyd's

    [14]   Beckerman, 'Procedural innovation and institutional changes', 228.
    [15]   *Dyffryn Clwyd Database*, GC1 #185, SC2/215/70 m.184.
    [16]   Ibid., GC1 #380, SC2/215/72 m.1.
    [17]   D. Pratt, 'Medieval Bromfield and Yale', 52.

courts appears to have been reserved for questions arising on the day of court, and then only in relatively serious cases such as land disputes or theft.

Some evidence suggests that a stage of curial development existed in the great court of Ruthin during which a certain level of criminal seriousness could warrant an examination of a presentment jury's findings by 'the country' when they were contested, but this threshold must have been eclipsed in or soon after 1312. In the surviving great court of Ruthin record, persons were allowed to have the question of their guilt or innocence put to the country only three times in the entire period before the Black Death of 1348–9, and not once after October 1312. In all three instances the accused were pleading in opposition to indictments presented against them, twice in denial of potentially capital offences, and in all three of these instances the accused party or parties were acquitted.[18] Just prior to this change, in a case of April 1312 when two young women were indicted by presentment for stealing some yarn of 'cheap clothes' (*de filo telarum vilierum* [*sic*] *furato*) and offered to put themselves on the country, the accused were 'not admitted against the inquisition of indictments'.[19] Ultimately amerced the small sum of *6d.* each, their crime was apparently not considered serious enough to warrant questioning the authority of the indictment and, in years following, the finality of the presentment jury's decisions became more entrenched.

Beckerman, who has looked broadly at procedural innovation in the manor courts of England, is 'uncertain whether trial juries (representing "the country") ordinarily were related to juries of presentment in manor courts'.[20] But in the great court of Ruthin it is clear that presentment juries

[18] *Dyffryn Clwyd Database*, GC1 #423, 424, 430; SC2/215/72 m.1. Two requests by accused persons to have their cases put to the country originated from the same community scandal, involving the theft of books later hidden in the church of Llanrhydd. The first accusation was of trafficking in the stolen books, a potentially capital crime. The second request was made by the same party denying a claim of harbouring and feeding the original identified thief of the books. The third (later) request to have a case put to the country revolved around the unrelated theft of an unspecified amount of money, another potentially capital offence.

[19] Ibid., GC1 #287; SC2/215/71 m.14d.

[20] Beckerman, 'Procedural innovation and institutional change', 215.

evolved to supersede completely trial by a jury of the court's suitors in prosecuting the borough's criminal offences.[21] Thus, ultimately, as Beckerman concludes, 'tasks previously discharged collectively by the suitors came to be initiated by the presenting jurors'.[22]

By the 1320s the grand, or presentment, jury of Ruthin was making uncontested presentments on the most serious of capital crimes, homicide.[23] With the accused denied the right to put themselves on the country in refutation of presentments, there is no evidence that after 1312 any great court of Ruthin grand jury indictment was overturned by any means. This inability to contest presentments includes denial by compurgation, the process of twelve or more men, including the defendant, swearing an oath of innocence on the defendant's behalf; a practice normally admissible in some interpersonal litigation.[24] The growing finality of presentment jury indictments throughout the period is best expressed by a court roll entry from April 1317, in which Ednyfed ap Bleddyn was amerced 'because he habitually challenges jurors of the inquisition on articles concerning peace in other inquisitions'.[25] With free rein to amerce its vocal opponents, what hope of acquittal could the presentment jury have left to those it accused?

Not only did the authority of the presentment juries grow throughout the decade 1312–21, but so also did their significance within the context of the great court of Ruthin. During these years the focus of the court was changing. In 1312 around 22 per cent (25 of 112 entries) of the great court of Ruthin's business was taken up by interpersonal litigation in

---

[21]   It is unclear when in Ruthin 'the country' ceased being all the court's suitors together and became a special jury of twelve men. There is little evidence of Ruthin's presentment jury attempting to involve itself systematically in distinctly 'civil' litigation, such as contract or debt disputes. See also, below, chapter III, for the use of presentments in some 'civil' versus 'criminal' litigation, such as theft.

[22]   Beckerman, 'Procedural innovation and institutional change', 242.

[23]   *Dyffryn Clwyd Database*, GC1 #1974, 2084; SC2/216/4 m.30, SC2/216/5 m.10.

[24]   This finding is in agreement with Beckerman, who argued that 'no denial of a jury's presentment could be proved by compurgation' (Beckerman, 'Procedural innovation and institutional change', 238).

[25]   *Dyffryn Clwyd Database*, GC1 #1273, SC2/215/76 m.14d; (*quia custumarie est calumpniare iuratores inquisicionis super articulis pacem tangentibus in aliis inquisicionibus*).

the form of licences to concord (that is, to come to an agreement) in pleas of debt, pledge and trespass, as well as some
occasionally more serious crimes such as bloodshed. These
licences to agree, which effectively sidestepped the use of a
jury by allowing disputants to settle out of court, would not
appear out of context in the records of the more regular
monthly borough court of Ruthin and by their nature typically
do not mention, nor would we expect them to involve, a
presentment jury. By 1317 the portion of business absorbed by
concords had dropped by over half to approximately 9 per
cent (5 of 54 entries).[26] Then in the great court of Ruthin
spring session of 1318 no licences to agree were recorded, and
none thereafter in the decade ending in 1321.

In 1312 around 21 per cent (23 of 112 entries) of the court's
business was linked to presentments, indictments and breaches
of various assizes brought by the grand/presentment jury of
the great court of Ruthin. By 1318 its work had increased to
encompass around 66 per cent (31 of 47 entries)[27] of the
court's business, and for the great court of Ruthin's spring
session of 1319 only a handful of entries was recorded that were
not expressly worded as presentments (around 18 per cent, or
7 of 38 entries).[28] Notably this same session, of spring 1319, is
also that for which the first list of presentment jurors survives.

On a comparative basis, the development of Ruthin's judicial system lagged behind that of parts of England (and
possibly Wales) regarding the use of presentments. Whereas
presentments did not become the principal means by
which business was brought before the great court of Ruthin
until 1318–19, it was already the dominant procedure in
Rickinghall (Suffolk) in the 1280s.[29] It is suggested in unpublished research as part of the *Dyffryn Clwyd Court Roll Database*
project that the decisive shift towards the use of presentment
in the great court of Ruthin which took place in 1318–19 may
have been an innovation prompted by the appointment of a

[26] The records of only one (of two) great court of Ruthin session survive from
this year.

[27] *Dyffryn Clwyd Database*, GC1 #1974, SC2/216/4 m.30.

[28] Ibid., GC1 #2084, SC2/216/5 m.10.

[29] L. Poos, Z. Razi and R. Smith, 'The population history of medieval English
villages: a debate on the use of manor court records', in Z. Razi and R. Smith (eds),
Medieval Society and the Manor Court (Oxford, 1996), p. 302.

new constable of the lordship between Michaelmas 1318, when John de Bekeringe was constable, and Michaelmas 1320, when Alexander de Saunterdon was constable.[30]

In 1322 the great court of Ruthin dealt with only 50 per cent as much business as it had in 1312 (52 as opposed to approximately 112 entries),[31] but in 1312 jurors had been responsible for only 22 per cent of that work. Ten years later, 100 per cent of the court's business was the prosecution of presentments. By 1322 all interpersonal litigation had been relegated to the monthly borough court of Ruthin (for which there was no presentment jury), and all presentments in the great court of Ruthin revolved around criminal acts, ranging from petty breaches of assize to homicide. This means that as the total volume of cases it handled fell, the focus of the court's proceedings narrowed. Meanwhile, the importance of the presentment jury became greater, as the volume of cases dealt with by presentment rose by about 30 per cent over the decade. Presentment jurors' decisions thus affected around 30 per cent more persons than at the start of the decade, while the nature of their work became both more authoritative and refined.

In conjunction with this, as the great court of Ruthin's civil litigation was shifted to the more frequent borough court of Ruthin, the inquest jury, which normally investigated the details of specific cases arising from interpersonal litigation, also disappeared from the great court of Ruthin (though it continued in use in the borough court). While some overlap remained between the great and borough courts, these changes left presentment juries as the sole fact-finding institution in the great court of Ruthin, the borough's primary venue for dealing with serious criminal charges.

The importance of these evolutionary aspects of the great court of Ruthin, in relation to the social status of its jurors, can hardly be overstated. By the 1320s, presentment juries'

---

[30]   This was brought to my attention by Professor Schofield. *Dyffryn Clwyd Database*, GC1 #1370, SC2/216/1 m.19d (Bekeringe) and GC1 #1494, SC2/216/3 m.18 (Saunterdon).

[31]   The 1322 case load of fifty-two is a calculation based on the twenty-six entries present in the one surviving great court of Ruthin for 1322 (there normally having been two sessions per annum).

members wielded potent powers of incrimination within the community which they seem not to have possessed twenty years before. Jury membership enabled a man effectively to pass judgment on his neighbours, determining the nature and extent of his fellows' legal infractions against one another and shaping the community's nascent perceptions of the public good.[32] Jury presentments typically included setting the value of damages due to victims by the perpetrators of legal infractions (trespass, bloodshed, purpresture, housebreaking, theft, etc.), the terms by which payment of such damages would be made and how future infractions would be dealt with (pledges for future good conduct, the threat of ejection from the town, etc.). There is a possibility that presentment jurors also acted as the court affeerors in this period, setting the value of amercements or fines to be paid to the court by offenders. The borough charter of Ruthin states that 'when (those) burgesses fall into amercement in this way (through "transgressions, pleas, disputes and contracts of all secular kinds"), they shall be amerced by their peers according to the gravity of the offence and their usual practices'.[33] While no more specific mention is made in the borough's charter or court rolls as to who were those 'peers' charged with setting amercements in the great and borough courts of Ruthin, it is likely that in a period when the power of the court as a community-collective institution was fading, tasks which could have been assigned to a presentment jury would have been so delegated.

It is only at this point that we can begin to reflect fully on the comparable, but later, range of court records available for Caernarfon borough and Wrexham bailiwick. In the court records of each of these localities by the 1360s and 1340s respectively, there appears in full bloom a similar two-tier system of biannual superior courts and inferior courts at three to four weekly intervals. Likewise, in each locality the superior court appears to have established itself as a venue solely for the reporting of criminal offences by a presentment jury, with interpersonal litigation relegated to the inferior court.[34]

---

[32] Such ideas of 'public good' and social control are dealt with in M. McIntosh, *Controlling Misbehaviour in England, 1370–1600* (Cambridge, 1994).

[33] R. I. Jack, 'The medieval charters of Ruthin borough', *DHST*, 18 (1969), 18.

[34] D. Pratt, 'Medieval Bromfield and Yale', 43–6.

Reasoning that an individual's inclusion on a presentment jury was an affirmation of his social standing or influence within the community, it follows that by the time Ruthin's clerks began consistently to record jury lists in 1319, jurors would have been key figures within the community. At the very least, jurors would have been men exercising important powers of social control, chosen to serve in that capacity because they were men most likely to have been '*au courant* of village affairs', and able to stay informed of the day-to-day events on which great court of Ruthin presentments were predicated.[35] For example, if we expand our focus period to include a jury list of 1323, it is notable that included in the first and last jury lists of the 1319–23 period are Richard *forestarius* and Hugh *faber*. Among borough property owners, these men paid respectively the fourth and twentieth highest levels of rent per annum (out of forty-eight levels), according to the Ruthin rental of 1324, and were engaged in the potentially lucrative activities of office holding and smithery.[36] Thus, both men were occupied in activities which would potentially have brought them in regular contact with a significant number of fellow townsmen.[37] Making similar observations of Wrexham bailiwick, Pratt has asserted that by 1339–40 'jurors had become, or were becoming, a select class, juries continually being made up of the same men', a development mirrored in Caernarfon by the 1360s.[38]

In this context, that of the presentment jury's waxing authority in policing and regulating the community, the extant jury lists of Ruthin have been employed in this chapter as a means by which to understand the town's social relationships. What follows is an analysis of the qualities and activities of those few in whose hands these powers were placed.

[35]   S. Olson, 'Jurors of the village court: local leadership before and after the plague in Ellington, Huntingdonshire', *JBS*, 30 (July 1991), 241. A 1391 set of jury instructions from the neighbouring marcher lordship of Bromfield and Yale states that the jury 'shall enquire diligently concerning the capital prerogatives' of the lord (D. Pratt, 'Medieval Bromfield and Yale', 51).

[36]   For wealth ranking within Ruthin, as portrayed by the 1324 rental, see chapter I.

[37]   The prominent court profile of Ruthin's foresters and parkers, as well as their ownership of multiple burgages, clearly indicate that these men's official duties by no means isolated them from town life.

[38]   D. Pratt, 'Medieval Bromfield and Yale', 45; *Caernarvon Court Rolls*, pp. 5–6.

The great court of Ruthin presentment jurors

Jury membership lists for this period exist for spring 1319, autumn 1320, spring 1321, autumn 1322 and spring 1323.[39] The fact that a different list exists for each session of court for which the record survives after 1319, be it a spring or autumn session, indicates that for each six-month period between courts new jurors were appointed, men who would then make presentments at the end of their half-year term.[40] Each of these surviving jury lists records the participation of twelve men almost equally divided between English and Welsh, ethnically distinguishable by naming practice and supplementary court roll evidence.[41] This either reflects an attempt to imitate on a smaller scale the lordship's supreme curial body, the great court of Dyffryn Clwyd, which had two juries of twelve, one English and one Welsh, or simply reflects the near-even ethnic division of property ownership and owners within the borough. In either case the status afforded to each ethnic group through jury membership was equal.

Of the two persons whose names appear in all five jury lists, one is a Welshman, Ieuan ap Einion ap 'Deen', and the other an Englishman, Hugh *faber*.[42] Of those persons appearing three or four times, five are Welsh and three English. Of those names which appear on at least two jury lists, five are Welsh and four are English. Lastly, of those persons whose names appear only once, one is Welsh and six are English. Taken as a whole, this indicates that with the status-affirming position of juror, as was case with the property market, there was a higher turnover among English than among Welsh one-time jurors. This greater turnover among English jurors is possibly a reflection of their proportionately greater wealth in the community as evidenced in table 1.1 above, allowing for a larger number of relatively affluent Englishmen who might

[39]   Jury lists: *Dyffryn Clwyd Database*, GC1 #1421, 1692, 1723, 1969, 1996; SC2/216/2 m.6, SC2/216/3 m.23, SC2/216/3 m.22, SC2/216/4 m.30, SC2/216/4 m.31.

[40]   See note 14 and accompanying text above for further details.

[41]   The ethnic composition was as follows, 1 May 1319 – 6 English and 6 Welsh, 21 October 1320 – 5 English and 7 Welsh, 19 May 1321 – 6 English and 6 Welsh, 19 October 1322 – 6 English and 6 Welsh, 12 April 1323 – 6 English and 6 Welsh.

[42]   'Ap Deen' is an unusual appellation, specific to this individual, sometimes written as 'ap Dean'.

vie with one another to take the post of juror. Viewed conversely, if a conscious effort were indeed made to balance juries between English and Welsh, the smaller pool of wealthy Welshmen eligible to serve as jurors would inevitably have led to their more frequent reappointment as jurors.

The position of juror was also firmly focused on those whose propertied interests lay primarily within the town. At least two-thirds of those appearing in the great court of Ruthin jury lists prior to 1323 had the majority of their holdings in the borough.[43] There was also only a very limited exchange of jurors between the great court of Ruthin and the great court of Dyffryn Clwyd. Of the twenty-six individuals identifiable in the five surviving jury lists of the great court of Ruthin for the period 1312–23, only one, Almary de Marreys, also acted as a juror in the great court of Dyffryn Clwyd. Far and away the wealthiest man to own property in the borough, Almary's primary landed interest lay in the commote of Llannerch. It is likely to be an indication of the great court of Ruthin's more formalized and possibly more socially influential activities after 1319 that he served on its jury in April 1321, rather than that he was an example of a burgess rising to be among the most appropriate men to represent the lordship as a whole.

If the use of jury membership as an index of social status is extended to encompass the most powerful court of the lordship, the great court of Dyffryn Clwyd, it appears that burgesses did not generally rank among the social elites of the lordship as a whole. Juries from the great court of Ruthin were consistently composed of borough office holders and tradesmen, whose names are largely familiar as borough property accumulators and high rent payers. They were not typically men with extensive holdings outside the borough (see table 2.1 below).

No less than 50 per cent of jury members can be identified as tradesmen or local office holders and, given the number of local officials rarely identified in the extant record but mentioned in at least a cursory manner, such as *subforestarius* (subforester) or *escaetor* (escheator), it is possible – if not likely

---

[43]   This is true as far as can be confirmed by the 1324 rental and surviving reliefs prior to 1323.

– that more jurors may have engaged, at one time or another, in the duties of minor office holding. Similarly, further jurors may have been tradesmen but managed to avoid repeated litigation closely associated with a particular trade. This office holder and tradesman profile is also reflected in later evidence of presentment jurors elsewhere, as at Caernarfon borough, where fourteen of fifteen known town bailiffs in 1361–1402 acted as presentment jurors, one of them an armourer (or specialized smith).[44] Lastly, for only four Ruthin presentment jurors does no record survive of their having owned any property within the borough before, or in, 1324, but at least two of these persons were office holders and it is unlikely that they would not have had some vested, if not propertied, interest in the town.

Presentment jurors and the community: personal pledging, 1312–21
How, then, did these presentment jurors conduct themselves in the community? As the great court of Ruthin was held only twice annually, the monthly borough court of Ruthin provides more rewarding material for statistical study. Virtually all varieties of litigation found in medieval manor courts, civil and criminal, appear in the borough court of Ruthin. Though the bulk of the borough's serious criminal litigation was dealt with in the great court of Ruthin, the broader variety of the borough court's diverse litigation, especially interpersonal or civil litigation, provides a much more robust body of data for study, with the borough court each year hearing approximately double the number of cases heard by the great court of Ruthin.[45]

Analysis of presentment jurors' activities in the borough court during 1312–21 is based on the data recorded in table 2.1. What stands out most clearly in this table is the number of times jurors acted as pledges, or sureties, in relation to other borough court activities. As recorded in the bottom right of table 2.1, jurors engaged in pledging around five times as

---

[44] Other Caernarfon jurors of 1381–1402 included a second armourer ('le Fourbour'), three spicers, a fletcher, a mercer, a mason and a dyer ('heuster'); *Caernarvon Court Rolls*, pp. 4–8.
[45] The borough court of Ruthin typically heard around two hundred cases each year, while the great court of Ruthin heard around one hundred cases each year.

Table 2.1. Great court of Ruthin jurors, 1312–21

Juror	Times on jury list	Welsh / English	Town based	Trade / office	Appears as plaintiff	Appears as defendant (because of failed duty as pledge)	Appears as pledge	(breakdown of cases as defendant)		
								Failed duty as pledge	Responds to common plea‡	Interpersonal litigation
Hugh *faber*	5	E	Yes	Smith	7	–	11	–	–	–
Ieuan ap Einion‡	5	W	No	–	1	–	1	–	–	–
Adam de Verdon	4	E	Yes	The lord's squire	2	5	10	–	2	3
William de Rowehull‡	3	E	No	–	7	8 (2)	11	2	3	3
Robert de Haggele	3	E	Yes*	–	2	15 (10)	41	10	5	3
William *saer*	3	W	Yes	Carpenter	6	3 (1)	27	1	1	1
Madog ap Dafydd Foel	3	W	Yes	–	8	5	1	1	2	3
Cynwrig *cissor*	3	W	Yes	Tailor	9	9 (3)	45	3	1	5
Adda Fychan	3	W	Yes	Bailiff	6	24 (12)	65	12	1	11
Iorwerth ap Bleddyn	3	W	No	–	13	6 (5)	69	5	1	–
Richard *forestarius*	2	E	Yes	Forester	1	3 (2)	12	2	1	–
John de Prez‡	2	E	No	Bailiff	–	6 (4)	41	4	–	2
Robert *faber*	2	E	No	Smith	10	6	18	–	3	7
John de Helpston	2	E	Yes	–	–	2 (1)	21	1	–	7
Ednyfed ap Bleddyn	2	W	Yes	Catchpoll/bailiff	6	22 (12)	51	12	3	7
Llywelyn Llwyd	2	W	U**	–	1	7 (5)	7	5	3	1
Ieuan Potel	2	W	Yes	Ale-taster	2	5	6	–	4	–
Jenkin Messor	2	W	Yes***	Hayward	1	1	2	–	1	–
Cadwgan Crum	2	W	Yes****	Butcher	2	6 (3)	6	3	3	1
John de Rouhul	1	E	Yes	–	3	5 (1)	4	1	3	–
Almary de Marreys	1	E	No	–	3	5 (1)	37	1	2	–
William de Thelewalle	1	E	Yes*****	–	1	3 (1)	6	1	1	1
Geoffrey *sutor*	1	E	Yes******	Cobbler	4	2 (1)	1	1	–	1

Richard de Prez	1	E	Yes	–	11	11 (5)	29	5	2•	4
Hugo de Wympton	1	E	Yes	Constable	8	3 (1)	–	1	–	2
Dafydd Goch‡	1	W	No	Ale-taster	6	17 (2)	23	2	8	7
Totals:	26 persons appearing 60 times	12W/14E 46%/54%	16 Yes 8 No 2 Unknown	15 Yes 11 Unknown	120 14%	181 22% (72)(9%)	545 64%	72 40%	48 26%	61 34%

$$
\begin{array}{r}
181 \\
- \ 72 \\
\hline
109 \\
- \ 48 \\
\hline
61
\end{array}
$$

61 times responding to other persons

$$
\begin{array}{r}
545 \\
+ \ 72 \\
\hline
617
\end{array}
$$

617 times known to have acted as pledge

Source: jury lists, as in note 3 above; other information drawn from sessions of the borough court of Ruthin, TNA, SC2/215/71–SC2/216/3.

‡ This designates an individual for whom there is no evidence that they owned property in the borough.

† This study defines 'common pleas' as any non-felony complaints (including presentments) brought by the lord, or on his behalf by his officials, and resulting in an amercement, excluding amercements arising from failing in one's duty as surety, or 'pledge'.

* Robert and his wife owned at least ½ acre in the borough in 1321 (TNA, SC2/216/3 session 6).

** In 1312 Llywelyn and his brother Madog were co-heirs of a large tract of land in Llannerch for which they paid 10s. in entry fines (*Dyffryn Clwyd Database*, Reliefs #89, SC2/215/71 m.16). Llywelyn also held property in the borough, 1/4 burgage on Welsh St which he purchased in 1317 (Ibid., Reliefs #318, SC2/215/76 m.1d.), and one burgage on Welsh St which he held in 1321 (TNA, SC2/216/3 session 8) but does not appear in the rental of 1324.

*** Jenkin does not appear in the rental but owned a tenement in Ruthin in 1316 (*Dyffryn Clwyd Database*, Reliefs #281, SC2/215/74 m.3)

**** Cadwgan owned at least one-third of a cottage in Ruthin in 1313 (Ibid., Reliefs #181, SC2/215/71 m.15d.)

***** William owned at least one burgage in Ruthin in 1312 (Ibid., Reliefs #78, SC2/215/71 m.16), is also referred to as 'lord' and had lands in other places (Ibid., Reliefs #139, SC2/215/72 m.15)

****** Geoffrey held at least 1/3 burgage in Ruthin in 1314 (Reliefs #192, SC2/215/73 m.1)

• Not counted here is an instance in which Richard was compelled to pay to have the lord's suit relaxed in a felony case of homicide until he could prove his innocence (TNA, SC2/216/2 session 9).

frequently as they appeared as plaintiffs, and ten times more often than they responded to the complaints of others in the same decade. This latter 10:1 ratio has been reached by sifting through the gross number of times great court of Ruthin presentment jurors appeared as respondents in the borough court, in order to ascertain the number of times jurors were directly confronted with the accusations of their fellow townsmen. For example, great court of Ruthin presentment jurors appeared in the borough court as respondents 181 times. From those 181 appearances have been subtracted seventy-two instances when the amercements were the result of having stood surety for someone who, when required to do so, did not attend court. From the remaining 109 appearances as respondents can also be subtracted the forty-eight cases in which they themselves responded to presentments by borough officials for such offences as escaped animals, trampling the lord's corn, gathering wood without permission and other similar activities. This leaves about sixty-one instances in which jurors were the subject of independent complaints by other individuals appearing in the borough court. By comparison, if the aforementioned seventy-two instances in which jurors were amerced for having failed in their duty as pledge are added to the surviving direct records of jurors acting as pledges, jurors appear to have served as sureties over 600 times.

Unlike many English and some Welsh communities at this time, Dyffryn Clwyd did not have an organized system of tithing, or frankpledge, which could have accounted for this pledging. Where the frankpledge system existed, as in the neighbouring marcher lordship of Bromfield and Yale, all free and servile men were pledged to one another in small groups, usually of ten men, providing mutual surety. In each of those groups, or tithings, there were one or two chief pledges responsible for the behaviour of those in their tithing.[46] But, given the absence of such organization and the chief pledges it provided, jurors' performance as pledges in

---

[46]   For a general survey of the frankpledge system, see W. A. Morris, *Frankpledge System* (New York, 1910); for an in-depth examination of aspects of the frankpledge system, see P. R. Schofield, 'The late medieval view of frankpledge and the tithing system: an Essex case study', in Z. Razi and R. Smith (eds), *Medieval Society and the Manor Court* (Oxford, 1996), pp. 408–49.

Ruthin represents an active role by jurors in the socio-pastoral care of the community. This care would then in turn have reaffirmed the role of these individuals as social elites.

The need for persons amerced in court to find surety was an immediate one. Ruthin's borough charter expressly guaranteed that 'none of them (persons amerced by the court) shall be imprisoned while he can find sufficient pledges, save for homicide, theft or other felony for which he cannot be reprieved'.[47] This provision also meant that persons not able to find a pledge, typically a pledge to ensure their payment of an amercement or fine, could be and regularly were lawfully imprisoned until they found surety or paid their amercement. This rule was most commonly enforced in cases of serious theft, but occasionally applied in various petty circumstances. In April 1312, for example, Adda Drukumero was initially to be imprisoned over a $12d.$ fine for removing boulders from one of the borough's parks, until later in the same session of the court he found a pledge.[48] Furthermore, when such circumstances arose it was typically a great court presentment juror who acted as surety. In this particular case, the juror William *saer* (as in table 2.1) served as Adda's pledge.

Unfortunately, no similarly robust body of data exists for any other Welsh town with which to contextualize the activities of Ruthin's jurors as sureties and their relationship with the wider community. However, similar English sources exist, and over recent decades historians of medieval England have given an increasing amount of attention to the social significance of these relationships, reflected by and arising out of the maintenance of this system of pledging. In particular, historians of the 'Toronto School', principally Ambrose Raftis and his students, have examined pledging in search of a sense of solidarity within rural communities.[49] In a recent response

---

[47]   Jack, 'The medieval charters', 18.

[48]   TNA, SC2/215/71 session 4.

[49]   The work of Raftis and his students is best summed up by E. DeWindt, 'Introduction', in E. DeWindt (ed.), *The Salt of Common Life: Individuality and Choice in the Medieval Town, Countryside, and Church: Essays Presented to J. Ambrose Raftis* (Kalamazoo, 1995), pp. xi–xvii. A good selection of this work is available in J. Raftis (ed.), *Pathways to Medieval Peasants* (Toronto, 1981), and a relatively comprehensive list of 'Toronto school' publications as of 1995 is included in DeWindt, 'Introduction', *Salt of Common Life*, pp. xii–xiii.

to this work, David Postles has compiled a set of core questions with which to approach pledging in any medieval
society: 'Could pledging have had alternative symbolic meanings, how personal was the commitment, and how inclusive was
pledging within the community?'[50]

Each of these questions can be applied to medieval Ruthin,
but with two principal reservations. Ruthin was probably more
urban than rural in character by the time of this study. Ruthin
was also a relatively volatile society, incorporating a newly
founded English settler community, as well as a more established Welsh community, and neither one of Ruthin's ethnic
groups possessed more than one generation's experience of
working within the framework of the borough's courts.

Previous studies have generally shown that in English
communities without a frankpledge system the majority of
sureties tended to be drawn from social elites, as at Ruthin.
But, if we begin our investigation by applying Postles's questions to the extant literature on medieval pledging, it becomes
apparent that two differing trains of thought have emerged as
to the overall significance of pledging. The first is that encompassing the conclusions of Edwin DeWindt and Sherri Olson,
of the 'Toronto School', and of Zvi Razi who have independently postulated that pledging across status and wealth
divisions indicates communal solidarity.[51] The second view is
that of Richard Smith, Martin Pimsler and Postles himself,
who have expressed the opinion that patterns of pledging
reinforced social differences.[52] In Ruthin, evidence points to
this latter conclusion's holding true, with implications for
assumptions about pledging in other locations.

[50]   D. Postles, 'Personal pledging: medieval "reciprocity" or symbolic capital',
JIH, 26 (1996), 421.

[51]   While agreeing with DeWindt and Olson on this point, Razi has been
an outspoken critic of the Toronto School's interpretation of court roll evidence
(Z. Razi, 'The Toronto school's reconstruction of medieval peasant society: a critical view', *PP*, 85 (1979), 141–57). See E. DeWindt, *Land and People at Holywell-
cum-Needingworth: Structures of Tenure and Patterns of Social Organisation in an East
Midlands Village* (Toronto, 1972); Z. Razi, 'Family, land and the village community
in later medieval England', *PP*, 93 (1981), 3–36; and Olson, 'Jurors of the village
court', 237–56.

[52]   R. Smith, 'Kin and neighbours in a thirteenth-century Suffolk community',
JFH, 4 (1979), 219–56; M. Pimsler, 'Solidarity in the medieval village? The evidence
of personal pledging at Elton, Huntingdonshire', *JBS*, 17 (1977), 1–11; and Postles,
'Personal pledging', 419–35.

As a point of comparison, let us take Olson's work on Ellington in Huntingdonshire, as her conclusions promote the idea of personal pledging as an expression of social solidarity. She states that critical to a presentment juror's credentials were social activities, such as pledging, which brought him into contact with many men not related to him from across the social spectrum; this was true in Ruthin.[53] She maintains that 'these ties did not perish with the termination of a particular association but survived by fostering long-term, even reciprocal, relationships between individuals'.[54] This was not the case in Ruthin, where relationships, while often long term, were distinctly one sided. Nor would we expect reciprocity and solidarity between elite sureties and their poorer neighbours to be the norm in Ruthin, where a fluctuating English immigrant element and ethnic inequalities of wealth would have made the practical aspects of social or fiscal reciprocity untenable.

For Olson, and other historians with similar views, a juror or frequent pledge was a man whose 'activities ... bound him to the great majority of the members of the community'.[55] The criterion which has justified this interpretation, that acting as a pledge bound the amerced and his surety, is the perceived personal commitment this relationship entailed on the part of the surety.[56] They would argue that this commitment was freely entered into, even though it was fraught with the danger of fiscal censure. Razi, for example, observed that at Halesowen (Shropshire) pledges were routinely fined $2d.$ to $4d.$ should their principal not make suit when required or lose his case.[57] Welsh evidence indicates even higher fines, as at Aberystwyth, where pledges were routinely amerced $6d.$ per instance of non-appearance by their principal.[58] Additionally, at Ruthin pledges could be held responsible for the debts of their principal, as specified in the particular case in which they had acted as a pledge. Compensation was regularly

---

[53] Olson, 'Jurors of the village court', 254.
[54] Ibid., 255.
[55] Ibid.
[56] Postles, 'Personal pledging', 419.
[57] Ibid., 422; Razi, 'Family, land and the village', 360–93.
[58] TNA, SC2/215/20 m.1.

extracted from the pledges of recalcitrant debtors at Ruthin by means of a plea of pledge.

Olson reasons that a willingness to enter into such a relationship demonstrated solidarity, and that jurors were chosen from the community, at least in part, because they perpetuated social solidarity in this way. She would have us believe that social climbers built up a relationship with the broader community through pledging and the personal relationships it generated as a prerequisite for jury selection and borough office holding. Comparative evidence from Ruthin suggests that Olson has perhaps viewed this system in reverse. Ruthin's jurors were not those most willing to bind themselves charitably to their social inferiors as pledges, but those most able to shoulder the risk of acting as a surety for personal gain and the better maintenance of their social status.

For the entire decade 1312–21, pledging is mentioned in Ruthin's surviving borough court rolls 1,631 times. Not all of these specify the pledge by name. One hundred and seventy-three court entries, especially those towards the end of the decade, simply appear in the form 'X is amerced *per plegium*' and the name of the pledge is not given. Additionally, in forty-six instances 'the bailiff' acted as the surety, but as there were concurrently Welsh and English bailiffs of the borough, many of whose identities we do not know, it is impossible to say who was being referred to at any given time. Leaving aside these ambiguities, in 1,412 instances, about 66 per cent of all court roll entries, a clearly identifiable individual or individuals stood surety in the borough court of Ruthin record between 1312 and 1321. In 617 of these instances the person standing surety was, at some point between 1319 and 1323, a great court of Ruthin presentment juror, that is for 44 per cent of the time.

Within the decade 1312–21, extant rolls show that about 1,200 individuals appeared in the borough court of Ruthin, of whom the twenty-six jurors in table 2.1 represent only 2 per cent. This means that if the amercement demanded of someone by the court was large enough in relation to his wealth to necessitate a surety of payment, a member of the tiny 2 per cent social elite who acted as great court of Ruthin presentment jurors served as that person's pledge on nearly half of all such occasions.

Proportionally, the amount of pledging carried out by Ruthin's jurors, as opposed to the jurors of Ellington (the Huntingdonshire shire community studied by Olson), was the greater. In Ellington less than 18 per cent of the known male population were identified as jurors who carried out 69 per cent of the community's pledging between 1280 and 1315.[59] In Ruthin the 2 to 4 per cent of residents (not all court litigants having been residents) who can be shown to have acted as jurors performed 44 per cent of pledging between 1312 and 1321. By Olson's reasoning this would indicate a higher, more focused, degree of social solidarity between jurors and the wider community in Ruthin than in Ellington. This is unlikely, as Ellington was a very long-established rural community and Ruthin a very young and fast-changing urban environment.

Olson tells us that Ellington's stable dominant families 'enjoyed virtually institutionalized status, according to the evidence, in the complementary functions of pledging and office holding', and yet Ellington's social power base was more diffuse than Ruthin's. Surely, if the charitable provision of surety by social climbers was a viable avenue into community leadership, then in a young urban settlement where village leadership was not yet institutionalized, numerous individuals would have been trying to scale the social ladder by this means at any given time. Yet, in Ruthin, there was only a handful of persons influential enough to be jurors, and pledging was firmly focused on these men.

This social anomaly makes more sense if we view pledging as 'the arrogation of power facilitated by economic stature and self-interest among a self-conscious village oligarchy'.[60] As a more fluid society than the long-established rural village of Ellington, Ruthin would have had a smaller pool of established families capable of, or willing to shoulder, the risky responsibility of regularly acting as pledges. The exceptional risk involved in being a pledge in Ruthin is embodied in the seventy-two instances set out in table 2.1 and in which pledges were amerced due to the failure of those they pledged to appear at court. This rate of default left regular sureties with

[59]   Olson, 'Jurors of the village court', 244–6.
[60]   Ibid., 239.

something between a 1:8 and 1:9 chance of being amerced every time they acted as pledge. Similarly, it is conceivable that those most in need of surety in Ruthin would regularly have been immigrants, a fairly large but unstable portion of the borough's population.[61]

In this environment the tiny minority of wealthy, established individuals able to contemplate the financial risks of acting as a surety could have and did use their economic stature to dominate personal pledging (as in table 2.1) and to perpetuate their narrow oligarchy. There is no evidence that they were offering their services in a show of solidarity, or as a means of establishing themselves in Ruthin's social hierarchy. Harking back to the recent origins of Ruthin's courts, it is likely that as the system in the 1320s was developing, those already in possession of substantial wealth entered it from the top. Even in the decade 1312–21, significant wealth would already have been a necessary prerequisite to afford entry into Ruthin's personal pledging market.

The record of Ednyfed ap Bleddyn shows how great the investment made by regular sureties was. He is known to have been amerced eight times totalling 2s. in the seven court sessions of 1316 for which records survive.[62] In each instance the person for whom he had provided surety failed to appear in court when required to do so. If one considers that in a typical year Ruthin's borough court was held at least twelve and sometimes as many as fifteen times per annum, his losses in this year alone may have totalled 4s. This was a sum greater than the annual property rents paid by himself and at least 55 per cent of his fellow burgesses.[63] In the short run such ongoing expenditure would have been practical only when offset by the profits of office holding, for he was described as bailiff in July 1316.[64] But, in the long run, this not insignificant investment in the affirmation of his social status served Ednyfed well, for he was again described as bailiff in October 1320.[65] Likewise, he was a great court of Ruthin presentment

[61]   R. I. Jack, 'Welsh and English in the medieval lordship of Ruthin', *DHST*, 18 (1969), 39.

[62]   TNA, SC2/215/75 sessions 1, 2, 3, 4 and 6.

[63]   See table 1.1.

[64]   TNA, SC2/215/75 session 6.

[65]   TNA, SC2/216/3 session 1.

juror in 1319 and 1322,[66] and was recorded in the rental of 1324 as a property accumulator holding two and three-quarters burgages in Ruthin.[67]

By means of investments akin to those made by Ednyfed ap Bleddyn, elites could have demonstrated and perpetuated their social dominance, and, taken to an extreme, hindered the attempts of others to gain the same social significance by monopolizing the personal pledging market. Admittedly this line of reasoning, like Olson's, involves a degree of speculation, but it would explain why in Ellington, where there resided a much larger number of long-established families competing for the same market, such narrow dominance could not have been achieved to the same degree. It may be that more intense competition in a less risky pledging market, rather than a large scale 'spirit of cooperation', may explain why Ellington, though longer established, had a more diffuse social power structure than did Ruthin.[68]

In this light, the greater amount of pledging performed by just a few men was unlikely to have been an expression of more intense social solidarity in Ruthin, as Olson's reasoning would suggest, but, rather, a flagrant expression of power by a more narrowly defined oligarchy. Some of the motives for such dominance have already been hinted at. Not least among these would have been the social affirmation necessary to maintain a position as a great court of Ruthin presentment juror, exercising all the responsibilities entailed in that position. Second is the strong correlation between pledging and the income from wider borough office holding. Lastly, there is the possibility put forward by Pimsler that pledgees may have made payments to their pledges in many instances in return for their services.[69] In this latter circumstance, which may well have existed at Ruthin, the giving of surety by elites may not have been motivated by charitable aims but, rather, by intentions which were overtly entrepreneurial.

The small elite which served as great court of Ruthin presentment jurors, who so often acted as pledges for the

---

[66] *Dyffryn Clwyd Database*, GC1 #1421, 1969; SC2/216/2 m.6, SC2/216/4 m.30.

[67] Ibid., Rental #55, 56, 57; m.7r; Jack p. 15.

[68] Pimsler first described pledging as a sign of solidarity in terms of expressing a 'spirit of cooperation': Pimsler, 'Solidarity in the medieval village?', 5.

[69] Ibid.

amerced, may also frequently have been those borough court of Ruthin inquest jurors or borough officials whose reports to the court had occasioned the amercement of their pledgees in the first place. While lists of inquest jurors were not kept in a similar fashion to those which record the great court of Ruthin's presentment jurors for this period, 202 unique lawsuits (approximately 13 per cent of the borough court's business) were resolved by the decision of an inquest jury during the decade 1312–21. Additionally, 396 cases from that decade (about 25 per cent of the borough court's business) were uncontested presentments to the borough court by individual borough officials as a result of which persons were amerced for escaped animals, trampling the lord's corn, gathering wood without permission and other infractions. Together these comprise nearly 40 per cent of cases brought before the borough court and resulting in an amercement between 1312 and 1321.

As shown in table 2.1, the extant record expressly notes eight of the twenty-six great court of Ruthin presentment jurors identified during the same decade as borough officials. It is possible that other presentment jurors also held office, but happen never to have been described as such in the extant record. Four more presentment jurors were fined between 1312 and 1321 for failing to come to inquest when called in the borough court of Ruthin, presumably to act as inquest jurors in the borough court.[70] And in the only court roll entry in this period to list the members of a borough court inquest jury, dated 1321, at least five members of that inquest jury had already served as presentment jurors in preceding years, namely, Robert *faber*, Iorwerth ap Bleddyn, Richard de Prez, John de Prez and Dafydd Goch.[71] A much earlier recorded inquest jury of 1296 also includes the names of two present-

---

[70]   William de Rouhul, TNA, SC2/216/1 session 6; William de Thelewalle, John de Rouhul and Robert *faber* TNA, SC2/216/3 session 8. These entries are each worded as '(NAME) *in misericordia quia non venit quando vocatus fuit ad inquisicionem*'. An alternative reading is that these persons were fined for not coming to answer to an inquest jury rather than to take part in one, but as this type of plea occurs only five times in the decade, and in four of these instances the person involved is a socially prominent great court of Ruthin juror, it is likely that these are fines for not serving on the inquest jury.

[71]   TNA, SC2/216/3 session 9.

ment jurors during 1312–21, namely, William de Rowehull and Ieuan Potel, attesting to the longevity of these men's public lives.[72] Moreover, close parallels are to be found in the court rolls of Wrexham bailiwick from October 1349 to September 1350, when seventeen of a possible thirty-six places across three recorded inquest juries were filled by men who acted as presentment jurors during the same twelve-month period.[73] And in Caernarfon, of the twelve men named in the town's earliest surviving inquest-jury list of 1365, at least nine would also act as presentment jurors within a few years, and three of these would serve as bailiffs.[74] Insufficient evidence survives to quantify the number of amercements levied in the borough court of Ruthin based on information provided by great court of Ruthin jurors. But it is likely that a significant proportion of those persons appearing in the borough court were reliant for their sureties on the same local social elites who determined their guilt or innocence, and their amercement.

Such circumstances would have deepened social divisions, accentuating the dependency of those regularly 'in mercy' on those in positions of influence. Thus, the butcher Nicholas de Schelton, most commonly known as Nicholas *carnifex* (butcher), paid the assize of meat to practise his trade throughout the entire decade,[75] and in 1321 he owned at least one burgage in Ruthin.[76] Between 1312 and 1321 Nicholas appeared in the borough court of Ruthin thirty-nine times in connection with thirty-three unique pleas. Nicholas was a successful plaintiff seven times, an amerced defendant in twenty-five cases and is never directly recorded as a pledge. The only surviving indication that Nicholas ever acted as a pledge comes indirectly from one court roll in which he is recorded as being amerced for his failure to deliver to the court a person for whom he had acted as surety. Nevertheless,

---

[72] TNA, SC2/215/66 session 1.
[73] TNA, SC2/226/17.
[74] *Caernarvon Court Rolls*, pp. 5–6, 24.
[75] *Dyffryn Clwyd Database*, GC1 #408, 482, 732, 794, 1014, 1070, 1276, 1383, 1718, 1743, and 1756; SC2/215/72 m.1, SC2/215/72 m.2d, SC2/215/73 m.26d, SC2/215/73 m.27d, SC2/215/74 m.16d, SC2/215/74 m.17d, SC2/215/76 m.14d, SC2/216/1 m.20, SC2/216/3 m.23, SC2/216/3 m.22, and SC2/216/4 m.1
[76] TNA, SC2/216/3 session 9: Nicholas does not feature in the rental of 1324.

despite being such a frequent loser in the courts (nearly four times as often as he found himself a beneficiary of the court), on at least four occasions a bad debtor and at least once causing his pledges to be amerced for refusing to appear in court, he successfully found a surety or sureties to stand on his behalf no less than twenty-eight times.[77]

Between 1312 and 1321 eleven persons acted as pledge for Nicholas *carnifex*, seven of whom were jurors. The juror Almary de Marreys stood for Nicholas eight times, Adda Fychan did so twice, Richard de Prez twice, Richard *faber* once, Cynwrig *cissor* (tailor) three times, Robert de Hageley twice and Hugh *faber* once. The minority of persons who acted as surety for Nicholas, but are not identifiable as jurors, were the common surety Bleddyn ap Heilyn, the prominent official and pledge John *forestarius*, and Nicholas's fellow tradesmen Thomas *carnifex* and Philip Taylor. These latter pledges stood as surety three times, once, four times and once respectively. In total, of the twenty-eight separate pledgings on Nicholas's behalf in which the pledge's name is known, nineteen (68 per cent) were conducted by great court of Ruthin presentment jurors.

Concurrently, Nicholas's dependence on Ruthin's social elites to stand surety on his behalf, while quite possibly falling foul of their presentments, demonstrates the borough court's domination by a small group of individuals. Five of the twenty-five cases which resulted in Nicholas's being amerced were resolved by a borough court inquest jury, and one amercement came as the result of an unnamed parker's presentment. If we entertain the notion that borough court inquest jurors were typically great court of Ruthin presentment jurors and that Nicholas regularly paid pledges for their service, he may have been caught in this costly loop at least 28 per cent of the time he was amerced.

This is as far as the evidence may stretch. Even in the case of Nicholas *carnifex*, 32 per cent of his pledges were not known presentment jurors. Moreover, there was no absolute uniformity among the activities of jurors. Yet a study of sureties in

---

[77]   Nicholas as a bad debtor: TNA, SC2/215/74 session 6 (twice), SC2/216/1 session 6, SC2/216/3 session 7. Nicholas failing to appear in court: TNA, SC2/215/72 session 2.

Ruthin offers a compelling alternative view to the model of pledging as an instrument of solidarity put forward by DeWindt, Olson and Razi. Comparable with the findings of Smith, Pimsler and Postles, the present study suggests that pledging was motivated primarily by self-interest among those with the economic means and social standing to act as pledge in the first place. As Postles found in late thirteenth- and early fourteenth-century Kibworth Harcourt (Leicestershire), 'pledging helped to distinguish the core from the periphery and to confine hegemony; it was a non-affective institutional arrangement designed for control'.[78]

We may recall the broad questions posed by Postles and how they are answered by the evidence from early fourteenth-century Ruthin. 'Could pledging have had alternative symbolic meanings?'[79] In Ruthin pledging is likely to have represented the extension of power by dominant elites in the affairs of the broader community. 'How personal was the commitment?'[80] In the many instances where jurors stood as pledges, they made themselves personally liable for their pledgee's actions, and it is possible that a social dependency was formed between those regularly amerced and those elites who could provide surety.[81] On the other hand, there are few signs of reciprocity across wealth and status lines. Pledging relationships in Ruthin were decidedly one sided. 'How inclusive was pledging within the community?'[82] About 66 per cent of court roll entries mention a pledge and about 44 per cent of pledging was done by 2 to 4 per cent of the population. The need to secure regularly a pledge was widely inclusive, in so far as most townspeople would at some point in their life be amerced by the court, but the initiative and wealth required regularly to take the substantial risks involved with pledging left the market for repeated surety dominated by a small number of self-motivated individuals. Closely connected with presentment-juror status, members of this elite were just as likely to be Welsh as English.

[78] Postles, 'Personal pledging', 435.
[79] Ibid., 421.
[80] Ibid.
[81] See below for a more detailed example.
[82] Postles, 'Personal pledging', 421.

Table 2.2. Random sample of non-juror court activities, 1312–21

Burgess, non-juror	Welsh / English	Appears as plaintiff	Appears as defendant / (because of failed duty as pledge)	Appears as pledge	(breakdown of cases as defendant)		
					Failed duty as pledge	Responds to common plea†	Interpersonal litigation
Nicholas Taylor	E	2	–	1	–	–	–
William Bunnebury	E	–	–	–	–	–	1
Rodger Burgess	E	2	2	5	–	1	1
Richard Carpenter	E	–	–	–	–	–	–
John de Fabrica	E	–	–	–	–	–	–
Rodger le Mon	E	–	1	1	–	1	–
Peter *faber*	E	3	4	1	–	–	4
Roger de Carlton'	E	–	–	–	–	–	–
Walter Hokedy	E	–	–	–	–	–	–
Adam de Hunte	E	–	–	–	–	–	–
Subtotals for English:	10E 100%E	7 32%	7 32% (0%)	8 35%	– 0%	2 29%	5 71%

	W							
Martin Goch	W	–	1	–	–	–	–	1
Heilyn *molindinarius*	W	–	1	(1)	1	1	–	–
Einion Bole	W	1	2	–	2	–	–	2
Hywel *saer*	W	3	4	–	–	1	1	3
Dafydd ap Bleddyn	W	–	2	(1)	4	1	–	1
Iorwerth ap Einion	W	2	3	–	–	–	–	–
Iorwerth *clericus*	W	–	1	–	2	–	–	1
Rhirid ap Llywelyn Llwyd	W	–	–	–	–	–	–	–
Ieuan ap Bleddyn ap Heilyn	W	4	2	–	–	–	1	1
Gronw ap Einion ap Hwfa	W	2	2	–	7	–	–	2
Subtotals for Welsh:	10W 100%	12 26%	18 39%	(2) (4%)	16 35%	2 12%	2 12%	14 76%
Totals:	10E/10W 50%/50%	19 28%	25 37%	(2) (3%)	24 35%	2 8%	4 16%	19 76%

Source: TNA, SC2/215/71–SC2/216/3.

† This study defines 'common pleas' as any non-felony complaints (including presentments) brought by the lord, or on the lord's behalf by his officials, and resulting in an amercement, excluding amercements arising from failure of surety.

Jurors' interpersonal litigation and common pleas

The court as an institution cannot be shown to have given special exception to jurors. Jurors' status, while reinforced by and creating authority through the provision of opportunities to act as presenters or personal pledges, was no universal protection against either interpersonal litigation or common pleas brought on behalf of the lord by his officials. Jurors were regularly amerced for common pleas such as escaped animals and trampling the lord's corn, as well as failing in their duties as a pledge.[83] It is either a sign of minimal corruption in the borough court or a hallmark of self-interest among those borough officers who stood to profit in some way from the prosecution of these pleas that jurors were as vigorously amerced for common offences as were other burgesses. As a point of reference, table 2.2 has been compiled in order to test these assumptions.

If the data derived from the random sample group of non-juror burgesses appearing in the rental of 1324, table 2.2, are compared with the data in table 2.1, it becomes apparent that jurors were more likely to be amerced in the borough court than were the non-juror burgesses in the sample group. This was the case even excluding the large number of amercements of jurors acting as pledges. As demonstrated by table 2.1 and table 2.2, there are numerous exceptions to this generalization, but on average jurors were around nine times more prone to be amerced for common pleas and over two and a half times more likely to be the subject of interpersonal litigation than were non-jurors.

This is at least partially explicable in terms of wealth. A significant number of the common pleas brought against great court of Ruthin presentment jurors was in response to livestock escaping into the lord's parks or trampling his corn. From this we may conclude that, not unexpectedly, jurors were men of such wealth as to afford more livestock than their neighbours and thus more likely to have had stray animals. In turn, the familiarity with the court which these amercements imply would have left jurors better equipped and perhaps

[83]   Nevertheless, where in table 2.1 the number of times a juror found himself a respondent was unusually large, his amercements were typically the result of numerous persons for whom he had pledged not attending court as required.

Table 2.3. Jurors compared with non-jurors, 1312–21 (average no. of appearances *per capita*)

(sample size)	Plaintiff	Defendant in pleas unrelated to pledging	(breakdown of cases as defendant)*	
			Responding to common pleas	Responding to interpersonal litigation
(26) Jurors	4.62	4.19	1.85	2.35
(20) Non-Jurors	0.95	1.25	0.2	0.95

Source: 'jurors' and 'non-jurors' results derived from data in table 2.1 and table 2.2 respectively.
* Only cases unrelated to pledging.

more willing to utilize the borough's judicial system. Hence, as Schofield found of interpersonal litigation in Hinderclay (Suffolk), a 'large number of pleas involving relatively few villagers almost certainly reflects economic and social where-withal'.[84]

Such social wherewithal probably also explains why jurors more regularly fell foul of common pleas brought on behalf of the lord for what we might view as 'white collar' crimes. For example, three of the borough court's four surviving instances of harbouring a known criminal in the 1312–21 period were brought against jurors.[85] While interesting in itself, this is a tantalizing hint as to the less quantifiable nature of an elite's or juror's role in the community. Conversely, of the eighty-two amercements levied for brawling (*brothergauetheu*) during the decade, only once was the offence committed by a known juror.[86]

As well as avoiding physical strife with non-jurors, jurors managed to avoid legal contests with one another. Of the sixty-one times in the surviving record of 1312–21 when jurors found themselves subject to interpersonal litigation, in only two suits was the plaintiff also a juror.[87] A later survey (1361–72) of litigation among Caernarfon's ten most frequent

[84] P. R. Schofield, 'Peasants and the manor court: gossip and litigation in a Suffolk village at the close of the thirteenth century', *PP*, 159 (1998), 14.
[85] Versus Almary de Marreys, TNA, SC2/215/73 session 1; William *saer*, TNA, SC2/216/2 session 11; and Madog ap Dafydd Foel, TNA, SC2/216/2 session 11.
[86] Ednyfed ap Bleddyn, TNA, SC2/215/75 session 7.
[87] SC2/215/71 session 1, SC2/215/71 session 2.

presentment jurors suggests a lack of inter-juror litigation may have been common to small-town life; Caernarfon jurors acted as plaintiffs or defendants in seventy-seven cases of inter-personal litigation without ever suing one another.[88] This is most notable because it is counter-intuitive, for, as well as being those best equipped to use the court, wealthy jurors would also have been those most worth litigating against. As Schofield has asserted, 'investment in law could be as real as investment in land' should the defendant be wealthy and prosecutable, but 'the plaintiff who sued the impecunious defendant could be wasting his or her time and money'.[89] Furthermore, the lack of this kind of adversarial interaction between jurors in Ruthin's curial setting is juxtaposed with their willingness to employ one another as sureties; sixteen of the twenty-six known jurors in question used one of their fellows as a pledge within the decade.[90]

There were almost certainly contributing factors which made Ruthin an environment conducive to this apparent soli-darity among jurors, as opposed to one characterized by the inter-elite litigation that Schofield's work suggests. Though not readily measurable, perhaps the culture of litigiousness that Schofield identified at Hinderclay had not yet emerged in Ruthin's relatively young institutions; while English immi-grants to Ruthin are likely to have had previous experience with manorial courts, Welsh townsmen of the 1310s would only have been working with these institutions for a genera-tion or so. Another influence, contributing to differing practices in Hinderclay and Ruthin, may have been Ruthin's urban, as opposed to Hinderclay's agricultural, character. It may be that in Ruthin, the existence of a middling social stratum comprised of tradesmen and women who would have had access to capital the year round (and so been worth liti-gating against) meant that litigious jurors would not necessarily have been inclined to litigate against one another. This is different from the environment revealed by Schofield's assessment of Hindeclay, as an agricultural community very

[88]   *Caernarvon Court Rolls*, pp. 6, 15–84.
[89]   Schofield, 'Peasants and the manor court', 15.
[90]   Four others either never found themselves as respondent in a suit or never had need of a pledge.

much composed of 'haves' and 'have nots' whose access to capital would have been more intimately tied to the agricultural cycle.[91]

In contrast to the way in which jurors avoided litigation with other jurors, they were liable to respond to suits brought by non-jurors, and were often compelled to do so. Richard de Prez, for example, as in table 2.1 above, has as typical a court profile as any juror. He was never litigated against by another known juror but was nonetheless subject to common pleas and interpersonal litigation with moderate frequency. In 1313 and 1314 he was amerced for damaging the lord's corn with a cart and for the escape of three of his pigs into the lord's corn.[92] In July 1319 Richard even found himself paying for the lord's suit to be relaxed concerning accusations of William Peysant's homicide, until he could find witnesses to place him elsewhere at the time of the crime.[93] Richard was also amerced three times between 1312 and 1321 as the result of interpersonal litigation brought by non-jurors. Henry le Messager, Malin the wife of William le Barker, Emma le Walkere with Henry Taylor (together) and Henry Taylor (alone), all successfully sought satisfaction against him. Richard was amerced in pleas of impediment, false claim (twice) and trespass respectively.[94] Moreover, the broad commonality of Richard de Prez's experience in a curial system common to Welsh towns is emphasized by a review of the activities of frequent presentment jurors at Caernarfon, who over a similar period, 1361–72, though refraining from litigation among themselves, spent at least 20 per cent of their time in court answering common pleas and 15 per cent of their time answering the suits of their non-juror neighbours.[95]

[91]   P. R. Schofield, 'Dearth, debt and the local land market in a late thirteenth-century village community', *AHR*, 45 (1997), 1–17.

[92]   TNA, SC2/215/72 session 2; SC2/215/73 session 7.

[93]   TNA, SC2/216/2 session 9.

[94]   TNA, SC2/215/73 session 2, SC2/215/73 session 5, SC2/216/1 session 1, SC2/216/1 session 4. It is possible that Richard was actually amerced for two separate instances of trespass in this last session. The roll is badly damaged at this point but it seems that the same plea of 'Henry le Taylor' versus Richard de Prez in a plea of trespass appears twice on the roll. This is possibly a scribal error; such duplication sometimes takes place, often one entry later being crossed out or *vacat*.

[95]   Based on Caernarfon's ten most frequent presentment jurors of 1361–1402 who, in the extant record of 1361–72, made 98 appearances, 62 as plaintiffs, 21

This type of apparently unfettered litigation between non-jurors and jurors seems to reinforce the assertion that there was no alliance between the court as a whole and the borough's social elites which would have sheltered them from interpersonal litigation. If non-jurors sought to pursue social elites in the borough court, there may have been nothing to deter them, except corruption in a system where inquest jurors may have been in a position to deliberate in cases involving fellow great court of Ruthin presentment jurors. Suggestive is a borough court roll entry of 1314, when a case in which Almary de Marreys (the richest man to own a burgage in Ruthin) had been indicted was respited until the following court because of defaulting jurors, and the case did not appear in the following court session.[96] But there survives from Ruthin no record of incidents such as that noted on a Caernarfon court roll of 1370, detailing both the amercement of a man for speaking with a member of an inquest jury 'without licence' after it had been called, and the amercement of the juror with whom he spoke.[97]

Nevertheless, we do know that even Nicholas *carnifex*, who was so unlucky in litigation, occasionally made a bid to sue known jurors, for tactical purposes at least. In July 1315, finding himself accused by Adda Fychan of owing 20*d*., Nicholas replied in the same session of court by accusing Adda of owing him 2*s*. 3*d*.[98] Each litigant was then to 'make his law', in defence, by finding eleven men to join him in swearing an oath of innocence at the next court, in August. When the court reconvened, Nicholas, unable to find eleven oath-helpers, failed in his defence, while Adda, who succeeded in finding eleven oath-helpers, so 'made his law'. As a result, Nicholas was defeated and amerced twice, once concerning Adda's debt plea and again for his own 'false claim', or accusation, that Adda had owed him 2*s*. 3*d*.[99] The outcome was unfortunate for Nicholas, but the significance of

answering common pleas, and 15 answering litigation by non-jurors: *Caernarvon Court Rolls*, pp. 6, 15–84.
[96]   TNA, SC2/215/73 session 3.
[97]   *Caernarvon Court Rolls*, p. 59.
[98]   TNA, SC2/215/74 session 5.
[99]   TNA, SC2/215/74 session 6.

this exchange is that Nicholas was willing to bring a plea against Adda at all. It is unlikely that someone such as Nicholas, with much experience of litigation, would have brought a plaint against Adda if there had not been at least a possibility of success. Nicholas had previously been amerced for a false claim against Thomas Skinner in July 1312, and must have known that failure against Adda would inevitably lead to an additional amercement for false claim.[100]

The relationship between Nicholas and Adda was not permanently damaged, however, for within nine months of the above dispute's resolution Adda was standing surety for Nicholas in another plea of debt, in May 1316.[101] As already suggested, this cycle of strife and later collusion was common in the borough court of Ruthin. Individuals appearing in court with even moderate regularity often built up an association with a particular member of the social elite and, while occasionally falling out with that person, just as often found themselves again dependent on them within a year or two.

This idea of dependency, already hinted at by the phenomenon of criminals seeking refuge in the homes of prominent jurors, contrasts with the comparatively high frequency with which jurors were defendants in cases of interpersonal litigation in the borough court (more than twice as often as non-jurors, as in table 2.3). Yet, these two findings are not contradictory. In fact they accord with the reality of a community and court system *within* the boundaries of which certain individuals strongly dominated an effective dispute-resolution system, but were neither immune nor excused from its principles and procedures. Presentment jurors in the great court of Ruthin may indeed have manipulated the system to their own ends, but they worked primarily within, rather than outside, its structures.

As is evident from table 2.3, jurors were over four and a half times more likely to initiate litigation than were non-jurors, and they brought that litigation almost exclusively against non-jurors. They too had to defend and/or press their rights in the borough court. For example, between 1312 and 1321

---

[100] TNA, SC2/215/71 session 4.
[101] TNA, SC2/215/75 session 3.

the juror and sometime constable Hugo de Wympton began litigation against men for offences ranging from unjust detention to deforcement and trespass.[102] Similarly, the bailiff Ednyfed ap Bleddyn brought before the court suits concerning trespasses, false claims and unjust detentions.[103] Even office holders of significant social standing – including Ednyfed, one of the court's most active pledges – were compelled regularly to seek satisfaction in the court in at least a proportion of their disputes. Again, they were obliged to do so, not when facing fellow jurors, but primarily non-jurors.

Conclusions about status

The cumulative impression of status in the borough, as revealed by the borough's court rolls, is one of division as well as solidarity. Even within the brief focus period of this study, the nature of the court system was changing. Many powers of the great court of Ruthin, including presentation and the regulation of assize, were coalescing in the hands of a few persons. Taken as a whole, men who were of such a status as to afford them places as jurors in the great court of Ruthin had a prominent role in the regular proceedings of the borough court of Ruthin. They dominated the personal pledging system and were the court's most frequent litigators, but they nevertheless worked *within* the framework of judicial practice available to other townsmen and women. They were regularly compelled to respond to the pleas of their neighbours at the same time as pursuing their own complaints. The practical application of their shared, elevated social status as presentment jurors (in addition often to being prominent office holders or tradesmen) contributed to their similar use of the court and tendency not to litigate against one another, but it did not afford them any special privileges or protection from the complaints of their fellow burgesses.

Given the intimate knowledge of community affairs necessary to make presentment jurors aware of the occurrences which they presented, it is likely that the great court of Ruthin presentment jury was an institution composed of socially

---

[102]   TNA, SC2/215/72 session 2, SC2/215/73 session 6, SC2/216/2 session 9.
[103]   TNA, SC2/215/71 session 4, SC2/216/1 session 7, SC2/216/3 session 6.

significant figures from its inception. Prominent members of the community, entering this institution at the top, would have developed similar court profiles characterized by the pledging activities which served to perpetuate their status. Furthermore, there followed some very limited degree of solidarity. In the extant 1312–21 record there are only two instances of inter-juror litigation, both appearing in the early months of 1312 prior to the point at which the names of presentment jurors begin to be recorded.[104]

Broadly speaking, there are similarities with the activity patterns among the wealthiest community members identified by Smith in his detailed analysis of Redgrave in Suffolk. In Ruthin town, as in the rural community of Redgrave, the upper ranks of society were at the centre of dense social networks represented by their frequent curial activities (as in table 2.1).[105] Simultaneously, they were the persons most likely to be self-reliant in society, tending to offer only dyadic relations of a patron-client type when other groups of society sought pledging and support from them.[106] While they generally refrained from pursuing each other in the courts, presentment jurors of the great court of Ruthin also refrained from regularly colluding in any way reflected in the borough court record.

The court profiles of presentment jurors, so often similar, may have served to set them apart from non-jurors, and their common curial interests appear to have promoted some degree of solidarity among Ruthin's elites. But it is hard to imagine that any solidarity would not have been tempered by the disparate extra-curial interests of the known jurors. If we take into consideration the various trades and backgrounds appearing in table 2.1, it is clear that within the borough high social status was enjoyed by widely dissimilar people. It follows that such a pattern would have been an important factor in determining with which groups of less publicly prominent individuals a particular juror would have been keen to interact. These differences are illustrated by a comparison of the jurors Almary de Marreys and Hugh *faber*.

---

[104] TNA, SC2/215/71 session 1, SC2/215/71 session 2.
[105] Smith, 'Kin and neighbours', 240.
[106] Ibid., 245.

Almary de Marreys was far and away the wealthiest man to own property in the community and simultaneously one of those most involved in the borough court, but as mentioned earlier his vast propertied interest lay outside the borough in the agricultural lands of Llannerch. As one of the lordship's great land holders, by 1320 Almary was regularly a great court of Dyffryn Clwyd presentment juror.[107] He appears as a great court of Ruthin presentment juror only in 1321, after already appearing in the borough court of Ruthin as a pledge at least thirty-six times during the preceding eight years. When Almary occasionally initiated pleas in the borough court, they tended to concern such matters as deforcement from common pasture or personal defamation.[108] An outsider maintaining only a single burgage in Ruthin, possibly a sublet property or secondary residence, Almary thus became a great court of Ruthin juror only after a long period of activity and involvement as a regular surety in the borough court.[109]

By contrast, Hugh *faber* is listed as a juror in the earliest surviving jury list and all four surviving lists thereafter, up to and including the year 1323. Like Almary de Marreys, he appears most commonly in the court record as a pledge, but in contrast to Almary he infrequently participated in litigation or the provision of surety. As shown in table 1.3, Hugh was one of the borough's prominent property accumulators, as well as an active tradesman, maintaining a forge on Mill Street ('Mulnestrete').[110] A borough juror at least as early as the spring of 1319, Hugh's more limited activity in the borough court (less than half that of Almary de Marreys) was perhaps simply a by-product of his participation in the trading community. On five of the seven occasions when we know Hugh to have appeared in the borough court of Ruthin to make a plea between 1312 and 1321, the pleas he brought were debt related.[111]

---

[107]   GC1 #1577, SC2/216/3 m.21.

[108]   TNA, SC2/215/73 session 6, SC2/215/75 session 8.

[109]   *Dyffryn Clwyd Database*, Rental #50; membrane 7d.; Jack p. 15.

[110]   Ibid., Rental #19; membrane 7d.; Jack p. 14.

[111]   TNA, SC2/216/1 session 4, SC2/216/3 session 1, SC2/216/3 session 5, SC2/216/3 session 9.

Nevertheless, this contrast of personal interests outside the court does not account for the occasional strong variances of litigation and suretyship rates appearing in table 2.1, nor are those variances clearly associated with ethnicity or wealth. If we compare Almary de Marreys with Cynwrig *cissor*, for example, the 1324 rental indicates that Almary de Marreys paid £3 7*s.* 8*d.* per annum in rents, the highest rent paid by any of Ruthin's burgesses. Cynwrig paid the nineteenth highest rent among Ruthin's burgesses, a comparatively paltry 5*s.* 6*d.* per annum. Yet, as in the data displayed in table 2.1, the two have a very similar profile of court appearances. Both men were a surety much more often than a plaintiff or defendant, infrequently failed in their duties as pledge and avoided inter-personal litigation. All the same, Almary was an English settler and Cynwrig a Welshman. While some sound hypotheses may be generated along ethnic lines (as with the distribution of wealth, discussed in chapter I), the overall impression given by the data at hand is that no strong correlation existed between the ethnicity of a juror, or social elite, and his activities in the court.[112]

To reconcile these images of a similar yet different group requires very careful handling of the available evidence. Given their differing interests, it would be inappropriate to assert that jurors, as men of high social status, were necessarily a close-knit group. Rather, and more accurately, it may be said that despite their diversity they acted as members of a loosely affiliated, mutually self-interested, social stratum with enough self awareness to avoid internal strife and to act in a commonly supportive manner regarding legal surety.

CREDITORS AND DEBTORS

Creditors in the community

It is probable that the great court of Ruthin presentment jurors shared enough common characteristics both within

---

[112] While, as stated here, the overall frequency with which jurors used the court bears little relation to ethnicity, there are differences in the frequency with which members of each ethnic group, jurors included, acted as plaintiffs or defendants with regard to a few specific pleas, in particular debt and unjust detention, as discussed below.

and outside the court setting to be regarded as socially distinct from their neighbours. Inevitably, however, the twenty-six jurors identified by the surviving jury lists of 1312–23 do not represent a comprehensive record of Ruthin's social elites. Not all persons who were influential in the community would have acted as jurors. In this section on creditors and debtors, Ruthin's society is inspected from another angle, in order to test some of the conclusions so far reached as well as to offer an alternative measure by which to identify men of potentially influential social status.

Those who held the financial reins of the borough were just as distinct a group within the community as were the great court of Ruthin presentment jurors. The volume of court roll entries in which creditors and debtors are represented will always be fewer than those associated with more ubiquitous activities such as pledging, for only a fraction of debts ever reached the borough court. Many small interpersonal debts within the community were undoubtedly incurred by friends or associates, neither occasioning a desire to have the debt recognized before the court at its outset nor actioned upon default.[113] Those cases most explicitly concerned with the lending of money, and which found their way onto Ruthin's borough court rolls, were those listed as either *placitum debiti* (plea of debt), that is a plea brought against an uncooperative or insolvent debtor regarding his or her failed obligation to repay a debt, or *iniuste detinet* (unjust detention), a plea brought against an individual for failing to produce monies, goods or services when required to do so.[114] What the court rolls contain is a record only of bad debts.

As a result, the credit-related litigation in the court record can at best be seen as a representative sample of the community's credit network. Additionally, it is worth remembering that only approximately half of borough court records survive, further limiting the volume of cases available for analysis. The

---

[113] R. Britnell, *Growth and Decline in Colchester, 1300–1525* (Cambridge, 1986), p. 103. For a good general discussion see C. Briggs, *Credit and Village Society in Fourteenth-Century England* (Oxford, 2009).

[114] The difference between these two pleas is rather ambiguous, but in Ruthin the sense of 'debt' was one of 'owing', while the sense of 'unjust detention' was one of 'withholding'.

figures in table 2.4 are thus likely to represent 50 per cent of that litigation which once appeared in the full court record, and even those comprised only a base number in need of multiplication to express fully the figure of large and small credit transactions which actually occurred in Ruthin between 1312 and 1321. That said, table 2.4 is based on the 341 cases of debt and unjust detention which appear in the extant borough court of Ruthin record between 1312 and 1321, from which have been identified the twelve persons most commonly appearing.[115] These persons are arranged in the table from top to bottom in descending order according to the combined number of times they appear as plaintiff in debt and unjust detention pleas.

Several points are apparent from an examination of table 2.4. The credit market in Ruthin was dominated by three persons; Ruthin's large-scale creditors were English; and the minority most heavily involved in lending were not necessarily the wealthiest persons to hold property in the borough. Of the 341 individual cases of debt and unjust detention appearing in the borough court of Ruthin between 1312 and 1321, either William *parcarius*, Felicity his wife, or Stephen *janitor* was the plaintiff in forty-two instances, or 12 per cent of all unique cases. While significant, this does not assign creditors a place in society as pervasive as that enjoyed by jurors of the great court of Ruthin. Nor is there any indication that a substantial enough group of persons was engaged in large-scale moneylending as to form a distinct social stratum, as was the case with regular jurors. Moneylenders like William *parcarius* and Stephen *janitor* are better compared with certain groups of Ruthin tradesmen, such as Hugh *faber*, Peter *faber*

---

[115] As was the case when compiling the data for table 2.1 and table 2.2, evidence from the great court of Ruthin and great court of Dyffryn Clwyd has been excluded from table 2.4. Given the comparative irregularity of surviving records from these courts and the unpredictable amount of interplay between them (especially the risk of double counting cases appearing in multiple/different courts) the best accuracy attainable in compiling table 2.4 has been achieved by working strictly on the evidence provided by the borough court record. The impact of including the available data from these other courts would be limited and mainly supportive. The most significant alterations to table 2.4 would be to ascribe an additional five debts and two unjust detentions to William *parcarius*, four debts and two unjust detentions to Stephen *janitor* and to exchange Robert *faber* for Hugh *parcarius* as the least active man included in the table by a margin of just one or two court actions.

and Robert *faber*, who were members of the same wider social elite as the jurors but whose significance within the community stemmed from a different social role.

Like Ruthin's presentment jurors (table 2.1) and property accumulators (table 1.3), most of those persons who regularly extended credit were local officials or tradesmen. At least eight of the twelve persons listed in table 2.4 were described as such in the court record (if we include John de Tilton, prior of the collegiate church of St Peter, Ruthin).[116] Moneylending often evolved from tradesmen's other business dealings and a close familiarity with their patrons.[117] But, most importantly, successful tradesmen and office holders were groups in possession of a steady income.

As was the case with property accumulators, only a small minority of the borough's creditors were Welsh. The explanation for this probably lies with the availability of capital. At the head of any 'pyramid of debt' needed to be a reliable source of wealth on which the creditor could draw, whenever it should be advantageous to do so. This assertion is an extension of the reasoning employed by Nightingale in her discussion of the mercantile credit relationships of London grocers in the later fourteenth century, namely, that the growth and stability of a credit network were underpinned by continued access to capital, particularly in coin rather than kind.[118] The application of this reasoning to the small credit market of medieval Ruthin risks misrepresenting Nightingale, but her general conclusion that (on the macro scale) credit provided primarily in kind could not support long-term economic expansion is borne out (on the micro scale) in Ruthin, where the rapid expansion of the borough and its economy gave way by the 1320s to an emergent focus on a few wealthy officers likely to have been in possession of capital in coin, in addition to the borough's more diffuse credit market spread thinly across a wide variety of tradesmen who could have provided credit in kind.

There is no sign that legal restrictions of any kind were in place to prevent Welshmen from becoming frequent, or

---

[116]   TNA, SC2/215/76 session 1.

[117]   Britnell, *Growth and Decline in Colchester*, p. 104.

[118]   P. Nightingale, 'Monetary contraction and mercantile credit in later medieval England', *EconHR*, 43 (1990), 560–75.

Table 2.4. Frequent borough court of Ruthin debt litigants, 1312–21

	(Creditor's details)					(as plaintiff)				(as defendant)		
Litigant	Wealth ranking (1s–48th)†	Rent paid	Welsh / English	Gross number of entries concerning debt and detention	Unique debt and detention cases	Acted as plaintiff	Cases withdrawn before pleading	'Debt' and 'detention' cases pursued	(Cases lost) ♦	Acted as defendant	Cases withdrawn before pleading	(Acquittals) ♦
William *parcarius* / Felicity his widow	NA*	–	English	33	29	29	2	27	(1)	–	–	♦
Stephen *janitor*	29th**	–	English	14	14	13	–	13	–	1	–	–
William le Serjeant	35th	2s. •	English	6	6	6	–	6	–	–	–	–
Nicholas *carnifex*	NA*	–	English	15	10	5	–	5	(1)	5	–	–
Iorwerth ap Bleddyn	(3rd–4th)‡	19s. 4d.	Welsh	9	5	5	–	5	–	–	–	–
Robert Box	NA*	–	English	6	5	5	1	4	–	–	–	–
Ednyfed ap Bleddyn	27th	3s. 5d.	Welsh	7	7	5	2	3	–	2	–	–
Walter de Lodelow	NA*	–	English	4	4	4	–	4	–	1	–	(1)
John de Tilton	NA*	–	English	6	5	4	1	4	–	–	–	–
Hugh *faber*	20th	5s. 4d.	English	5	4	4	1	3	–	–	–	(1)
Robert *faber*	6th	10s. 9d.	English	8	7	3	1	2	–	4	–	–
Totals			9 English 2 Welsh	113	96	83	7	76	(2)	13	–	(2)

Source: TNA, SC2/215/71–SC2/216/3.

♦ Due to missing or damaged judgements/outcomes the *Cases lost* and *Acquittals* indicated here are not comprehensive totals.

• Estimated rent based on a similarly sized holding in the same location.

• Comparative wealth ranking among those known to have held at least some land in Ruthin town (see chapter I).

‡ Iorwerth did not hold lands within the town of Ruthin, but by comparison with those who did, his relative wealth would have placed him between the third and fourth wealthiest.

* Does not appear in the 1324 rental.

** Wealth calculated by that of his heir *post mortem*.

semi-professional, creditors who regularly supplemented their income by extending credit to their fellow townsmen and women. But, having typically experienced diminished access to the most profitable of local offices (for example, parker/ forester), and less frequently having participated in some of the borough's most lucrative trades (for example, metal-working), Welshmen were not generally in a position to access or accumulate capital as regularly as were their English neigh-bours.[119] In moneylending, even more so than in other occupations, the availability of capital was the prime deter-minant of participation and exclusion.

Ruthin's credit market in perspective
To understand the significance of William *parcarius*, his wife Felicity (who would outlive him) and Stephen *janitor* as community lenders, we need to consider the credit market more broadly than table 2.4 allows. While there is a natural break between Stephen *janitor* and other lenders in table 2.4 based on the number of pleas he initiated, any distinction between those creditors appearing towards the bottom of the table and the other 240 or so persons identifiable as initiating debt or unjust detention pleas between 1312 and 1321 is far less sharp. Approximately 40 per cent of credit-based law suits were brought by one-time plaintiffs, and this broadly based commu-nity credit structure tapers down to the 4 to 6 per cent of suits initiated by those persons responsible for four or five pleas, before jumping back to the disproportionate 12 per cent of litigation emanating from the tiny minority represented by William, Felicity and Stephen. The overall impression this creates is of a community with primarily horizontal credit rela-tions, complemented by a very small number of frequent, or semi-professional, creditors at the top of the credit structure's natural pyramidal hierarchy.

No comparable study of a similar small borough in Wales or elsewhere has yet been published but, despite Ruthin's burgeoning urban rather than rural character, the commu-nity's credit structure was not dissimilar to that which Elaine

---

[119] As shown in chapter I, parkers, foresters and smiths were prominent among the town's most affluent burgesses.

Table 2.5. Borough court of Ruthin debt and unjust detention plaintiffs, 1312–21

Number of pleas initiated	Number of unique persons	Percentage of all pleas they represent*
6 or more	3	12%
5	4	6%
4	3	4%
3	14	12%
2	36	21%
1	135	40%

Source: TNA, SC2/215/71–SC2/216/3.
*Plaintiff unclear in about 5 per cent of cases due to damage to the original record.

Clark identified in the records of the fifteenth-century rural community of Writtle (Essex).[120] This was a system in which the dominant type of credit relationships to be found in the community were arranged in a socially horizontal manner, with persons of similar wealth and social status acting as creditors for one another. In contrast to this overall pattern, at Ruthin there were certainly some very specialized lenders, as exemplified by William *parcarius*, Felicity his wife and Stephen *janitor*, but they were an exception to the social norm.

There also were commonly enduring relationships between the same creditors and debtors over time, as was the case between frequent sureties and defendants, despite the influence of any individual creditor on his or her debtor having been potentially far more intimate than the influence of socially elite sureties on the persons for whom they pledged. For example, two of the four cases initiated by Hugh *faber* (in table 2.4) were against the same Meurig *cocus* (cook), separated by just under three years.[121] The same is true of Robert Box, who initiated and then withdrew a plea of debt against Thomas le Hare in August 1317, only to be his creditor again by February 1321.[122] This was the case with Walter de Lodelow, who had to seek legal recourse against Nicholas *carnifex* in

[120] E. Clark, 'Debt litigation in a late medieval vill', in Raftis (ed.), *Pathways to Medieval Peasants*, pp. 247–79.
[121] TNA, SC2/216/1 session 4, SC2/216/3 session 5.
[122] TNA, SC2/215/76 session 4, SC2/216/3 session 5.

March 1313 and found himself in the same position by July 1318.[123]

In this manner, Ruthin's borrowers tended to accumulate debt, despite a propensity to borrow from relative social equals, a point on which Ruthin's credit relations differed from those studied by Clark at Writtle. Clark somewhat ambiguously suggested that debt was most frequently comprised of reciprocal or potentially reciprocal agreements in which two persons borrowed from one another whenever they found it mutually beneficial to do so.[124] Ruthin's debts tended more toward the type of accumulation noted in a similar study by Briggs of Oakington, Cottenham and Dry Drayton (Cambridgeshire).[125] A very good example of this appears in the Ruthin borough court roll of March 1314:

> iii *d*. —— Roger *cirothecarius* [glover] and Agnes his wife complain of Thomas le Taskere concerning a plea that the said Thomas unjustly detained from them xxi*s*. ix*d*. which the said Agnes before she was contracted in marriage to the said Roger handed over to him [Thomas] through parcels underwritten. Namely in pence, vi*s*. in the first instance, iii*s*. vi*d*. on another occasion and iii*s*. vi*d*. on a third occasion, and ii quarters of oats valued at viii*s*. and iii hopes of wheat valued at xxi*d*. to the damage of Roger and Agnes etc. And the said Thomas comes and totally denies all of this and says that he received v*s*. from which he bought a tunic from the said Agnes and iii*d*. which gained interest (*approviavit*) to xii*d*. and this he handed over to the said Agnes and concerning this he places himself on the country. And the said Roger and Agnes say that he has paid nothing to them of the said money and according to this has unjustly detained (these things from them). And concerning this they put themselves on the country. And the Jury says that the said Thomas has paid nothing of the said money whence damages are assessed at ii*s*. Therefore the decision is that the said Roger and Agnes are to recover the said money and the said Thomas is in mercy per a pledge.[126]

---

[123]   TNA, SC2/215/72 session 2, SC2/216/1 session 6.

[124]   Clark, 'Debt litigation', pp. 265, 270.

[125]   C. Briggs, 'Creditors and debtors and their relationships at Oakington, Cottenham and Dry Draton (Cambridgeshire), 1291–1350', in P. R. Schofield and N. Mayhew (eds), *Credit and Debt in Medieval England, c.1180–c.1350* (Oxford, 2002), pp. 127–48.

[126]   TNA, SC2/215/73 session 5.

Here is demonstrated the reality of debt accumulation between two persons, revealing the intimate relationships involved. We do not know over what period of time Thomas acquired so many notable debts to Agnes but collectively they represent a very substantial sum. This kind of scenario may have led to numerous debts being noted in the court record by less full entries.

It is also likely that in Ruthin debts of account, like that exemplified here by Thomas le Taskere's ongoing dependence on Agnes, represent the 'lower tier' of a two-tier debt system. This lower tier was occupied by cyclically exploitative relationships typically existing between a financially secure individual and someone not greatly less affluent but regularly less solvent. For example, none of the creditors specifically mentioned thus far – neither Agnes, her husband Rodger *cirothecarius*, Hugh *faber* nor Walter de Lodelow – was respondent to a debt or unjust detention plea in the extant borough court records of 1312–21. Alternatively, all the respondents specifically mentioned – Thomas le Taskere as well as Meurig *cocus* and Nicholas *carnifex* – were repeat borrowers. While these creditors and debtors were relative social equals, it is not suggested that this lower tier of credit relations represents 'social solidarity', as the creditor/debtor relationships appear to have been one sided.

The upper tier of Ruthin's debt system was comprised of a tiny group of specialized, semi-professional creditors. In the 1312–21 period these were William *parcarius*, his wife Felicity and Stephen *janitor*. Like great court of Ruthin presentment jurors, this probable social elite did not litigate between themselves, and are likely to have been those from whom persons sought aid (in this case financial) if otherwise frustrated.

Conclusions on creditors and debtors in Ruthin's society
The patterns of social structure and interaction revealed by an examination of Ruthin's credit market, and those persons it brought to the fore, are compellingly similar to those already revealed by reviewing the actions of Ruthin's jurors. Just as the personal pledging market was dominated by a very narrow social elite, so too does there appear to have been a narrow hierarchy of elite persons atop Ruthin's credit market

(table 2.5). Those few individuals most disproportionately involved in lending, William *parcarius*, his wife Felicity and Stephen *janitor*, are likely to have been established social notables extending their influence into the credit market from above. William and Stephen bear the hallmarks of other members of the borough's social elite previously discussed in this chapter. William, as well as being a parker between 1312 and disappearing from the court record after June 1316, was a prolific litigator, his name appearing in the court record of 1312–21 no less than thirty-four times.

Similarly, Stephen *janitor* (castle porter, or gate keeper) was active throughout the decade and maintained more than an honorary role as an office holder, since he appears in a record of goal delivery for Dyffryn Clwyd from Michaelmas 1320 as having been attacked by night in his chamber at the castle.[127] He was active in the borough court until April 1321 and must have been a property accumulator, as his son and heir Hugh appears in the rental of 1324 holding three burgage plots in the borough.[128] Together, these roles of office holder and property accumulator probably provided the social status and capital necessary to be a prominent creditor.

It may further be observed that most persons who appear in table 2.4, while not acting as creditors frequently enough to warrant identification as socially dominant lenders (on the same scale as William, Felicity and Stephen), also have names recognizable from earlier sections of this study that set them apart as members of the borough's social elite.[129] As with Ruthin jurors' prominent role as sureties, the borough's creditors controlled a disproportionate share of the market. Twelve per cent of Ruthin's debt and unjust detention suits were brought by 0.5 to 0.6 per cent of the borough's population.

As was the case with property accumulation, the opportunity to prosper as a semi-professional, upper-tier creditor was both conceptually and ethnically unrestricted, yet somewhat practically limited by the amount of capital necessary to enter the market. Ruthin's most prominent creditors were not the

---

[127] *Dyffryn Clwyd Database*, GC1 #1555, SC2/216/3 m.19.
[128] Ibid., Rental #17, membrane 7d, Jack p. 13; Rental #18, membrane 7d, Jack p.13.
[129] See table 2.6 below.

borough's highest rent payers but both William *parcarius* and Stephen *janitor* were office holders. It is also likely that, as was the case with property accumulators, creditors may have used office and high-value trade revenues as a resource, allowing them to generate an income higher than the amount they paid in rents would suggest. Thus, it is not surprising that by this measure, too, Welshmen, themselves less often office holders or metalworkers, are not as well represented as their English counterparts.

The overall picture of the credit market in Ruthin is that it was beginning to be used and commercially exploited by a few persons who were already by 1321 influential social figures, but not yet numerous enough to comprise an independent social elite. During the period of this study, Ruthin was dominated by intimate credit relationships, maintained between individuals of similar wealth. While credit was more typically extended in only one direction within these personal relationships, making indebtedness more prone to accumulation than to reciprocation, the bulk of relationships are not shown by the borough court record to be of a highly formalized or professionalized nature. As of 1321, this predominance of one-to-one indebtedness was more likely to have fostered intimate (if unequal) interpersonal ties among town dwellers of the same social stratum than the exclusivity perpetuated by jurors within the personal pledging market. But, as the examples of William *parcarius* and Stephen *janitor* show, seeds of specialization and juror-like dominance were present within the community's credit network.

CONCLUSION

Nothing quite so developed or homogeneous as a 'social class' existed in Ruthin at this time, but we can nonetheless identify groups of borough residents which comprised 'social strata'. Indeed, there were at least two distinct social strata present in early fourteenth-century Ruthin. The topmost, or most socially elite, of these was composed of men entering it from different points and inevitably sharing common interests and activities, such as great court of Ruthin presentment jury duty, service as borough court inquest jurors, property accumulation/speculation, money lending, surety provision and office holding. The second social stratum was composed of everyone else of sufficient affluence to be picked up by the court record, essentially those who could afford to litigate or those against whom another individual (or even the court) deemed solvent enough to warrant litigating. Almost certainly, alongside these existed a third stratum whose gender, absolute poverty, or 'marginal' status allowed them to escape the written record.

Within the borough and encompassed by this social hierarchy were two populations, a Welsh community focused on Welsh Street and a growing English community focused on the adjoining Castle Street. Probably by 1312, and almost certainly by 1321, these two communities were engaged in the process of integration, with Welsh and English living side by side throughout the rest of the town. When examined through the prism of property ownership and investment (from within as well as without the town), jury service and non-professional moneylending, Welshmen and Englishmen can be seen engaging in the same types of behaviour. The only exception to this was large-scale, semi-professional moneylending.

Measured by these social indicators, Welshmen were to a degree less prevalent or materially affluent than their English counterparts. For this, there are two likely explanations, both revolving around the availability of capital. First, the borough of Ruthin was an English foundation essentially placed on top of a Welsh community, and as English settlers arrived to take up either permanent or temporary residence within the borough they would have brought with them capital with which to establish themselves. This capital allowed them to settle in a more affluent manner than that of their Welsh counterparts. Secondly, those who would become the English component of Ruthin's upper social stratum, or elite, capitalized on the borough's wealth-producing potential in ways which Welshmen did not or could not readily grasp. These Englishmen tended to be tradesmen in lucrative industries such as metal working, and held lucrative offices such as that of borough parker or castle porter, both occupational groups which were largely English preserves. In these ways, Englishmen, with more capital on arrival and from their commercial and official activities, were able to perpetuate their higher degree of affluence within the community.

However, ethnicity should not be overemphasized; the socially pervasive levelling factor of prosperity, regardless of ethnicity or background, was available capital. No legal restrictions can be shown to have been placed on Welshmen within the borough. Welshmen with dispensable capital, such as William *saer* and Ednyfed ap Bleddyn, a tradesman (carpenter) and Welsh bailiff respectively, met with success equal to that of any Englishman in maintaining their status and prosperity within the community. Furthermore, as can be determined from the borough's court rolls, the broad intra-curial interests and activities of Ruthin's upper stratum were homogeneous and regardless of ethnicity.

Table 2.6 provides an example of the continuity and cross-ethnic unity of activity among Ruthin's elite social stratum between 1312 and 1321. Were this table expanded, an even greater degree of continuity would be apparent. In table 2.6 English names appear twenty-eight times and Welsh names appear twenty times. Among these forty-eight table entries, are the names of only nineteen individuals. To put this in perspective: if, as is surmised, the borough contained around five hundred residents, and were table 2.6 expanded to encompass a slightly wider range of persons identifiable as members of the borough's social elite (around twenty persons for the sake of easy division), Ruthin's upper social stratum would only include about 5 per cent of the borough's population as a whole.

Finally, the actions of these elites rather than ethnic divisions tell us most about Ruthin's social organization. In the borough environment there were two social systems at work, one of unity and another of dichotomy. Unity is suggested by the high proportion of personal credit relationships, roughly 61 per cent as indicated by debt litigation records, which were distributed across a broad swathe of the community, that is to say, credit relationships which were between debtors and non-professional creditors who initiated only one or two debt suits between 1312 and 1321 (see table 2.5).[130] Unity is also

---

[130] It is important to recognize the difference between unity and solidarity here. Unity was expressed by persons of similar wealth and status forming credit relation-

suggested by the fact that, despite 44 per cent of all pledging being done by a small social elite, the majority of identifiable sureties in 1321 was still a diverse group composed of unremarkable persons from Ruthin's non-elite social stratum who stood surety for their kin, friends, neighbours and acquaintances. Similarly, there existed unity of action, and some evidence of solidarity, in the upper social stratum, as is conveyed by table 2.6.

The other side of this coin is the social dichotomy indicated by the 2 to 4 per cent of persons who dominated 44 per cent of Ruthin's personal pledging. Dichotomy is visible in the controlling influence this minority must have exerted in the community, as great court of Ruthin presentment jurors, property accumulators and landlords, borough officials and probably even as borough court inquest jurors. Further to the 44 per cent of personal pledging undertaken by this group, just three likely members of Ruthin's top social stratum dominated at least 12 per cent of the community's credit market. While members of Ruthin's elite social stratum were as dissimilar in background as they were similar in the way they used the borough's courts, making suggestions of a 'class' inappropriate, many of their interests and concerns cannot have been entirely incongruous.

This image of the community is most illuminating when used to contextualize an event, such as the rebellious attack on the castle of Ruthin which occurred in May 1321. During that month a group of at least 125 Welshmen, later charged in a special court, assaulted the castle 'by unanimous assent out of aforethought malice (*ex malicia precogitata*)', plundered the town, killed two Englishmen and burnt the house of Ieuan Potel.[131] As local men of significant status, we would expect that any one of the twelve Welshmen who had served as a great court of Ruthin presentment juror during the preceding decade would have made a natural, popular leader of revolt within the community. However, none of these men joined in the uprising. In fact, it is unlikely to have been a coincidence that the Welshman Ieuan Potel, twice a juror as well as an

ships among themselves. These relationships were not mutually beneficial, and do not necessarily express any solidarity of the variety discussed elsewhere in this study.

[131] *Dyffryn Clwyd Database*, GC1 #2014, SC2/216/4 m.32.

Table 2.6. Elites by indicator*

	Top 11 credit litigators	Top 11 wealthiest by rental (in borough)	Top 10 most frequent jurors	Top 11 most frequent pledges	Top 6 most prolific property accumulators
1.	William *parcarius* and Felicity his wife/widow	Almary de Marreys	Hugh *faber*	Iorwerth ap Bleddyn	Richard *forestarius*
2.	Stephen *janitor*	Hugh *parcarius*	Ieuan ap Einion	Adda Fychan	Hugh *parcarius*
3.	William le Serjeant	Dafydd ap Bleddyn	Adam de Verdon	Bleddyn ap Heilyn	William *saer*
4.	Nicholas *carnifex*	Richard *forestarius*	William de Rowehull	Ednyfed ap Bleddyn	Dafydd ap Bleddyn
5.	Iorwerth ap Bleddyn	Henry le Messager	Robert de Haggele	Cynwrig *cissor*	Hugh *faber*
6.	Robert Box	Robert *faber*	William *saer*	Robert de Haggley	Stephen *janitor* (per his son Hugh)
7.	Walter de Lodelow	Iorwerth ap Ieuan	Madog ap Dafydd Foel	John de Prez	
8.	John de Tilton	Richard de Prez	Cynwrig *cissor*	Almary de Marreys	
9.	Ednyfed ap Bleddyn	Peter *faber*	Adda Fychan	Richard de Prez	
10.	Hugh *faber*	Ieuan ap Philip Culla	Iorwerth ap Bleddyn	William *saer*	
11.	Robert *faber*	Ieuan ap Heilyn	John *forestarius*		
Persons not appearing in another column	7	5	4	3	0
Number of Welsh and English in each column	9 English 2 Welsh	7 English 4 Welsh	6 Welsh 4 English	6 Welsh 5 English	4 English 2 Welsh

Source: TNA, SC2/215/71–SC2/216/3; *Dyffryn Clwyd Database*, 'Rental'; TNA, WALE 15/8/1, Jack 'Records of Denbighshire lordships II'; and as above table 1.3, table 2.1, table 2.4.

*The number of names placed in each column was dictated by a natural break in each respective data-set; that is, when the activities of persons decreasingly well suited for inclusion in a particular column varied suddenly and significantly from their better suited fellows. This has been done in order to keep the size of the table manageable.

office holder in preceding years, found his home targeted in the raid's only incidence of arson.

The attackers were mostly, but not exclusively, from the outlying lands of 'Edeirnion, Ardudwy, Penllyn and Merioneth', beyond the borders of Dyffryn Clwyd, and if they had hoped that the Welsh of Ruthin would rise up to help seize the castle they were mistaken. By 1321 the vested interests of the borough's Welsh elite lay in the community's better maintenance and trade with their English neighbours, not in the town's destruction. Social elitism as expressed by the opportunity to dispense justice as a juror, or prosper through various entrepreneurial activities, rested in the hands of men whose future lay in stability and the better protection of their social status through prudent action. In early fourteenth-century Ruthin, social standing was a more potent factor in determining a person's actions than ethnicity or social background.

Part 2

WOMEN IN THE BOROUGH: ACCESS TO CAPITAL AND OCCUPATION

Part 2 tests the ideas presented in Part 1 through a case study of Ruthin's women, as they appear in the borough's early fourteenth-century court rolls. In summary, these ideas are: that access to capital was the prime determinant of the range of occupations open to any particular group of urban dwellers; that there was a very close association between occupation and social status; and that a degree of mutual and self-protection was consciously exercised by trade and status groups across the wealth spectrum. In conducting this case study, Englishness versus Welshness has been considered throughout, but issues of ethnicity have only been given particular focus where it appears that the Welsh cultural context had an especially strong role to play. Pride of place has instead been given to the cross-cultural consequences of social and economic dislocation caused by the great famine of 1315–22 and, to a lesser extent, the tendency towards 'lawlessness' in the Welsh March.[1]

The following chapters are designed to construct a relatively comprehensive, if necessarily representative, image of urban women in the early post-conquest Welsh March. Chapter III begins with an examination of the nature of female representation in the court record and how this relates to women's general role in the community, before considering those townswomen with the highest levels of investment capital, Ruthin's brewsters. The activities of townswomen with moderate levels of investment capital are detailed in chapter IV by, first, concentrating on the borough's bakeresses, and then by offering a more general assessment of other skilled tradeswomen. Finally, chapter V considers the range of women who possessed little or no investment capital – the

---

[1]   R. R. Davies, *Lordship and Society in the March of Wales, 1282–1400* (Oxford, 1978), pp. 3–11.

borough's female victuallers, cloth workers and service women – and ends with conclusions about women in the borough. In these chapters, examining in detail Welsh urban life in the first half of the fourteenth century, we are almost totally dependent on the records of Ruthin and English sources, as no contemporary source material survives from elsewhere in Wales.

III

CURIAL REPRESENTATION, BREWSTERS AND WOMEN WITH HIGH LEVELS OF INVESTMENT CAPITAL

WOMEN'S ACCESS TO THE COURTS

With the notable exception of a small group of writers, including Jeremy Goldberg, Judith Bennett and Maryanne Kowaleski, the historiography of the medieval economy has been overwhelmingly subject to a 'one-sex model' in which the day-to-day labours and aspirations of medieval women have been largely neglected.[2] This inequality of treatment is partly due to the general inability of most centrally produced documents, such as the records of the chancery or exchequer, to offer explicit information about the role of women in the medieval economy. It is only recently that historians of medieval women have directed their attention to the more voluminous, though less accessible, local records (especially manorial and borough court rolls) in which the actions of women are more frequently detailed. At the same time, the significance of women's appearances in these local documents, which were produced by institutions in which the role and status of women are often unclear, is not easy to identify.

The use of Ruthin's female, rather than male, residents in this case study of the borough's society and economy is an attempt to redress this historiographical imbalance and to contribute to an emerging field of enquiry. But inherent in the use of Ruthin's court rolls in this way is the problem of deducing the manner and extent to which Ruthin's women made use of the courts. It is essential to look beyond the

---

[2] N. Partner, 'Introduction', *Speculum*, 68 (1993), 306 (this volume is a special edition dedicated to the historiography of medieval women's history); P. J. P. Goldberg, *Women, Work and Life Cycle in a Medieval Economy: Women in York and Yorkshire, c.1300–1520* (Oxford, 1992); J. Bennett, *Women in the Medieval English Countryside: Women's Work in a Changing World, 1300–1600* (Oxford, 1996); M. Kowaleski, 'Women's work in a market town: Exeter in the late fourteenth century', in B. Hanawalt (ed.), *Women and Work in Preindustrial Europe* (Bloomington, 1986), pp. 145–64.

narrow, literal interpretation of women in the court record as governed by a doctrine of female disability in an overtly masculine environment, and to attempt to qualify and quantify this disability so as to lay the foundations for an empirical study of the borough's women.[3]

Under English common law as practised in the king's law courts at Westminster, and ostensibly imported to the new boroughs of Wales, women were subject to a variety of gender-specific personal limitations collectively referred to as coverture.[4] In summary, the common law concept of coverture held that a woman was subject to the legal guardianship of her father until she married, at which time she passed to the guardianship of her husband, and would only come to enjoy legal autonomy, should she outlive her spouse, as a widow. In theory, non-widowed women could therefore not independently possess property, make contracts, hold public office, or represent themselves before the courts. In reality, local legal practice often deviated, sometimes quite significantly, from the strict observance of coverture. At Ruthin, as will be shown, non-widowed Welsh and English women possessed property, transacted local business and were often before the borough's courts.

Moreover, for all social groups, and especially widely under-represented groups such as women, the court record is merely one area in which a high concentration of some varieties of social dispute found their way into the legal record. Other kinds of business may have been spread across a variety of agencies. As Roberts argues of dispute resolution in pre-modern courts, there is always a 'disparity between the form in which a dispute appears in the court and the "real" substance of the quarrel which gives rise to it … and that disputants will probably know this and present the matter in such a way that the court is prepared to hear it'.[5] Hence as long as those legal devices employed by under-represented groups such as

[3]   Bennett, *Women in the Medieval English Countryside*, p. 38.

[4]   For an overview of the rights of women in the royal courts, see F. Pollock and F. W. Maitland, *The History of English Law Before the Time of Edward I*, vol. 2, 2nd edn (Cambridge, 1968), pp. 403–5.

[5]   S. Roberts, 'The study of dispute: anthropological perspectives', in John Bossy (ed.), *Disputes and Settlements; Law and Human Relations in the West* (Cambridge, 1983), p. 22.

Ruthin's townswomen were applied consistently, and we are aware of the manner in which women's litigation was brought before the court, we need not consider the evidence of women in the courts to be any less reliable or informative than that pertaining to men.

Subject to a theoretical lack of independent recognition before the common law (in so far as it seems to have been observed in Ruthin), both in their minority and while married, women are chronically under-represented in Ruthin's court record. In the years 1312–21 approximately 246 women and 948 men are named in the borough court of Ruthin and approximately 193 women and 240 men, not present in the borough court's records, are named in the great court of Ruthin. While the use of non-specific names renders these figures imprecise (persons identifiable in the borough court may have appeared under a different name in the great court), a cumulative total would be approximately 1,627 persons, of whom 27 per cent (439) were women and 73 per cent (1,188) were men.[6] However, despite this under-representation, the manner and extent to which these women can be shown to have utilized the courts were consistent and explicable.

Borough court of Ruthin versus great court of Ruthin
Across the ten years 1312–21, the proportion of great court of Ruthin and borough court of Ruthin court roll entries citing at least one female 'litigant' is virtually identical (table 3.1 (A)).[7] This is despite the great court of Ruthin's having been

[6]   Similarly, Razi found of persons named in the courts of Halesowen in five-year sample periods: 1301–5, 24 per cent women, 1311–15, 30 per cent women, 1321–5, 29 per cent women (Z. Razi, *Life, Marriage and Death in a Medieval Parish: Economy, Society and Demography in Halesowen, 1270–1400* (Cambridge, 1980), p. 25). Poos and Smith observed that in the records of Great Waltham and High Easter in the later fourteenth century, married women in particular were less than half as likely to be named in local court rolls than were their husbands (L. Poos, Z. Razi and R. Smith, 'The population history of medieval English villages: a debate on the use of manor court records', in Z. Razi and R. Smith (eds), *Medieval Society and the Manor Court* (Oxford, 1996), pp. 307–8). (Note, however, that this book does not attempt to generate demographic data based on these figures.)
[7]   Here the term 'litigant' is used to denote a named participant in either actual or implied litigation. Actual litigation encompasses interpersonal pleas, including 'common pleas'; implied litigation encompasses disputes which have followed a different course, for example, to presentment. The emphasis of these definitions of the terms 'litigant' and 'litigation' is on female agency in the legal process

what one may loosely refer to as a higher court, and more frequently concerned with relatively high value, interpersonal litigation and felony cases than was the borough court. The nature of women's participation in these courts differs in the frequency with which they used this judicial machinery, rather than in being subject to it. Women less frequently initiated pleas in the great court of Ruthin than they did in the borough court. In fact, women's 'entry-appearances'[8] as plaintiffs in the great court of Ruthin account for only about 38 per cent (66 of 176) of those entries featuring at least one female litigant, as opposed to around 50 per cent (202 of 405) at the borough court level. This is contrary to the trend among male litigants, for whom the portion of entry-appearances in which they acted as plaintiff was higher in the great court of Ruthin at 59 per cent (294 of 499) than at the borough court level at 42 per cent (945 of 2,247).

Nevertheless, we should not read too much curial 'disability' into the reduced proportion of female plaintiffs in the great court of Ruthin as opposed to the borough court. This imbalance (table 3.1) is primarily a result of two circumstances, which combine to give the misleading impression that women were poorly equipped to access the borough's higher court. First, only a relatively low number of women initiated many of those varieties of civil litigation most common to the great court of Ruthin, such as high value debt, unjust detention and contract cases. In each of these pleas, women were less likely than men to make entry-appearances as plaintiffs and slightly more likely to appear as defendants than as plaintiffs. Across the decade 1312–21, these pleas accounted for 36 per cent (105 of 294) of entry-appearances by male plaintiffs and 34 per cent (101 of 294) by male defendants; while in contrast only 15 per cent (10 of 66) of entry-appearances were made by female plaintiffs and 26 per cent (17 of 66) of entry-appearances by female defendants.

Secondly, women were less often plaintiffs in the great court of Ruthin because they were disproportionately unlikely

irrespective of procedural developments, such as those that affected Ruthin's great court which moved steadily toward a presentment-based system throughout the 1312–22 decade.

[8]   See table 3.1 for the definition of 'entry-appearances'. See above, chapter II, for more on presentments in Ruthin's courts.

Table 3.1. Women in Ruthin's courts, 1312–21

		Borough court of Ruthin		Great court of Ruthin	
(A)	Proportion of all court roll entries citing a female 'litigant'	405 of 1702 Approximately ¼		176 of 680 Approximately ¼	
(B)	Entry-appearances[†]	Answering common pleas / regulatory presentments[*] 60		Answering common pleas / regulatory presentments[**] 53	
		Interpersonal litigation 407		Interpersonal litigation 154	
		As plaintiffs	As defendants	As plaintiffs	As defendants
	Versus men	143	146	35	57
	Versus women	59	59	31	31
	Subtotals (% of A)[•]	202 (50%)	205 (50%)	66 (38%)	88 (50%)
	Portion of all inter-persona entry-appearances	50%	50%	43%	57%
	Total entry-appearances	467		207	

Source: TNA, SC2/215/71–SC2/216/3.

[†] 'Entry-appearances' have been calculated as the number of court roll entries in which one or more members of a particular gender group (either men or women) are present among plaintiffs and/or defendants. This is a measure of representation in the court record by female and male gender groups, not a per capita measure of the individuals involved. The focus is therefore on the number of cases in which one or more women acted as plaintiffs, and the number of cases in which one or more women acted as defendants. For example, if we had the court roll entry 'female A and male A appeared versus female B and female C', this single court roll entry would account for one entry-appearance by men and two entry-appearances by women, once in the role of plaintiff and once in the role of defendant. This system obviously only allows a maximum of two entry-appearances per gender group per original court roll entry.

[*] This includes entry-appearances by women in response to common pleas and presentments brought directly by the court, or through its officials, for such acts as forestalling, gleaning, the escape of animals and other crimes against the community.

[**] Amercements for baking and brewing have been specifically excluded here because their uniquely formalized and impersonal nature leaves them more accurately viewed as a record of indirect taxation than of peasant litigation (see below, and chapter IV). The inclusion of the large number of female entry-appearances arising from these assizes would be misrepresentative of female curial activity as a whole.

[•] Percentages in this row relate to the portion of court roll entries naming a female litigant in which there was a female entry-appearance as plaintiff or defendant (for example, of the 176 great court roll entries which name at least one female litigant, 66 (38 per cent) contain a female entry-appearance as plaintiff). The presence of cases in which women litigate against other women means that the percentages in this row under the great court column do not amount to 100 per cent.

to be plaintiffs in criminal cases of theft, which comprised just 2 per cent (42 of 1,702 entries) of the borough court's business but 8 per cent (53 of 680 entries) of the great court's business. Theft held a unique position in Ruthin's legal system, prosecuted in both of the borough's courts and being treated at times as a crime against the community but more often as an interpersonal plea (that is, between the victim and the accused, though decisions were often recorded as present-ments). A perpetrator's punishment for theft was sometimes the provision of compensation to the victim, sometimes a period in the pillory or village stocks and occasionally both, though the pillory could be avoided by making a fine.[9] There were nineteen theft cases involving women before the great court between 1312 and 1321, recorded as: nine personal pleas (or presented resolutions thereof); three presentments on behalf of 'neighbours'; and seven presentments in which the agency behind the initiation of the plea is unspecified, though it is often clear that a specific individual lay behind the litigation.[10] Women were plaintiffs in only 16 per cent (3 of 19) of the great court of Ruthin's female entry-appearances arising from these theft pleas, and defendants in the other 84 per cent (16 of 19) of entry-appearances. Hence women's overwhelming tendency to answer but not initiate pleas in this significant sector of female 'litigation' directly contributed to their proportionally poor showing as plaintiffs in the great court of Ruthin.

By comparison, men were involved in numerous theft pleas, and were named as defendants in a modest majority, 60 per cent or so (39 of 62), of their related great court of Ruthin entry-appearances. But, unlike women, men were also prone to initiate high-value civil litigation in the borough's great court. Cases relating to theft accounted for about 7 per cent (42 of approximately 645) of great court of Ruthin cases involving a male litigant, compared to 11 per cent (19 of 176) of cases involving a female litigant. The smaller majority of

---

[9]   For example, *Dyffryn Clwyd Database*, GC1 #1061, SC2/215/74 m.17d.
[10]   An example of this latter case is the brief entry 'Alice le Blowestere was indicted for stealing malt, value 3*d*.' Ibid., GC1 #1078, SC2/215/74 m.18. The cause of this ambiguity is that, as Baker explains, while we now discern civil law as 'designed to provide private redress for wrongs to individuals' and criminal law as 'concerned with public order and the treatment of offenders against that order ... there was a time when the notion of public order was so underdeveloped or weak that no such distinction could be made' (J. Baker, *An Introduction to English Legal History* (London, 1979), pp. 411–12). In England, the statute of Winchester 1285 had made the people of each hundred answerable for all robberies in their hundred, requiring that persons be selected from within the community to make presentments on infractions (ibid., p. 23). See chapter II for comments on the increasing use of juries of presentment in Ruthin.

male theft defendants and their more voluminous alternative litigation diminished the impact of their entry-appearances relating to theft on the overall proportion of entries in which men acted as defendants.

Nevertheless, women's smaller proportion of entry-appearances as plaintiff in the borough's higher court as arising from these pleas does not necessarily imply curial disability. Instead, we should view women's low number of entry-appearances as plaintiff in theft pleas as an indication that women did not always need to initiate litigation in their own names in order to receive justice. In cases of theft concerning those items most commonly stolen either from or by women – usually small quantities of foodstuffs or house-hold goods – the related pleas or presentments almost always express the crime in terms of the household from which the goods were taken. Furthermore, goods being most commonly stolen from the home, and most heads of household being male, this system normally recorded male plaintiffs, though in reality the dispossessed party in stolen property cases may often have been a woman. For example, in a plea of November 1314, Malin the wife of William Tanner was amerced for stealing moist oats from the household of Robert *faber*, though the grain in question would almost certainly have been taken from Robert's wife, one of the town's most prolific commercial brewsters (for moist grain was used for brewing).[11] Brewing in particular, as famously conveyed by the exploits of the mystic and would-be alewife Margery Kemp, was one area in which medieval women often had a separate economic identity.[12]

Only when a woman's personal effects were stolen, or in pleas where the victim of a theft was a single woman living alone, does the court record expressly name a woman as a plaintiff, or injured party. In two of the three great court of Ruthin cases in which a woman initiated theft litigation, the

[11]   *Dyffryn Clwyd Database*, GC1 #986, SC2/215/74 m.16; see table 3.6 for details of the wife of Robert *faber*.

[12]   In her early fifteenth-century autobiography Margery says that she would not follow her husband's advice, 'and out of pure covetousness' she took up brewing but 'lost a great deal of money ... the loss of her goods'. *The Book of Margery Kempe*, ed. B. Windeatt (London, 1985), p. 44.

item stolen was an article of clothing (hood) or personal
effect (kerchief) likely to have been taken outside the home.[13]
In the third instance the items taken (fence posts) were,
broadly speaking, taken from the home, but the woman
affected was a widow and so she initiated litigation on her own
behalf.[14] As a result of these proceedings, all three female litigants appear to have been successful. Two of the persons
accused of theft were amerced, and an order was given to
arrest the third, the detail of whose ultimate fate has been lost.

The overall impression that these records give of women in
theft litigation is not that they lacked the capacity to seek or
attain legal redress in these pleas, but only that the court's
clerical conventions often did not allow for the identification
of female plaintiffs in the written record. In the few great
court of Ruthin theft cases which do specify a female plaintiff,
the plaintiffs were successful. While this tendency not to identify directly female plaintiffs of theft was the single biggest
contributor to the low level of named female plaintiffs in the
borough's higher court, there is no evidence that the handling
of cases in which women were either actual or implied plaintiffs was prejudiced.

Likewise, the statistic that women did not initiate as many
high-value civil pleas in the great court of Ruthin as those to
which they responded may be related to a similar tendency for
men to initiate such pleas when they related to household
enterprises, coupled with nothing more sinister than a reduced
need for women to initiate such pleas.[15] The nature of female
trade, as will be discussed later in part 2, was no less diverse
than men's work, but typically revolved around lower-value
goods. While wives in particular did occasionally initiate or
respond to high-value civil litigation alongside their husbands
(see table 3.4 and comment), most women may simply have
had less need to seek recourse in the great court of Ruthin
than in the borough court.

---

[13] *Dyffryn Clwyd Database*, GC1 #1262, 1454; SC2/215/76 m.14d; SC2/216/2
m.6.
[14] Lucy the widow of Martin *parcarius*, ibid., GC1 #1702, SC2/216/3 m.23.
[15] See above in this section, and also table 3.2 with accompanying text, for
comparative borough court evidence.

Finally, it must be stressed that, across the range of pleas involving female litigants in Ruthin's courts, women generally were equally empowered to bring pleas before either the borough court or the great court of Ruthin. All four pleas already discussed (debt, unjust detention, contract and theft), and which were examined because of their unique impact on the proportion of great court of Ruthin entries in which women acted as plaintiffs, cumulatively comprise less than one-third of the higher court's business. An examination of the other two-thirds of pleas initiated by women in both courts show virtual equality in the proportion of entry-appearances in which women acted as plaintiffs in each court.

By way of illustration, women were just as likely to bring pleas of violence before the great court of Ruthin as before the borough court when the gravity of their litigation warranted the higher court's consideration. For the years 1312–21, court roll evidence indicates that an equal portion of each court's business was taken up by violence against and between the borough's women.[16] The plaintiff, or victim, in about 20 per cent (60 of 297 entries) of all entry-appearances concerning physical violence recorded in the borough court of Ruthin was a woman. Likewise, around 19 per cent (18 of 96) of those violence-related entries in the great court of Ruthin record involved a woman as the plaintiff or victim on whose behalf the case was heard. Hence, while women may have had cause less frequently to access the great court of Ruthin to resolve certain varieties of litigation, they were generally no less successful in utilizing the borough's higher court when the need to do so arose.

There is a subtle difference here between instances in which a female plaintiff actively brought a case to the attention of the court and instances in which an act of violence may have been independently cited and prosecuted by a presentment jury on behalf of a passively involved female 'victim' (from a curial standpoint). The former circumstance indicates female agency facilitated by independent access to the

---

[16] Entries pertaining to violence are those describing beating/striking, brawling, bloodshed, choking, threatening/attacking with a weapon and other similar acts. Excluded from consideration here are cases of defamation and other non-physical disturbances not involving a weapon.

court; the latter implies an indeterminate level of dependency on the agency of court officials. While there is evidence of women as both active plaintiffs and passive victims in the records of the borough's courts, the majority of women seem to have been directly involved in pleading their own cases. In both courts, prior to 1319, approximately 25 per cent of violence cases were recorded as presentments (by either inquest juries or great court of Ruthin presentment juries), approximately 35 per cent as personal 'pleas', and approximately 40 per cent as non-detailed records of amercements. As a result of administrative changes early in 1319, as reflected in the greatly increased use of both presentment juries in the great court of Ruthin and the making of presentments by juries of inquisition in the borough court of Ruthin, a majority of violence-related entries in both courts are recorded as presentments rather than pleas.[17] It is unlikely, however, that this immediately affected the agency used by persons attempting to bring their complaints to the notice of the court but, rather, that it hinders our ability to extract from the court record a good sense of the role played by personal initiative.

This procedural shift towards an increased use of presentment juries is a common feature of late thirteenth- and early fourteenth-century manorial courts, and has been observed by Smith and Poos. For example, in the records of Rickinghall, Suffolk, they have observed that the principal means by which infringements were brought into the court changed from personal initiation in the 1270s to presentments in the 1280s. Likewise, a similar shift was taking place in Halesowen between 1276 and 1307.[18] This change affected the number of persons named in the court record, as entries arising from presentments typically cite fewer persons than do interpersonal pleas. However, it is hoped that, as the comparisons in this chapter are made between sample groups (of men and women), concerning each of which the data have been collected across the period of procedural change in Ruthin, any effects these changes may have had on each group's observable representation in the courts will have influenced the sample groups in the same manner.

[17]   See above, chapter II.
[18]   Poos, Razi and Smith, 'The population history', pp. 302, 342–3.

Household versus public sphere

There is a clear link between women's representation in the borough's courts and their most common roles in the community. Less active than men in pursuits that regularly took them outside the borough, such as field work, cattle dealing, or long distance trade, women are more frequently represented in the court rolls as engaging in activities focused on the home and the immediate community. Writers such as Judith Bennett, Barbara Hanawalt and Jeremy Goldberg have suggested that as a rule the social activities of women in rural English communities prior to the Black Death (1348–50) were particularly narrow and orientated toward family members.[19] Bennett in particular argues that as women in rural England 'failed to profit from the social prestige and economic opportunity of official service' – not being allowed to hold office (as was the case in Dyffryn Clwyd) – they developed certain economic, political, legal and social disabilities which further limited the capacity of those women who did succeed in accessing the court to use it effectively.[20]

However, it is equally possible that this interpretation of women in the community is unnecessarily severe and makes assumptions that do not hold true of Ruthin's emerging urban society. For example, it is immediately apparent from a survey of the borough's court rolls that Ruthin's female litigants did not feel the need to employ the legal aid of a male member of the community in order to overcome whatever social disabilities they may have faced in the courts. Of the 389 women appearing in the 1312–21 records of the borough court and great court of Ruthin, 153 are described using the phrase 'X the wife of Y', and yet the vast majority do not appear as litigants in conjunction with their husband. This is a striking proportion considering the theoretical inability of married women to conduct themselves independently of their spouse in a legal setting. It also sets the stage for a much more

---

[19] B. Hanawalt, *The Ties that Bound: Peasant Families in Medieval England* (New York, 1986); P. J. P. Goldberg, 'The public and the private: women in the pre-plague economy', in P. Cross and S. Lloyd (eds), *Thirteenth Century England III: Proceedings of the Newcastle Upon Tyne Conference* (Woodbridge, 1991), and Bennett, *Women in the Medieval English Countryside*.

[20] Ibid., p. 38.

liberal interpretation of the nature of Ruthin's judicial practice than Bennett found appropriate to her own source material.

While a clear majority of women's interpersonal entry-appearances in the biannual great court of Ruthin came in response to accusations made against them (table 3.1), in records of the monthly borough court of Ruthin women were defendants in only about half (205 of 407) of their total inter-personal entry-appearances. In the other half (202 of 407), women acted as plaintiffs.[21] By comparison with Bennett's find-ings for the English manorial court of Brigstock (a rural equivalent of Ruthin's borough court), Ruthin's urban women were more progressive in utilizing the court. In pre-plague Brigstock, between 60 and 62 per cent of women appearing in the court did so as defendants, and no more than 40 per cent were plaintiffs or victims.[22] This difference between Ruthin and Brigstock may be explicable either in terms of rural/urban circumstances or in Welsh/English social contexts. Brigstock's manorial court is equivalent to the borough court of Ruthin in so far as it was the lowest level of court accessible to residents of the community, typically dealing with petty regulatory offences (for example, gleaning, escaped animals etc.) and low-value interpersonal litigation (debts not exceeding 40s.). It differs principally in that Brigstock was an agricultural community with a stable population, while Ruthin was a rapidly expanding settler community highly dependent on urban economic

[21]   The blanket term 'plaintiff' has been used here, though in 13 per cent (52 of 407) of these entry-appearances a verdict was presented by a jury of inquisition, making it difficult to gauge the level of female agency involved. Most of these presentments by inquisition, 77 per cent (40 of 52), are in cases of violence initiated after the administrative changes of 1319 (for these changes see chapter II).

[22]   The upper limit of female plaintiffs in Brigstock of 62 per cent is drawn from Bennett's sample of civil litigation. The lower limit of 60 per cent has been derived from Bennett's methodological appendix concerning criminal acts, in which she mentions 295 instances of litigation involving women: 176 (60 per cent) cases naming female 'criminals', presumably defendants; and 119 (40 per cent) 'victims'. Bennett's use of the terms 'criminals' and 'victims' arises from Brigstock's exclusive use of presentments in the prosecution and recording of criminal acts. However, parallel rates of representation among female 'criminals' as opposed to 'victims' (60 per cent, 40 per cent), and civil 'defendants' as opposed to 'plaintiffs' (62 per cent, 38 per cent), strongly suggests a similar degree of female agency in bringing criminal litigation to the attention of the court. Bennett, *Women in the Medieval English Countryside*, pp. 31, 215–16.

enterprises.[23] But, as has already been suggested, it is a contention of this case study that in both communities the level of direct female participation in the court is not necessarily an accurate representation of the social status and economic integration of women in their respective social environments.[24] As has been stressed by both Goldberg and Power, legal demands (as expressed in the written record) do not always correspond to wider social realities.[25]

Focusing on representation in Ruthin's borough court, this claim rests on two principal sets of evidence: comparative rates of certain pleas between or concerning men of the community in relation to those involving women, and extensive supportive evidence in the court record attesting to the high level of female involvement in low-level trade and commerce where that trade was not necessarily focused on the home. This evidence shows that while the nature and geographical extent of male and female social networks may have differed, the density and social significance of these networks were probably equal.

Table 3.2 lists the nine most common circumstances leading to court roll entry-appearances by women and men in the borough court of Ruthin during the period 1312–21. Of primary interest here are the rates of physical violence in relation to unjust detention (debt in default) pleas. Women were roughly twice as likely to appear in the court for violence as for unjust detention.[26] Alternatively, men were nearly one and a half times more likely to appear in the borough court in connection with unjust detentions than with violence. An obvious explanation for this would be, as Bennett has asserted, that women's social sphere was particularly narrow and orientated towards family members and so, while still prone to unavoidable social ills such as violence, women were not as involved in the credit market as men. Indeed, women only appeared in the court with one-fifth of the frequency of men.

[23] See Bennett, *Women in the Medieval English Countryside*, pp. 9–17.
[24] In this study, Bennett's statistical interpretations of her data have been accepted. But Goldberg has offered criticisms of Bennett's use of the court record. Goldberg, 'The public and the private', p. 83.
[25] Ibid., 83; E. Power, *Medieval Women* (Cambridge, 1975), p. 34.
[26] No women appear in records of this period charged with being scolds, or similar.

Table 3.2. Reasons for 'entry-appearances',[†] borough court of Ruthin, 1312–21

	Women				Men			
Rank	Charge	No. of appearances	% of all appearances		Charge		No. of appearances	% of all appearances
1.	Violence*	112	24.0	(3.)	Unjust detention		515	22.9
2.	Trespass	86	18.4	(2.)	Trespass		393	17.5
3.	Unjust detention	58	12.4	(1.)	Violence		374	16.6
4.	False claims	49	10.5	(4.)	False Claims		197	8.8
5.	Debt	30	6.4	(5.)	Debt		186	8.3
6.	Defamation	16	3.4	(9.)	Theft		62	2.8
7.	Contract	16	3.4	–	Escapes		61	2.7
8.	Land related	15	3.2	(7.)	Contract		59	2.6
9.	Theft	12	2.6	(8.)	Land related		50	2.2
	Other	73	15.6		Other		350	15.6
	Total	467	99.9%				2247	100%

Source: TNA, SC2/215/71–SC2/216/3.

† See table 3.1 for the definition of entry-appearances.

* 'Violence' includes principally, but not exclusively, instances where the terms *verberavit* (assault), *vulneravit* (wounding) and *sanguinem effusit* (bloodshed) appear in the court roll.

However, excluding this juxtaposition of unjust detention and violence, the overall distribution of cases in which they were directly involved is strikingly similar if numerically fewer. Women's involvement in the credit market generally followed the same pattern as did men's, displaying an elevated number of unjust detention and debt pleas during the worst years of the great famine, and a decreased number of violence-related pleas during the same lean seasons. Both sexes engaged in theft, made false claims against their neighbours and were responsible for the making and breaking of contracts (*conventiones*). Moreover, women were acting independently in the vast majority of these cases. In only 10 per cent (forty-eight) of all entry-appearances by women were they accompanied by a husband, father, or other guardian.

This raises two questions. First, is there a plausible reason why women may have been more under-represented in the court record concerning unjust detention pleas than violence pleas? To this an affirmative answer almost certainly lies with the theoretical inability of married women to possess capital, or 'coverture' under common law, making it the natural course of action for women to initiate suits through and against male heads of household.[27] In only two of the fifty-eight unjust detention entry-appearances made by women in the borough court during the sample decade did a married woman bring a plaint of unjust detention.[28]

By comparison, married and not-married women alike brought violence-related litigation before the court against other members of the community with relative impunity (table 3.3). Ruthin's borough court appears to have been liberal with regard to the servicing of violence cases, related pleas and the complaints of female victims. No record survives from the period 1312–21 of any woman's violence-related litigation being dismissed on grounds of her sex, and only in a handful of instances did a husband or guardian bring a plaint on behalf of a woman in either the borough court or the great court of Ruthin. Alternatively, it was not uncommon for

[27]   There is probably also an element of coverture at work with regard to the tendency for male heads of household to be recorded as plaintiffs in the theft pleas, though in practice this almost certainly excluded personal effects and foodstuffs.
[28]   TNA, SC2/215/73 session 1, session 8.

Table 3.3. Women in unjust detention and violence cases, borough court of Ruthin, 1312–21

	Unjust detention Entry-appearances / (unique cases)		Violence Entry-appearances / (unique cases)	
	As plaintiff	As defendant	As plaintiff	As defendant
Women vs. women	6 (6)[*]	6	26 (26)[*]	26
Women vs. Men	19 (15)	27 (23)	37 (35)	23 (22)
Not-married women vs. Men[**]	17 (13)	22 (18)	19 (19)	13 (13)
Wives vs. men[***]	2 (2)	5 (5)	18 (16)	10 (9)
Total		58 (44)		112 (83)

Source: TNA, SC2/215/71–SC2/216/3.

[*] In instances of women vs. women litigation, each case contains both one female entry-appearance as plaintiff and one as defendant.

[**] 'Not-married women' indicates both never-married and widowed women.

[***] Instances in which a mother and unwed daughter jointly initiated a plea versus a man have been tabulated in accordance with the mother's marital status, based on the assumption of matriarchal household authority over unwed daughters.

husbands or fathers to pay amercements on behalf of their daughters, wives and sometimes even their servants.

This raises a second question. Behind what proportion of debt, unjust detention and contract pleas initiated by men lie the extra-curial negotiations and arrangements of women? This is a much more difficult issue to resolve, and any attempt to answer this question must be more heavily reliant on illustrative examples than an analysis of interpretable data.

Foremost among those socio-economic agreements liable to have been orchestrated by women with much greater frequency than the court rolls reveal would have been small loans in coin or kind. Married women in particular are likely to have been some of the most financially secure and strongly positioned to engage in the urban economy. But, as the rolls themselves suggest, married women were some of those most likely to be under-represented in the courts, their financial dealings typically eclipsed in the legal setting by their husbands' curial presence (table 3.3). As Craig Muldrew has asserted of the early modern period, the legal reality of 'the husband', as the 'contracting agent' in debt litigation masks in the court record the participation of wives in the credit market.[29]

---

[29]   C. Muldrew, '"A mutual assent of her mind?" Women, debt, litigation and contract in early modern England', *HWJ*, 55 (2003), 49.

It may be that, while it was more common and perhaps socially preferable for men to plead cases related to members of their household, the high degree of engagement of women with the community as a whole meant that their curial presence could not be totally eclipsed by their male counterparts. The overall impression of women in Ruthin's credit litigation agrees with Briggs's findings for the rural Cambridgeshire manors of Oakington and Horwood, namely, that it was a general tendency of women to bring litigation before the court only as a last resort in especially intractable cases.[30] Hence it is conceivable that the 25 per cent of Ruthin's court roll entries relating to women may actually represent only a small part of the whole, rather than the whole of a small part played by women in the local community and economy outside the home.

Numerous entries that support this hypothesis appear throughout Ruthin's court rolls. One such is a plea brought in 1314 by Richard de Prez versus Hywel 'Kennyn' in which Hywel was amerced because he took away (*deducit*) some grain from a half-quarter of oats, the sale of which his wife had already negotiated with Richard for the price of 2*s*. 1*d*., thereby doing damage to Richard assessed at 3*d*.[31] More succinct is a court roll entry of 1317 in which it is recorded simply that 'Einion ap Goronwy ap Einion was attached to respond to William le Sergeant and his wife Agnes in a plea of debt'.[32] Similarly, we may consider an entry of 1318 which states that 'Cadwgan ap Ithel and his wife are at law *versus* Dafydd ap Madog that they did not warrant him concerning two bushels of wheat which they have sold (*vendiderunt*) to him'.[33] Thus, we need not understand the relatively small number of entries on the roll directly citing the involvement of women as proportional to women's (and especially wives') actual social and curial interests. Instead, they are probably a representative sample of the variety of cases in which wives

---

[30]   C. Briggs, 'Empowered or marginalized? Rural women and credit in later thirteenth- and fourteenth-century England', *CC*, 19 (2004), 26–7.

[31]   TNA, SC2/215/73 session 5.

[32]   TNA, SC2/215/76 session 4.

[33]   TNA, SC2/216/1 session 7.

were most likely to have been involved, or which they had chosen to bring to the court on their own behalf.[34]

Furthermore, this conclusion allows us better to understand the significance of the greater frequency of women's entry-appearances in violence-related pleas than in unjust detentions (table 3.2). For if we accept that violence cases relating to women were likely to be freely initiated by all female victims, while the financial disputes of a significant proportion of women were initiated through husbands or male heads of household, this imbalance is explicable in terms of curial representation rather than social participation. Hence we need not believe that women were necessarily more closely linked with the home than were men due to their more frequent entry-appearances in violence cases than in unjust detention pleas.

More broadly, the curial activities of Ruthin's female litigants do not correspond to Bennett's description of medieval women, for whom she asserts that adolescence represented 'a modest measure of public opportunity' and marriage 'the final destination ... dependence'.[35] Wives in particular, though representing only 39 per cent of Ruthin's known female litigants, comprised 49 per cent of female plaintiffs, relying (at least explicitly) on their husbands' assistance less than a quarter of the time (table 3.4). Wives in Ruthin had the legal option of pleading their cases through their husbands,

---

[34]　On this point, Briggs's position is in opposition to that presented here as to the extent of female under-representation. Briggs was able to find limited evidence suggestive of extra-curial credit arrangements by the married women of Oakington and Horwood, but these did 'not point in the direction of large numbers of hidden credit ties' (Briggs, 'Empowered or marginalized', 24). The basis of this conclusion was Briggs's inability to locate records such as that cited above, where a woman is described as having made credit arrangements but *not* as having acted as plaintiff during the prosecution of bad debtors in those arrangements. From his survey of the manorial court of Oakington and Horwood, 1291–1380, Briggs was able to locate only one such entry (ibid., 24). By comparison, there survives an average of one indirect reference to a female credit or contract arrangement per year in Ruthin's court record, though this number decreases as the wording of Ruthin's court roll entries becomes progressively more formalized during the early fourteenth century (see above, chapter II). This incongruity is due either to a difference in the way in which the court rolls examined by Briggs (Oakington, Horwood and elsewhere) were compiled, or more probably to the more pronounced urban character of Ruthin's courts in contrast to the rural courts of Oakington and Horwood.

[35]　Bennett, *Women in the Medieval English Countryside*, p. 100.

Table 3.4. 'Absolute-appearances'[†] in the borough court of Ruthin, 1312–21

All women named in borough court and great court of Ruthin 1312–1321	Identified as / by	Borough court Absolute-appearances			
		Plaintiffs		Defendants	
		alone	chap.[*]	alone	chap.[*]
153 (39%)	'the wife of'	113 (49%)	26	101 (39%)	22
141 (36%)	trade, location, or descriptive names	53 (23%)	–	87 (33%)	–
84 (22%)	'the daughter of'	54 (24%)	–	62 (24%)	1
11 (3%)	'widow of' or 'who was the wife of'	10 (4%)	–	11 (4%)	
389 (100%)		230 (100%)		261 (100%)	

Source: TNA, SC2/215/71 – SC2/216/3.
[†] 'Absolute-appearances' calculates each time a woman's name appears in the court roll, regardless of the number of roll entries. For example, if 'female A and male A appear vs. female B and female C', this roll entry would account for three absolute appearances by women, one in the role of plaintiff and two in the role of defendant.
[*] Chaperoned/represented by husband or father also appearing in the same entry.

and yet the court record suggests that they generally did not choose to do so.

For example, Agnes the wife of William le Sergeant was a plaintiff in five borough court cases between 1312 and 1321, jointly with her husband in three debt concords and independently in two trespass pleas.[36] Similarly, Amelia the wife of Robert *faber* was sole plaintiff in four pleas of trespass, battery and slander (twice) in the borough court during the same period, but also as a wife whose plaint was brought by her husband after Meurig *cocus* wounded her with a knife in December 1315.[37] Other wives only brought plaints independently of their husbands. Gwerful, the wife of Bleddyn ap Ieuan Foel, brought two plaints to the borough court, one of battery against Tangwystl, the wife of Maredudd ap Iorwerth de Yale, in 1317 and another of trespass against Cynwrig Goch de Llyn Cymer ('Lencumer') in 1321, in neither instance calling on her husband for representation.[38]

[36]   TNA, SC2/215/74 session 6 (two instances), SC2/215/75 session 4, SC2/215/76 session 4, SC2/216/3 session 8.
[37]   TNA, SC2/215/74 session 3, SC2/216/3 session 8. It is possible that Amelia was injured too severely to appear in court.
[38]   TNA, SC2/215/75 session 7.

We must again acknowledge that the form of the court record itself emphasizes the impression that women initiated their own litigation in pleas affecting their immediate person (theft of personal effects, violence, defamation, trespass, etc.) and for the court to record male plaintiffs on behalf of women in pleas regarding capital or household goods (debt, unjust detention and theft from the household). Equally, there must have been an underlying social ethos which shaped the preferences of the court, within the wider framework of what was legally acceptable. We know from cases such as that of 1315, in which Robert *faber* brought a plea of wounding on behalf of his wife, that it was acceptable for husbands to initiate lawsuits for their wives, yet it remains unclear why it was most common for wives to bring their own violence litigation (both interpersonal/actual and implied by related presentment) before the court.

Across the decade 1312–21, only for married women did the number of the absolute-appearances as plaintiff exceed the number of their absolute-appearances as defendant (table 3.4).[39] This suggests that for at least a certain segment of married women in the community, the court was probably not particularly intimidating or inaccessible. Married women like Gwerful, who appeared alone but whose pleas would have led to the amercement of their (and, by default, their husband's) household if their plea failed, must have had at least the acquiescence if not the support of their spouse in doing so. If the borough court was otherwise so biased as to preclude on grounds of gender the reasonable possibility of legal victory for women pleading alone, or so sophisticated as to render women technically less capable of pleading, then surely married women would not have appeared alone with the frequency they did. As Briggs found of the women of Oakington and Horwood, on bringing pleas before the court they tended statistically to be more likely to win than were male plaintiffs.[40]

Finally, a few difficulties encountered in researching women's representation in the courts need to be noted.

---

[39] This is especially remarkable given the exceptional circumstances surrounding married women and unjust detention cases, as already discussed.

[40] Briggs, 'Empowered or marginalized?', 26.

Foremost among these is the problem of identifying widows. It has been estimated that at least 10 per cent of medieval households were headed by widows, though only around 4 per cent of those persons appearing in Ruthin's rolls are identified as 'X lately wife of Y' or simply as 'X, widow'.[41] Part of this gap may be explained by the continued identification of women in the court roll as 'X the wife of Y' regardless of their husband's death. An example of this is Felicity, the wife of William *parcarius*, who was initially identified in the court record as 'Felicity who was the wife of William *parcarius*' at the time of her husband's death, in or around August 1316, but later came to be known simply as Felicity *parcarius* or Felicity *de le Parc* until the time of her last court appearance in October 1320.[42] Ruthin's low number of widows may also be attributable to the town's continued character as a settler community, in which an ongoing influx of immigrants, a group which may have been predominantly male in character, served to help absorb into matrimony a significant proportion of the borough's widowed. It must be acknowledged, though, that any movement of chiefly male immigrants into the borough's matrimonial market may very well have been offset, especially during the famine years, by an equal or probably larger volume of migrants (see below, this chapter), a group which Hilton suggested and Goldberg (among others) has convincingly argued was sometimes strongly feminine in character.[43]

Another difficulty is that of knowing the personal relationships which existed between individuals in the medieval community or household. For example, there are a few instances of widows appointing attorneys, such as Margaret, the widow of Hugh Scot, who did so in 1313, and Amy (*Amicia*), the widow of Roger de Chester, who did so in 1321.[44] Apart from

---

[41]   H. Leyser, *Medieval Women; A Social History of Women in England, 450 – 1500* (London, 1995), p. 166.

[42]   TNA, SC2/215/75 session 7, SC2/216/3 session 1. M. Kerr also noted this occasional anomaly in the records of thirteenth-century criminal proceedings before the king's justices. M. Kerr, 'Husband and wife in criminal proceedings in medieval England', in C. Rousseau and J. Rosenthall (eds), *Women, Marriage and Family in Medieval Christendom* (Kalamazoo, 1998), p. 246.

[43]   R. H. Hilton, *The English Peasantry in the Later Middle Ages* (Oxford, 1975), pp. 106–7; Goldberg, *Women, Work and Life Cycle*, pp. 280–304. 'Immigration' and 'migration' are employed here as in the preliminary Definitions page above.

[44]   TNA, SC2/215/73 session 1, SC2/216/73 session 9.

suggesting that not every woman felt that she had the legal expertise to pursue her own pleas, the court record does not explain why these women chose particular attorneys or the nature of their relationships with them. There is no evidence of professional attorneys acting in Ruthin. Likewise, when husbands did occasionally represent their wives, as Tudur ap Bleddyn did for his spouse in a 1312 plea of battery against Richard de Taperton, was this choice the product of a victim's anxiety about facing her assailant, a woman's belief that the court might favour the pleading of the case by her husband, or a reflection of a husband's distrust of his wife's curial competence?

Common sense dictates that familial discontent or a jealous household patriarchy may sometimes have repressed a woman's ability to find representation either through or apart from her father or husband. Likewise, as has been demonstrated with regard to the infrequency with which women were explicitly named as plaintiffs in cases of theft, while the court seems to have dispensed unbiased justice, social and curial conventions may have forced female litigants to negotiate more informal obstacles than those faced by their male counterparts. What Ruthin's evidence suggests, however, is a very strong role played by women in all aspects of life, with the potential to appear in the court record regardless of their chronic curial under-representation. While the legal environment of the community and court may have been inherently gender biased, access to the borough's judicial facilities was within the reach of Ruthin's townswomen. Lastly, there is no discernible difference in the court record between the litigation pattern of Welshwomen and that of Englishwomen.

Brewsters: investment, profit and market manipulation[45]

This section develops the argument that women may have had a stronger role within borough society than the current historiography suggests. It seeks to explore the possibility that, rather

---

[45] Parts of this section have been published in M. Stevens, 'Women brewers in fourteenth-century Ruthin', *DHST*, 54 (2005–6), 15–31.

than disabling social constructs and biased curial institutions, the factor which controlled female market participation was access to capital. Attempting to deconstruct the community along these lines, Ruthin's brewsters, as both the best documented and often the wealthiest of the borough's women, provide a good starting point.[46]

Almost exclusively the preserve of women in the pre-famine period, brewing ale was a feminine microcosm of the community's broader wealth structure, as well as a pale reflection of its masculine political hierarchy.[47] It was the preferred commercial activity of women with access to significant quantities of investment capital, and a focus of the struggle for market entry by those less fortunate. Hence, women's participation in the ale trade provides an opportunity to assess the level of female market awareness, and the importance of access to capital in regulating women's market participation in borough society.

Participation

As was common in communities throughout later medieval England and Wales, Ruthin's residents were subject to an assize of ale, or 'set of regulations specifying the quality, prices and measures to be observed by brewers – whose enforcement rested with local courts'.[48] Two minor officials, or ale tasters, were appointed to work together for six-month terms and charged with overseeing the assize's implementation. Usually wealthy burgesses, these officers' duties included tasting each brewster's ale for quality and strength, verifying that the measures used to sell it were of a standard size and ensuring that ale was sold for no more than regulation prices.[49] Ale tasters then presented at the biannual great court of Ruthin, at which

[46]   'In the thirteenth and fourteenth centuries only one drink – ale in English, *cervisia* in Latin – was prepared by England's [and Wales's] brewers', as distinct from beer, with hops, which was not widely brewed in England until the fifteenth century. J. Bennett, *Ale, Beer and Brewsters in England : Women's Work in a Changing World, 1300–1600* (Oxford, 1996), p. 79.

[47]   Bennett, Britnell and Goldberg have stressed the strong association between socio-economic prosperity and commercial brewing. Bennett, *Women in the Medieval English Countryside*, pp. 212–15; Bennett, *Ale, Beer and Brewsters*; Britnell, *Growth and Decline in Colchester, 1300–1525* (Cambridge, 1986), pp. 89–90; and Goldberg, *Women Work and Life Cycle*, pp. 111–17.

[48]   Bennett, *Ale, Beer and Brewsters*, p. 4.

[49]   These officers, their duties and price regulation are discussed below.

they 'listed all persons involved in the trade – not only those who had cheated in some manner but also those who had brewed and sold honestly'.[50] For this reason the assize of ale functioned not only as a corrective but also as a licensing tool, with even honest brewsters regularly paying as a small amercement an amount reflecting the frequency with which they brewed.[51] The survival of these assize lists has in turn provided a robust body of evidence by which to gain an insight into the nature of brewing in pre-plague Ruthin.

Brewing was the activity in which the broadest swathe of townswomen was engaged. As it was one of the most closely regulated of traditionally female activities in the borough, many of the women amerced for brewing for sale, thereby 'breaching' or 'breaking the assize of ale' (both phrases having the same meaning), were undoubtedly brewing largely for their own household's consumption.[52] Equally, many others seem to have been brewing as a commercial enterprise, implying habitual contact with the broader community to facilitate the regular sale of their commodity. Moreover, Ruthin's married women, rather than the unmarried or widowed women, dominated the ale trade. Even Bennett, who consistently views the lives of medieval women as particularly restricted, concedes that 'brewing represents one of the few known public arenas that was actually opened to women by marriage'.[53]

Thirteen lists of women and men amerced for breaching the assize of ale, 220 persons in all, appear in the surviving great court of Ruthin records of 1312–21.[54] Women dominate this group, brewing more than five times as often as men. Careful evaluation of women's brewing reveals three distinct

[50]   Bennett, *Ale Beer and Brewsters*, p. 4.
[51]   See below for amercement amounts in relation to brewing frequency. This use of assize as a form of regulatory taxation was common in most medieval English communities. See Bennett, Britnell and Goldberg (as above, note 47) for comparative observations on the assize of ale in Brigstock, Colchester and York, respectively.
[52]   To 'break' or 'breach' the assize was not to commit a crime, but simply to pay a small compulsory amercement for brewing ale for sale.
[53]   Bennett, *Women in the Medieval English Countryside*, p. 123.
[54]   *Dyffryn Clwyd Database*, GC1 #296, 437, 502, 746, 799, 1008, 1093, 1266, 1416, 1417, 1459, 1722 and 1744; SC2/215/71 m.14d, SC2/215/72 m.1d and 2d, SC2/215/73 m.26d and 27d, SC/215/74 m.16d, SC2/215/74 m.18, SC2/215/76 m.14d, SC2/216/1 m.20, SC2/216/2 m.6d, SC2/216/3 m.23d, SC/216/3 m.22.

levels of market participation, as shown in table 3.5. From the bottom, first are those women comprising group 1 who brewed only occasionally or on a very limited scale, accumulating less than five amercements or an average amercement of less than 6*d*. Second are those in group 2, whose records suggest five amercements and an average amercement of at least 6*d*. Last are those in group 3 who were amerced five or more times with an average amercement of 9*d*. or more, these divisions representing natural breaks in the data.[55]

These calculations are possible because the value of the amercement which an individual paid for breaching the assize of ale in Ruthin was directly related to the quantity of ale brewed. Presentments on the assize usually appear in Ruthin's court rolls only as long lists of names accompanied by each brewer's amercement. However, occasionally, as in May 1316 and April 1317, the scribe included a note indicating the frequency with which each amerced person brewed.[56] In April 1317, for example, having brewed 'often' occasioned an amercement of 12*d*., three or four times most commonly equated to 6*d*., and once or twice led to an amercement of only 3*d*.[57] Examples of other communities in which closely graduated amercements have been explicitly associated with brewing frequency are rare. Britnell found of Colchester that, though some brewsters were occasionally charged 6*d*. or even

[55]   The difference between an average amercement of 6*d*. and 9*d*. is much more significant than is immediately obvious, as typical fines (3*d*., 6*d*., or 12*d*.) increased incrementally by doubling, as opposed to increasing by sequential multiples of the 3*d*. minimum. Thus, attaining an average amercement of 6*d*. required an occasional or petty brewster to brew only a few large batches, while an average amercement of 9*d*. or more severely limited the number of times a generally productive brewster could reduce her market participation and still meet the group 3 criteria.

[56]   *Dyffryn Clwyd Database*, GC1 #1093, 1266; SC2/215/74 m.18, SC2/215/76 m.14d.

[57]   Ibid. There is some evidence in Ruthin to support May's often challenged position that manorial court fines were relative to the impoverishment of those amerced, for while the tripartite division of amercements in relation to the number of times the amerced brewed is generally consistent, there are exceptions. In May 1316 the wife of Hugh *faber*, one of Ruthin's wealthiest burgess, was amerced 6*d*. for brewing three times. On the same date, the wife of the less affluent Andrew de Landingate was only amerced 3*d*. for brewing three times. These data are problematic, at best. See A. N. May, 'An index of thirteenth-century peasant impoverishment? Manor court fines', *EconHR*, 26 (1973), 389–402, and J. B. Post, 'Manorial amercements and peasant poverty', ibid., 28 (1975), 304–11.

Table 3.5. All brewers, Ruthin, 1312–21

(Brewing frequency)*	Male brewers	Female brewers	Wives / widows	Daughters	Tradeswomen	Other
Group 3 (high)	–	25 →	20 / 4	–	–	1
Group 2 (moderate)	–	21 →	14 / 2	–	3	2
Group 1 (occasional)	39**	117 →	80 / 0	8	5	23
Total	39	163 →	114 / 5	8	8	27

Source: Dyffryn Clwyd Database, GC1 #296, 437, 502, 746, 799, 1008, 1093, 1266, 1416, 1417, 1459, 1722 and 1744; SC2/215/71 m.14d, SC2/215/72 m.1d. and 2d., SC2/215/73 m.26d and 27d, SC2/215/74 m.16d, SC2/215/74 m.18, SC2/215/76 m.14d, SC2/216/1 m.20, SC2/216/2 m.6d, SC2/216/3 m.23d, SC2/216/3 m.22.

* See below, 'Market dominance and manipulation', for calculation of brewing batch-size.

** Over 75 per cent of these men had wives who brewed occasionally, and on whose behalf it is likely they were being amerced.

1s., 'as a rule' the charge was 3d.[58] And in Brigstock amerce-ments were rigidly standardized: 223 of the 246 brewing amercements recorded there between 1326 and 1330 were assessed at 2d. each.[59]

The breakdown of brewsters by frequency in table 3.5 helps to distinguish between likely by-industrial and occasional producers, as well as emphasizing the strong link which existed between marriage and market activity. The vast majority of Ruthin's brewers were women, as in group 1, who brewed only small quantities and/or only occasionally dabbled in the market. The town's true ale-wives were predominantly those group 3 women wed to wealthy burgesses, through whom they may have accessed the capital necessary for buying the grain and equipment needed to brew with frequency and in quantity. In the early fourteenth century these married women worked as by-industrial brewers more often than did single women and widows because their domestic situations, work patterns and access to capital offered important advantages; among these, access to capital was most important.[60]

Table 3.6 shows that at least 60 per cent of group 3 brew-sters were the wives of prominent borough jurors and office holders. Similarly, 40 per cent of these brewsters' husbands who can be directly or indirectly traced in the 1324 rental were members of the borough's wealthiest 50 per cent of burgesses (judged by rents paid to the lord). This same wealth is likely to have been set against the financial outlays repeat-edly encountered by Ruthin's brewsters. In addition to the considerable cost of materials, at least four group 3 women paid nearly 10s. in amercements for breach of assize over the 1312–21 decade.

In May 1318, on the heels of the great famine's worst years, fifty-four women were amerced specifically for 'brewing malt wheat in breach of the prohibition'.[61] The four greatest offenders paid amercements of 12d. each, suggesting that they had brewed at least four times over the preceding six months, a period during which the value of a single hoop (*hope*, or

[58] Britnell, *Growth and Decline*, p. 89.
[59] Bennett, *Women in the Medieval English Countryside*, p. 208.
[60] Bennett, *Ale, Beer and Brewsters*, p. 55.
[61] *Dyffryn Clwyd Database*, GC1 #1417, SC2/216/1 m.20.

bushel) of wheat ranged from a high of 2s. to just over one shilling as the famine eased in 1318.[62] Even were these women to have brewed in such small quantities as to have utilized only one hoop or bushel of wheat per batch of ale, their grain costs alone would have varied between an additional 4s. and 8s. over six months. However, brewing such small quantities of grain would probably not have yielded more than a maximum of 36 gallons of weak ale per batch, a bushel being about the smallest quantity of grain one might expect to see utilized at any one time.[63]

It seems more likely that the quantities of ale produced by the borough's most busy brewsters, and their corresponding outlay for materials, would have been far greater. Bennett suggests that the upper limit of what could have been brewed at one time in the later Middle Ages was as much as eight quarters of grain, producing around five hundred gallons of very weak ale.[64] Alternatively, as brewed weekly in the noble Clare household in 1333–4, each batch of ale required a full eight quarters of barley but yielded only about sixty gallons of presumably very strong and high quality ale.[65] Regardless of how much ale was ultimately produced, and even were oats to have been brewed as a cheap mainstay with barley and wheat used only in small quantities for flavour, the initial outlay for the eight quarters of grain required to produce just one of

---

[62]   The size of a 'hope' in Ruthin is uncertain, but if it were about a bushel, which was an eighth of a quarter, it suggests that the value of a quarter of wheat ranged from 16s. to 9s. during this period. Such a price range makes sense in the context of J. E. Thorold Rogers, *A History of Agriculture and Prices in England* (Oxford, 1866), and so may be considered a reliable guide. The single exception to this is oats, which Rogers observed are in some instances measured in quarters of 16 bushels (Thorold Rogers, *A History of Agriculture*, p. 3). Alternatively, it has been suggested by D. Pratt that in Wrexham the 'hoop' or 'hobbet' was about half a 'milliet', a milliet being roughly equal to a bushel (D. Pratt, 'Wrexham's medieval market', *DHST*, 15 (1966), 13–14). However, there is no evidence of the milliet in Ruthin at this time, and if we assume that a hoop was equal to only half a bushel (effectively doubling the indicated value of grain by volume), the grain prices for hoops specified in Ruthin's court rolls are unrealistically at odds with both the prices specified for whole quarters of grain in Ruthin's court rolls and with those prices noted by Thorold Rogers (see note 66 below). TNA, SC2/215/76 session 1, SC2/216/1 session 3.

[63]   Bennett, *Ale, Beer and Brewsters*, p. 18.

[64]   Ibid., p. 20.

[65]   Ibid. Presumably Bennett refers to the household of the Clare earls of Gloucester, but she does not note her source.

these large batches of ale in Ruthin in 1317–18 would have been around 80s.[66]

These two examples stand at extremes; the actual quantity and strength of ale typically brewed by Ruthin's group 3 ale-wives at each breach of the assize must have been at a level within this range. The general thrust of these examples is to demonstrate that the burden of capital outlay to brew frequently was significant, and so it should not be surprising that those women engaging in brewing as a by-industry were necessarily those with wealthy backers. In addition, it would be foolish to assume that a woman's primary reward for brewing in the borough was high social status. Women were eager to gain market access, were aware of market forces and, for those who could raise the capital to do so, in coin or kind, brewing was potentially rewarding.

When a woman's husband or household could not afford the necessary investment, Ruthin's brewsters looked else-where for backing. Elena, the wife of David *sutor* (cobbler), a man who does not feature prominently in Ruthin's court record, brewed throughout the decade but generally only in small quantities. An exception to this occurred in April 1314 when, after a year's absence from the brewing lists, Elena was amerced the large sum of 1s. 6d. for breaching the assize of ale, one of only five in 105 amercements meted out in 1314 that were so large.[67] In the following list of brewers, in November 1314, she was amerced 1s. in association with Ieuan *molendinarius*, who was not a burgess of Ruthin and whose name appears to have been added to the membrane after the original compilation of the list. At no later time in the decade does Ieuan again appear on the list of assize breakers, nor was Elena again amerced more than 6d. for breaching the assize, most frequently attracting only 3d. fines.[68] However, the two appear together again in a great court of Ruthin entry for October 1320 when Ieuan, still not enjoying the liberty of the

---

[66]   TNA, SC2/215/76 session 1, four hopes worth 2s. 6d. (or 10s. per quarter); SC2/215/76 session 1, one quarter worth 13s.4d.; SC2/215/76 session 4, one quarter worth 12s. These values are equal to, or slightly greater than, those found in Cambridge at this time, the highest noted by Thorold Rogers, *A History of Agriculture*, p. 75.

[67]   *Dyffryn Clwyd Database*, GC #799, SC2/215/73 m.27d.

[68]   Ibid., GC #1008, SC2/215/74 m.16d.

Table 3.6. Group 3 brewsters, Ruthin, 1312–21

Ale-wives	Total brewing amercements in d.	Average amercement in d.	Husband was: Juror	Husband was: Office holder	Husband's wealth rank in rental / total rents in d.	Husband as frequent pledge (most active)	Husband / wife as credit litigator (most active)
The wife of Ieuan ap Heilyn	138	11.5	–	–	11th / 112.75	–	–
Tangwystl the wife of William *saer*	126	10.5	3 times	–	16th / 72*	10th	–
The wife of Madog ap Dafydd Foel	135	11.25	3 times	–	25th / 45.5	–	–
Lucy the widow of Martin *parcarius*	111	9.25	–	Parker	–	–	–
Felicity the widow of William *parcarius*	108	12	–	Parker	–	–	1st
Gwenllian wife of Bleddyn ap Heilyn	108	9.81	–	–	12th / 112.5*	3rd	–
Amy the wife of William de Rowehull	102	10.2	3 times	–	–	–	–
Emma the wife of John de Trigamonde	99	11	–	–	–	–	–
Cecilia de Chester	96	10.67	–	–	–	–	–
Dyddgu the wife of Cadwgan mab 'Crom'	96	9.6	2 times	–	–	–	–
Lleucu the wife of Madog ap Bleddyn ap Philip	96	9.6	–	–	24th / 46	–	–
Cecily the wife of John de Helpston	90	11.25	–	–	–	–	–
Isabel the wife of Henry le Messager (*nuncio*)	90	10	–	Messenger	5th / 159	–	–
The wife of Adam de Verdon	90	9	4 times	Lord's squire	17th / 68	–	–
Alice the wife of Iorwerth ap Bleddyn	84	10.5	3 times	–	–	1st	–
Edith the wife of Iocyn Messor	84	9.33	2 times	Hayward	–	–	5th
The wife of John *cissor*	81	9	–	–	–	–	–
Juliana the wife of Thomas Chamberlain (*camerarius*)	69	9.86	–	Chamberlain	–	–	–
Margaret the wife of Stephen *janitor*	60	12	–	Castle doorkeeper	29th / 36*	–	2nd
The wife of Richard *forestarius*	60	10	2 times	Forester	4th / 170.25	–	–
Angharad the wife of Bleddyn ap Philip	57	11.4	–	–	–	–	–
Amelia the wife of Robert *faber*	54	9	–	–	–	–	–
Gwerful the wife of Einion Goch mab 'Honor'	48	12	–	–	–	–	–
The wife of Ieuan Potel	48	6.9	2 times	Ale-taster	23rd / 51	–	–
Juliana wife/widow of Alexander de Sywelle	48	9.6	–	–	–	–	–

Source: Brewing – as in table 3.5; other information as in table 2.1; and *Dyffryn Clwyd Database*; 'Rental'; TNA, WALE 15/8/1, R. I. Jack, 'Records of Denbighshire lordships II – the lordship of Dyffryn Clwyd in 1324', *DHST*, 17 (1968), 7–53.

* Estimated by the heir's holdings in the 1324 rental, thus almost certainly underestimates.

borough, was found to have been once more brewing at the house of Elena (now the widow of David *sutor*), and hence had his *brasina* (brew or brew house valued at 5s. 4d.) confiscated.[69]

Such collusion or cooperation was uncommon but certainly not unique. In April 1312, Agnes, the daughter of Andrew, was amerced with Margery de Hassald, and in May 1313 Adam de Verdon with Dafydd Du and Andrew de Landengate with the wife of William de Bostok were amerced in pairs.[70] Significantly, such co-investment is not apparent in the lean years of the famine, but it does recur afterwards. In a court roll entry of 1324, the *brasina* of Einion Du de Ysgeibion is to be confiscated from the house of Gwenllian, the widow of Adam *sutor*, another small-scale occasional brewster, under the same conditions as had been applied to Ieuan *molendinarius* ten years earlier.[71]

Market dominance and manipulation
The absence of collaborative brewing during the famine period reflects the way in which Ruthin's women adjusted their involvement in trade in response to market forces. Britnell concluded, in his study of medieval Colchester, that in the first quarter of the fourteenth century statistics for brewing provide a better economic indicator than amercements in other areas of food production, such as milling; he pointed out that the portion of the market that any one brewster could command was comparatively small.[72] The general validity of Britnell's observation is tempered by our knowledge that a small core of women who brewed consistently accounted for a disproportionately large part of Ruthin's ale production. Nonetheless, it holds true with regard to the much more numerous body of inconsistently active entrepreneurial women whose lesser economic status probably made them only marginally capable of market participation. With this in mind, the pattern of activity shown in figure 3.1 is telling.

While market participation was restricted by the cost of materials during the famine years, especially in 1317 when

[69]   *Dyffryn Clwyd Database*, GC1 #1715, SC2/216/3 m.23.
[70]   Ibid., GC1 #296 and 502, SC2/215/71 m.14d and SC2/215/72 m.2d.
[71]   Ibid., GC #2091, SC2/216/5 m.10.
[72]   Britnell, *Growth and Decline*, p. 90.

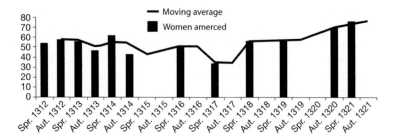

Figure 3.1. Ruthin's female brewers per biannual assize list, 1312–21
Source: as in table 3.5.

grain prices peaked in Ruthin, women had vigorously re-
asserted themselves by autumn 1320 to spring 1321, surpassing
the highest number of brewers in the pre-famine period by
more than 8 per cent. It is likely that while around 10 per cent
of the countryside starved during a famine in which rural
dwellers left their homes in search of food, the borough
swelled in numbers, maintaining the size of the ale market.[73]
Simultaneously, the profits to be made by those who could
afford to engage in brewing from 1315 to early 1318 are likely
to have been significant, encouraging poorer women to re-
enter the market as soon as possible thereafter.

This latter supposition runs counter to the comments of
both Bennett and Britnell, who believe that high grain prices
translated into nothing more than the smallest of profits in
famine years, and that the size of the market ensured that
there was no possibility for brewers to fix prices or quality.[74]
But their comments assume that both the number of women
participating in the market as well as the fixed and enforced
price charged per gallon (or other set quantity) of ale
remained relatively constant throughout such a crisis, both
assumptions which do not hold true of Ruthin. Figure 3.1
indicates that just over half as many women could afford to
enter the ale market in 1317 as had participated from 1312 to

[73]   Poorer women who would otherwise have brewed for household consumption, aiming to sell surpluses for additional income, would instead have been forced
to conserve grain for eating as bread or pottage. I. Kershaw, 'The great famine and
agrarian crisis in England, 1315–1321', *PP*, 59 (1973), 39, 47, 49. See below, chapter
IV, for a fuller discussion.
[74]   Bennett, *Ale, Beer and Brewsters*, p. 21; and Britnell, *Growth and Decline*, p. 90.

1314. Additionally, some 56 per cent of the women whose brewing persisted in 1317 were group 3 brewsters from wealthy households (as in table 3.6).[75] This contrasts with only 32 per cent in early 1314 and 26 per cent in late 1320.[76] The difference is significant, for while group 3 brewsters typically produced ale with greater frequency than other women, if one assumes a standard average batch size and compares the total number of batches brewed by group 3 brewers (in accordance with amercement values) in years like 1314 and 1320, they still produced the lesser part of Ruthin's ale. In years such as 1317 they produced the greater part, likely removing or greatly diminishing natural market controls on price and quality at a time when ale may have become more of a luxury.

As for official controls over the selling price and strength of ale, in a memorandum of 1296 'the twelve of Ruthin' had set the value of a gallon of ale 'however good it might be' at 1*d.*, and that of a gallon of 'less good ale (*peioris cervisie*)' at ½*d.*[77] Numerous amercements also indicate that gallon measures had to be sealed in accordance with the assize, proving that they indeed contained a full gallon. However, there is ample evidence to suggest that these regulations were only loosely enforced, at best. Ale tasters seem to have been appointed from 1296 onwards, and would theoretically have visited all known ale-wives at least once every six months to sample their ale. At least one additional amercement for bad ale appears in the earliest surviving list of assize breakers.[78] But in the decade 1312–21, alongside the hundreds of amercements imposed for brewing, only thirteen were issued for bad or unwholesome ale (*cervisia non sana*), seven of which were presented together at the spring 1312 great court of Ruthin.[79]

Evidence for the regulation of price per quantity is more abundant, but again smacks of sporadic enforcement. The first surviving amercement for either overpriced or deficiently

[75] *Dyffryn Clwyd Database*, GC1 #1266, SC2/215/76 m.14d.

[76] Ibid., GC1 #799 and 1722, SC2/215/73 m.27d and SC2/216/3 m.23d.

[77] Ibid., GC1 #24, SC2/215/66 m.1.

[78] Ibid., GC1 #27, SC2/215/66 m.1 mentions Hywel Goch, ale-taster (*cencator cervisie*), in 1296; and GC1 #96, SC2/215/69 m.3 includes an amercement for bad ale in 1306.

[79] Ibid., GC1 #296, 437, 799, 1722; SC2/215/71 m.14d, SC2/215/72 m.1d, SC2/215/73 m.27d, SC2/216/3 m.23d.

measured ale in Ruthin does not appear in the rolls until May 1313, over six years after the 1296 memorandum.[80] The record is then silent for eighteen months until November 1314, when nine ale-sellers were simultaneously amerced for selling ale at the inflated price of 1½d. per gallon.[81] Further amercement does not appear for another two years, until October 1316, when six persons were amerced for having false gallon measures and two were amerced for charging up to 2d. per gallon, twice the allowed price.[82] Enforcement then seems to have lapsed until the famine eased and another series of amercements appears in a borough court session of April 1318, when seven persons were amerced for false measures.[83] Between 1318 and 1321, no further amercements of this type appear in the records.

It may be that more groups of such amercements appear in the 40 per cent or so of the records of the borough court and great court of Ruthin which have not survived. However, it seems more likely to have been part of a broader pattern of borough administration: namely, that nothing was done about a problem until it became too great a nuisance to be ignored, at which time an atypical and relatively lengthy list of amercements was issued, after which nothing more is mentioned of the problem in the court rolls for months or even years.[84] This pattern of reactive administration was certainly also common in Caernarfon, where surviving records begin in the 1360s, and is no doubt just as familiar to many small-town residents of Britain today.[85] Meanwhile, the borough's ale tasters seem to

---

[80]   *Dyffryn Clwyd Database*, GC1 #480, SC2/215/72 m.2d.

[81]   Ibid., GC1 #1009, SC2/215/74 m.16d.

[82]   Ibid., GC1 #734–740, SC2/216/73 m.26d; TNA, SC2/215/75 session 8 (borough court).

[83]   TNA, SC2/216/1 session 4. Much later records of Caernarfon in the 1370s suggest that such false measures may have been Welsh measures used when selling ale to Welshmen, but there is no indication of this at Ruthin (C. Jones and H. Owen (eds), *Caernarvon Court Rolls, 1361–1402* (Caernarvon, 1951), p. 91).

[84]   Another good example of this is the clogging of the borough's streets with dung and wood heaps, which was combated with a sizeable group of amercements at the end of a borough court session in March 1313 and then all but forgotten for the remainder of the decade. TNA, SC2/215/72 session 2.

[85]   For example, an isolated block of amercements for non-burgesses selling their goods together with those of their burgess employers appears in a Caernarfon town court roll of 1365, followed by a conspicuous lapse of regulatory enforcement. Jones and Owen (eds), *Caernarvon Court Rolls*, p. 34.

have been apathetic, opportunistic, or simply corrupt. Rodger de Chester (possibly related to group 3 brewer Cecilia de Chester) was amerced in May 1313 for not performing his office of ale taster as he ought, along with the occasional brewers Tudur ap Bleddyn and '[Bleddyn] Bustagh', who were amerced for meddling in his office.[86] Again, in May 1321, ale tasters William de Wytemor and Dafydd Goch, respectively the town's most prolific baker and the husband of a group 2 brewster, were amerced because they 'in undue manner took with them three or four men to taste ale, to the impoverishment of many women'.[87] Given that this pair had previously been the borough's ale tasters from May to October 1320, and probably during the intervening period as well, it may be that their indiscretions spanned a notable period before any action was taken to curb their abuses.[88]

In the face of such weak regulation, Ruthin's brewsters seem to have had strong associations with one another. Of the nine persons amerced together in 1314 for charging ½d. more per gallon than was allowed by the assize, seven were group 3 and two were group 2 brewsters.[89] More explicitly, four of the six persons amerced for selling ale with false measures in 1316 were group 3 or group 2 brewsters, or their husbands, and all seven known pledges who stood as surety for those persons were themselves the husbands of group 3 brewsters.[90] Similarly, given the small pool of Ruthin's social elites from which these women were drawn, it seems unlikely that the issuing of their amercements as a group (in one court entry), and their uniform overcharging, was a coincidence. Only one other woman was amerced for overcharging in 1316, in the borough court instead of the great court of Ruthin, and for charging a different price per gallon; although this woman was a group 1 brewster, both of her pledges were the husbands of group 3 brewsters.[91]

Given the probability of lax regulation, if we cast our minds back to the fifty-four women amerced for brewing malt wheat

86 *Dyffryn Clwyd Database*, GC1 #496, SC2/215/72 m.2d.
87 Ibid., GC1 #1741, SC2/216/3 m.22.
88 Ibid., GC1 #1722, SC2/216/3 m.23d.
89 Ibid., GC1 #1009, SC/215/74 m.16d.
90 Ibid., GC1 #734–740, SC2/216/73 m.26d.
91 TNA, SC2/215/75 session 8.

contrary to the prohibition in 1318, it becomes apparent that even in the worst years of the famine their endeavours are likely to have been rewarded. Bennett has calculated that given grain and materials costs in relation to market prices in Oxford in 1310, returns per bushel of grain brewed may have ranged from a slight loss to a profit of 25d., depending on the mix of grains used and the strength of ale produced.[92] It seems reasonable to suggest that if a Ruthin brewster of 1318 had been inclined to keep to the selling price of 1d. per gallon, as specified in the 1296 memorandum, had brewed beer exclusively from wheat malt bought at the famine price of 2s. per bushel and had produced moderately strong ale at 24 gallons per bushel brewed, she would still have almost broken even on her investment.[93] If, more realistically, an evenly mixed bushel of wheat and oats were to have been brewed in the same year and sold at 1d. per gallon, the brewster could have expected profits of around 8d.–10d. In a year of more moderate grain prices, such as 1320–1, this profit per bushel would have been quite substantial, at around 1s. 2d.

Conclusion

Women of the community could not fail to have observed that, for those with capital to invest, brewing was profitable. Were lax regulatory enforcement to have allowed the sale of weaker brews and an inflation of prices during the famine (not least of all because Ruthin's ale tasters were almost exclusively men with a direct interest in the profitability of brewing), it is probable that Ruthin's brewsters enjoyed continued prosperity during these years. Moreover, it is no wonder that this prosperity, in the face of the subsistence crisis and the suffering of their neighbours, encouraged many women to try to enter the market as soon thereafter as they could raise the necessary capital. This explains both the quick recovery and rise in the number of brewsters immediately after the worst years of the famine, as is evident in figure 3.1, and throws into sharp relief the high level of market aware-

---

[92]   Bennett, *Ale, Beer and Brewsters*, p. 23.
[93]   Bennett does not specify how she arrives at the cost of additional materials which she incorporates in her calculations, but her corresponding table suggests that they were not great. Ibid.

ness and opportunistic participation exhibited by Ruthin's women. In short, the prime determinant of the varying levels of female participation seems to have been access to capital. Moreover, as was the case with the overall pattern of female activity in the courts, Englishness or Welshness seems to have been irrelevant: at least twelve of twenty-five group 3 brewsters were Welsh, or the wives of Welshmen.

IV

BAKERESSES AND OTHER SKILLED WORKERS: WOMEN WITH ACCESS TO MODERATE LEVELS OF INVESTMENT CAPITAL

FEMALE BAKERS: TRADE PARTICIPATION AND EXCLUSION

In chapter III women's market awareness and the importance of access to capital were illustrated by an examination of commercial brewing. However, the wealth of Ruthin's by-industrial brewsters and the female nature of brewing as a social and economic activity make the circumstances of ale production atypical. This chapter seeks to establish the relationship between access to capital and economic opportunity for the borough's more numerous middling women, those who most often worked as skilled labourers in the households of male tradesmen.

In nearly all areas of entrepreneurial endeavour other than brewing women were in the minority and at a theoretical disadvantage. In the case of married by-industrial brewsters, it was common for their husbands to be engaged in one trade while they worked at another, thereby establishing a degree of autonomy. By comparison, the unmarried brewster more often than not worked alone and in relative poverty, without the benefits enjoyed by her married counterpart of servants or children to aid her.[1] As brewsters, wealthy wives could be at the head of their own household economic and social hierarchy. Apart from commercial brewing, virtually no woman was likely to hold any better than a middling position within a complex household structure. Unmarried tradeswomen living alone were not usually wealthy enough to have hired or fostered servants.[2] And, with the exception of widows

---

[1] J. Bennett, *Ale, Beer and Brewsters in England: Woman's Work in a Changing World, 1300–1600* (Oxford, 1996), p. 38.
[2] Single women, however, would have avoided certain time-consuming domestic obligations such as food preparation and the rearing of children too young to contribute to the domestic economy.

continuing to work at their late husbands' crafts, women who lived in a complex household but were not focused on brewing were typically subsumed into a secondary role in their husband's or father's trade.[3]

In fact, as Helen Jewell relates, the contemporary perspective was 'that women's work was comparatively casual and amateur, and that they would have to be the flexible workers in any marriage partnership, turning their hands to different trades as opportunity arose or desperation drove'.[4] Excepting only the small minority of women with sufficient capital to engage in by-industrial levels of work (and perhaps then only in brewing), the nature of early fourteenth-century labour attributed to Welsh women by Llinos Smith, the English women of Exeter by Maryanne Kowaleski, of Shrewsbury by Diane Hutton and of York by Jeremy Goldberg is one of typically an economy of makeshifts personified by lower status and lesser pay than their male counterparts had.[5]

Only the overarching argument put forward by Rodney Hilton, and championed by Goldberg, that in the post-plague period a woman's position in the labour market was significantly improved as a by-product of labour shortages, runs contrary to this dismal appraisal.[6] However, even this positivist view of later medieval women has its detractors. Bennett in particular has argued that the subordination of women both before and after the plague was rooted in the household rather than the economy. Hence she asserts that in the

---

[3] It is likely that, in Wales, fosterage and servant-hood were intimately connected. For a fuller discussion see chapter V.

[4] H. Jewell, *Women in Medieval England* (Manchester, 1996), p. 93.

[5] Ll. B. Smith, 'Towards a history of women in late medieval Wales', in S. Clarke and M. Roberts (eds), *Women and Gender in Early Modern Wales* (Cardiff, 2000), pp. 38–9; M. Kowaleski, 'Women's work in a medieval market town: Exeter in the late fourteenth century', in B. Hanawalt (ed.), *Women and Work in Pre-Industrial Europe* (Bloomington, 1986), pp. 145–64; D. Hutton, 'Women in fourteenth century Shrewsbury', in L. Charles and L. Duffin (eds), *Women and Work in Pre-Industrial England* (London, 1985), pp. 96–7; and P. J. P. Goldberg, *Women, Work and Life Cycle in a Medieval Economy: Women in York and Yorkshire, c.1300–1520* (Oxford, 1992), pp. 86–7, 101.

[6] Caroline Barron has also developed this argument, applying the oft used expression 'golden age' to the period of increased economic opportunity afforded to women after the plague. C. Barron, 'The "Golden Age" of women in medieval London', *RMS*, 15 (1990), pp. 35–58; R. Hilton, *The English Peasantry in the Later Middle Ages* (Oxford, 1975); Goldberg, *Women, Work, and Life Cycle*.

fourteenth century 'the expansion of women's public activities was so limited and so ambivalent that it never substantially
changed the status of women', and that economic or labour
opportunities may have done little more than increase the
volume of low-status, low-skill jobs for women.[7]

This debate is too broad in scope to be adequately addressed
as a context of this book, but a study of Ruthin's skilled female
workers, Welsh and English, can make a modest contribution
to it. First, by a close examination of women in commercial
baking, this chapter assesses the extent of those opportunities
presented to women as a by-product of the great famine.
Secondly, it considers the nature of those opportunities and
their link with access to capital. For, if an increase in the visibility of women in these skilled jobs were due to the public
acknowledgment of pre-existing but previously unrecognized
labourers, then we might assume that these women experienced a legitimate improvement in their social status.
Likewise, evidence that women attempted market entry in
typically masculine areas of skilled production, such as
baking, as opposed to only 'low status, low skill jobs', would
imply that access to capital was potentially a more potent
determinant of women's social status than any overriding
ethos of female subordination.[8] The main purpose of this
examination is to understand the nature of Ruthin's economy
in relation to its middling women. But, in making a close study
of the impact of famine-crisis labour opportunities for
women, it is hoped that a valuable point of comparison may
also be created with the plague-crisis historiography of
medieval women in Wales and England.

Ruthin's 'middling women' with access to moderate
amounts of investment capital were a distinct group, neither as
destitute as the prostitute or spinster at her piecework, nor as
wealthy as the by-industrial brewer. Working in the shadow of
husband, father, or brother, the female baker is the best documented of these middling women.[9] While the survival of court

---

[7] J. Bennett, *Women in the Medieval English Countryside: Gender and Household in Brigstock Before the Plague* (Oxford, 1987), pp. 197–8.
[8] Ibid.
[9] See table 4.2 for a representative sample of the range of occupations of middling tradeswomen.

roll entries pertaining to the assize of bread is patchier than for the assize of ale, some details of the long-term significance of baking for Ruthin's women in the pre-plague period can be teased out. As with the assize of ale, baking presentments made to the great court of Ruthin record the names of all persons who baked bread for sale and thereby lawfully 'breached' or 'broke the assize' by doing so, not only the names of those sellers who violated market regulations.[10] Thus, assize lists, naming all those who 'breached' the assize by baking bread for sale during each six-month period between sessions of the great court of Ruthin, offer data which can be used to test certain propositions, which in turn illuminate the nature of life of many women in this middle stratum.

By Goldberg's reasoning, as long as labour opportunities presented themselves, women would enter an available trade and significantly delay marriage or remarriage in exchange for income and higher status within the economic community.[11] Once such a labour shortage had passed and these opportunities had disappeared, he suggests that women again fell prey to early marriage and lower status within a town's economy.[12]

Not immediately concerned with the implications of changing marriage patterns or long-term population growth or decline, the approach of the present discussion is three-pronged. First, it seeks to consider the possibility that, while the pattern of opportunistic female market participation suggested by Goldberg is valid for Ruthin, it does not apply exclusively to women in the post-plague period. Secondly, the more frequent amercement of women for trading offences does not always signify the difference between occupation and idleness, but rather a change in women's socio-economic status, from makeshift to legally recognized skilled labour input. Thirdly, this discussion explores the possibility that, while a need for labour may indeed have helped women enter

---

[10] Like the assize of ale, the assize of bread was largely used as a licensing tool. To 'breach' or 'break the assize' (both phrases having the same meaning) was not to commit a crime, but simply to pay a small compulsory amercement for baking bread for sale.

[11] Goldberg, *Women, Work and Life Cycle*, p. 7.

[12] Ibid., p. 437.

trades, it was access to, and maintenance of, capital which allowed a woman to perpetuate her trade participation and status within the community's socio-economic hierarchy.

Overview of baking
From 1306 to around 1321 the number of bakers typically amerced in the great court of Ruthin doubled, and the proportion of these who were women rose from 20 per cent to around 40 per cent (figure 4.1). As was the case with brewing, the early famine years from 1315 to mid-1318 stimulated opportunistic market entry by bakers from late 1318 onwards, as well as absorbing more female labourers into the trade. Just as these years may have encouraged the increased production of ale in the early 1320s, it is likely that, following the rural displacement of persons seeking food as the period of famine became more protracted, the borough would have played host to a growing number of consumers. The sudden need to meet the demand from these consumers, and the desire to profit from it, would in turn have created a skilled labour shortage which women were the first to fill.

Research on different parts of England has shown that famine conditions led to widespread urban population growth and an influx of paupers into large and small towns alike. As Smith has pointed out, crude 'subsistence' or 'push' factors were vital in dictating levels of migration in the early fourteenth century.[13] Thus, Kershaw observed a significantly increased number of surrenders of rural property in Hertfordshire and Cambridgeshire during the great famine, noting that subtenants and labourers must have been among those worst affected.[14] For the same period, Hilton noted that significant numbers of 'strangers' became more visible in the records of the small seignorial borough of Halesowen, where 'some two-hundred court presentments of residents lodging or receiving persons' were made between 1272 and 1349.[15]

[13]   R. Smith, 'Demographic developments in rural England, 1300–48: a survey', in B. Campbell (ed.), *Before the Black Death: Studies in the 'Crisis' of the Early Fourteenth Century* (Manchester, 1991), p. 75.
[14]   Kershaw, 'The great famine and agrarian crisis in England, 1315–1322', *PP*, 59 (1973), 36–9.
[15]   R. Hilton, 'Small town society in England before the Black Death', *PP*, 105 (1984), 64–5.

Likewise, for the large urban centre of Norwich, tithing roll evidence has been used to estimate a population increase of around 33 per cent between 1311 and 1333.[16]

Ruthin almost certainly underwent a similar substantial increase. By spring 1318, a toll had been imposed on the removal of foodstuffs from the borough.[17] Additionally, a ban on trading outside Ruthin's marketplace ensured that, at least for those in the borough's hinterland, the town was the only available venue for the legal purchase of victuals. For the poor or starving, the combination of these two ordinances had a magnetic effect, drawing them into the borough for the purchase of food and encouraging them to consume it there.

Under these conditions, an increasing number of women began to bake for retail sale as the famine briefly eased in late 1318 and early 1319, and managed to maintain their market position until around 1330. Unfortunately, this prosperity was short lived. After 1330, while the total number of bakers amerced declined slightly, the proportion of those who were female plummeted to the pre-1315 levels of only 15 to 20 per cent. In this way, the circumstances of female bakers, and presumably other less well-documented tradeswomen, follow the pattern of opportunity offered and then withdrawn that Goldberg describes for the post-plague period.

Makeshift and recognized skilled labour input
Unlike brewing, where the core of consistently active by-industrial producers (women with access to the most significant quantities of capital) was predominantly female and working in a mainly feminine trade, Ruthin's female bakers and other skilled labourers were engaged in typically masculine trades. By brewing, women with quantities of capital allowing them at least marginal market entry typically took up an occupation different from that of their spouse or guardian. Conversely, those women who, in increasing numbers, breached the assize of bread in the early 1320s were typically paying to work in conjunction with a male baker. Thus, for

---

[16] Based on tithing rolls, an increase from 16,627 to around 25,000 has been estimated. E. Rutledge, 'Immigration and population growth in early fourteenth-century Norwich: evidence from the tithing roll', *UHY*, 27 (1988), 15–30.

[17] TNA, SC2/216/1 m.20.

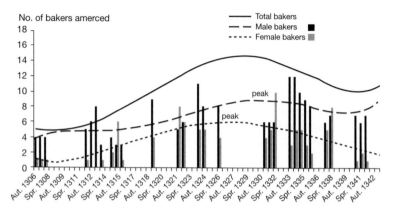

Figure 4.1. Number of Ruthin bakers amerced per biannual assize, 1306–42

Source: *Dyffryn Clwyd Database*, GC1 #95, 119, 217, 250, 291, 409, 490, 491, 500, 795, 1015, 1067, 1068, 1069, 1377, 1378, 1379, 1380, 1391, 1392, 1394, 1396, 1397, 1398, 1399, 1400, 1717, 1742, 1994, 2011, 2094, 2107, 2328, 2685, 2799, 2816, 3012, 3031, 3352, 3376, 3451, 3546, 3569, 3785, 3880, 3892, Roll1 #16 and Roll2 #100, 128; SC2/215/69 m.3 & 4, SC2/215/70 m.5, SC2/215/71 m.13 and 14d, SC2/215/72 m.1, SC2/215/72 m.2d, SC2/215/73 m.27d., SC2/215/74 m.16d., SC2/215/74 m.17d., SC2/216/1 m.20, SC2/216/3 m.22 & 23, SC2/216/4 m.30d & 31, SC2/216/5 m.10 & 11, SC2/216/6 m.1, SC2/216/9 m.18, SC2/216/10 m.26 & 27, SC2/216/12 m.14 & 14d, SC2/216/13 m.23 & 23d, SC2/216/14 m.24, SC2/217/1 m.12 & 13, SC2/217/3 m.11, SC2/217/4 m.16 & 16d., SC2/217/6 m.2, SC2/217/7 m.3 & 4.

women with anything less than large quantities of investment capital, the nature of market entry was far from clear cut or assured.

The children of the office holder and baker Thomas Chamberlain and his wife, Juliana the brewster, personify this market participation in the patriarchal sphere. Thomas Chamberlain was among those bakers amerced in each of the first seven consecutive surviving assize lists of autumn 1306 to spring 1313, and in each instance he paid the highest level of amercement charged by the court.[18] While Thomas appeared

---

[18]   Either 6*d.* or 12*d.* Amercements for breaching the assize of bread, like those for the assize of ale, were related to the quantity of work done. Baking amercements, like those of brewing, were most commonly subject to the tripartite divisions of 12*d.*, 6*d.*, and 3*d.* For an example and discussion, see *Dyffryn Clwyd Database*, GC1 #1994, SC2/216/4 m.30d; and below, table 4.1.

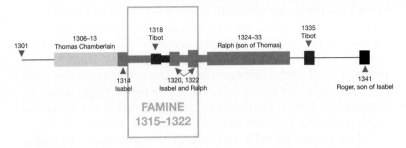

Figure 4.2. Timeline of Chamberlain family's baking amercements*
Source: as figure 4.1.
*Gaps between amercements, especially during the famine period, are mainly due to gaps in the court record. It is likely that, in these years, one family member baked continuously until succeeded by another. For example, Isabel probably baked continuously from 1314 until succeeded by Tibot in 1318. These periods, for which documentation is lacking, are represented by the narrower, shaded sections of the timeline.

in the borough court as late as September 1318, he was arguably less active in the courts after 1313 and was no longer amerced for breach of assize, quite possibly due to advanced age or decrepitude.[19] He was replaced by his daughter Isabel from autumn 1314, daughter Tibot in 1318, daughter Isabel and son Ralph together in 1320 and 1322, and finally by Ralph alone from 1324 onwards.[20]

Isabel's name did not again appear in connection with the assize of bread until her son Roger, 'son of Isabel Chamberlain', was amerced for baking in April 1341.[21] Her sister Tibot was amerced only once more after the famine period, in October 1335, when she was referred to as 'Tibot le Chaumb ...', one of several 'common [bakers]' in breach of the assize of bread.[22] Relative to these dates, the final appearance of 'Ralph *camerarius*' (later simply 'Ralph *pistor*') for

---

[19]   TNA, SC2/216/1 session 7; 'Thomas (Chamberlain) *pistor*' also appears in the earliest surviving great court of Ruthin, Easter 1296 (*Dyffryn Clwyd Database*, GC1 #20, SC/215/65 m.4), and may have been overtaken by old age or ill health by 1313. Having possessed a variety of burgage property as late as 1315 (Ibid., Reliefs #264, SC2/215/74 m.2d), his absence from the rental of 1324 almost certainly indicates his death before that date.

[20]   Source as in table 4.1.

[21]   *Dyffryn Clwyd Database*, Roll1 #34, SC2/217/6 m.1.

[22]   Ibid., GC1 #3569, SC2/217/1 m.12.

breaching the assize of bread, after eleven years of consecutive amercements for baking, came in April 1333, only eighteen months prior to Tibot's reappearance.[23] Afterwards, Ralph was amerced for non-attendance at the great court of Ruthin in April 1334 and subsequently his name was recorded only once more in the court rolls, on 13 October 1338, when an inquisition jury reported that he again did not attend the court, and that his lands were 'in the hands of the lord'.[24]

Tibot's and Isabel's continued identification by their father's title of 'Chamberlain', respectively twenty-seven and seventeen years after their first appearance in the court rolls (presumably at an age no younger than twelve) suggests that these women were still unwed in their thirties.[25] The 1341 record of Isabel's son Roger in the great court of Ruthin in association with his mother, rather than in association with the name of his father or trade, is further suggestive of Isabel's having borne an illegitimate child who in turn also entered the family business of baking. It is highly likely that throughout the decade of the mid-1320s to the mid-1330s both sisters continued to work in the household of their brother Ralph, opting for the economic security of labouring under the umbrella of his trade rather than seeking uncertain prosperity in marriage.

This chronology is also suggestive of the amercement of Isabel and Tibot for baking during a period of increased demand from 1318 to 1322, when they may have been afforded more direct involvement with the production and sale of bread, and/or during the time between their father's decline and their brother's majority. It is likely that both daughters had regular access to moderate amounts of capital, in cash or kind, for which they were responsible and which they manipulated to the benefit of the household. Tibot was

---

[23]   *Dyffryn Clwyd Database*, GC1 #3376, SC2/216/13 m.23d.
[24]   Ibid., GC1 #3873, 3461; SC2/217/4 m.16, SC2/216/14 m.24d. The significance of this entry for Ralph is unclear, but suggests that he had either died or committed a felony.
[25]   Razi in particular has based a great deal of research upon the assumption that young persons usually first appeared in the court record within a few years of turning twelve, and not often before that age. Z. Razi, *Life, Marriage and Death in a Medieval Parish: Economy, Society and Demography in Halesowen, 1270–1400* (Cambridge, 1980), pp. 3, 50–64.

amerced for faults in her 'bread powder' (or flour) in January 1318 and Isabel for forestalling in April 1323. That their probable unmarried status persisted over a decade later leads one to suppose that they continued at the family trade late into life, retaining access to the family's bakehouse, but for neither is there any curial indication of having attained a position of more than middling prominence in the community's socio-economic hierarchy.

Similarly, while their mother Juliana, wife of Thomas Chamberlain, was one of the borough's more prolific brewers (see above, table 3.6), neither daughter went on to brew regularly. No record of Tibot's breaching the assize of ale survives, and Ruthin's extant court rolls indicate that Isabel was only twice amerced for brewing in the 1312–21 period.[26] Here, too, Isabel at least seems to have been afforded access to, and responsibility for, enough household capital to participate in a trade, but not enough to achieve the independence or social standing of her brother or mother.

On the one hand, for young single women, earning money in any way that required significant capital outlay was clearly difficult. Therefore, as exemplified by both of Thomas Chamberlain's daughters, few could become brewsters or bakers in their own right until later in life, if ever.[27] On the other hand, it is clear that women of such moderate means as Tibot and Isabel Chamberlain were continuously involved in the borough's economy. As Hutton explains of medieval Shrewsbury, 'even periods of complete silence on the subject of women cannot be taken as an indication that women did not participate [in the urban economy]', and, as with Thomas Chamberlain's daughters, the record is almost never totally silent.[28] Given the available evidence, it is more realistic to conclude that women such as Isabel and Tibot worked at their craft throughout the early fourteenth century, but received legal recognition only when the crisis circumstances of the great famine elevated the social importance of their role. This

---

[26] Ibid., GC1 #1722, 1744; SC2/216/3 m.22, m.23d.

[27] H. Leyser, *Medieval Women: A Social History of Women in England, 450–1500* (London, 1995), p. 44.

[28] D. Hutton, 'Women in fourteenth century Shrewsbury', in L. Charles and L. Duffin (eds), *Women and Work in Pre-Industrial England* (London, 1985), pp. 83–4.

supposition is supported by a review of the other women who worked as bakers in the 1320s, most of whom are likely to have moved from the makeshift role of helper to that of skilled worker, only to return eventually to legal obscurity.

Capital and extended market participation
Table 4.1 refers to all women amerced for breaching Ruthin's assize of bread between 1306 and 1342, distinguishing those women for whom a familial connection to another assize breaker can be identified (group 1) from those who seem to be venturing alone into the trade (group 2).[29] This table conveys the strong impression that two distinct groups of women received legal recognition at about the same time as Isabel and Tibot Chamberlain. The first and larger group comprised the 60 per cent or more of female assize breakers who, like the Chamberlain sisters, were working in the household of a husband, father or sibling who also paid for the right to bake commercially during the same period. Like Tibot and Isabel, these women almost certainly worked consistently throughout the period but occasioned curial notice or censure only during the famine and immediate post-famine decades. The second were those women who attempted to enter the market at or around the point of its expansion in the 1320s and 1330s, without the benefit of other family members already baking commercially.

For these two groups the experience of baking for retail consumption must have been markedly different. Presumably, any woman would have needed access to at least moderate amounts of capital in order to generate a sufficient quantity of trade to warrant the notice of the borough's jurors, and merit an amercement for breaching the assize of bread. However, while the first group of bakers could draw on the resources of a household already functioning as a commercial unit, no doubt in some instances enjoying enhanced means of production such as a bakehouse, the second group must have been risking irreplaceable reserves of coin, kind or credit on

[29]   The general impression of the evidence is that at least a few more women than could be firmly linked to another baker were in fact functioning as part of a larger organizational unit; however, this suspicion cannot be substantiated by the evidence.

Table 4.1. Female bakers of Ruthin, 1306–42

	Appear once		Appear 2–5 times	Average total interval*	Appear > 5 times	Average once total interval*	
Group 1: Related to another baker	19 (61%)	→ 5 (26%)	12 (64%)	110	2 (10%)	147	= 100%
Group 2: No known relation	12 (39%)	→ 5 (42%)	5 (42%)	40	2 (6%)	159	= 100%
	31 (100%)	→ 10 (32%)	17 (55%)		4 (13%)		= 100%

Source: as figure 4.1; *Dyffryn Clwyd Database*.
* This is the average total interval (in months) between the first and last amercements paid for breach of assize.

basic materials and tools. As the merchant of Chaucer's 'Shipman's Tale' says of chapmen (and women!), 'hir money is hir plough'.[30] This difficulty is illustrated by the greatly reduced average interval of forty months between the first and last breaches of assize by women who were working independently, compared to 110 months for those with discernible relationships with other bakers (table 4.1).

'Related bakeresses' (group 1) are personified by women such as Tibot Chamberlain, whose amercements were spread across the period 1318–35, during which she was likely to have been working continuously as part of a larger household unit. 'Independent bakeresses' (group 2) are best represented by women like Isolda de Stretton, who was amerced for breaching the assize on only three consecutive occasions: in October 1331, April 1332 and October 1332.[31] Isolda entered the market for a short time during which she worked steadily, occasioning a middling amercement of 6d. at each relevant great court, and then chose to withdraw from the trade, so ending her commercial venture.

Isolda is also representative of independent bakeresses with regard to her curial background. While most female bakers related to other assize breakers were infrequently involved in borough court litigation, and almost never in trade-related disputes, independent bakers like Isolda were much more likely to be party to a variety of commercially orientated pleas. For example, the independent bakeress Alice le Blake, who was amerced for breaching the assize of bread in October 1320, was also cited by Ruthin's courts of 1312–21 for forestalling 'small foods'.[32] Independent bakeress Olive, the wife (and eventual widow) of Roger *cirotecarius* (glover), who breached the assize of ale on four occasions, was recorded in Ruthin's surviving rolls of the same decade not only in connection with baking but also when pursuing a plea of unjust detention.[33] Furthermore, Isolda herself appeared in

---

[30] G. Chaucer, *The Canterbury Tales: A Selection*, Penguin Popular Classics edn, (London, 1969), p. 151.

[31] *Dyffryn Clwyd Database*, GC1 # 3012, 3031,3352; SC2/216/12 m.14 & 14d, SC2/216/13 m.23.

[32] Ibid., GC1 #1721, SC2/216/3 m.23.

[33] TNA, SC2/216/3 session 8.

Ruthin's borough courts of 1312–21 not only for baking but also when pursuing debt and unjust detention pleas against Einion ap Cynddelw and a prominent borough juror, William de Rowehull.[34]

By contrast, the related bakeress Amy, wife of baker William de Helpston, was amerced four times for breach of assize, but only appeared in the borough courts of 1312–21 three further times: in connection with pleas of defamation, battery and concord (though the subject of this agreement is lost).[35] Maud, the wife of the baker Walter de Lodelow, who broke the assize of ale on four occasions, only appeared in court in one non-assize-related plea, when bringing a charge of blood-shed against the son of Walter *carectarius* (carter).[36] And the regular bakeress, Agnes, the wife of baker William de Flittewyk, appeared in the borough courts only in response to five breaches of the assize of bread.

It is possible that this pattern is to some extent related to the high proportion (around 52 per cent) of women among related bakeresses regularly identified as 'the wife of' or 'the daughter of' a male member of the community. This contrasts with just 33 per cent of independent female bakers who were routinely referred to with reference to a male member of the community. But, as is argued in chapter III, there was little correlation between marriage and a woman's capacity to access the courts in Ruthin. The most credible explanation is simply that as long as related bakeresses were working with capital drawn from a larger household unit, they were less able to invest that coin, kind or credit in the variety of ways open to independent bakeresses. One may perhaps liken the related bakeress to a member of a single-craft corporate enterprise, and her independent counterpart to a freebooting entrepreneur who sometimes chose to invest in baking. This latter woman, even if married, would probably have enjoyed a degree of autonomy more akin to that of the borough's prosperous brewsters than to that of her related bakeress counterparts.

---

[34] TNA, SC2/215/74 sessions 5 & 6, SC2/215/74 session 8.

[35] TNA, SC2/216/2 session 8, SC2/216/3 session 2.

[36] *Dyffryn Clwyd Database*, GC1 #1706, SC2/216/3 m.23.

However, in neither group in table 4.1 did more than a couple of women appear as regular members of the baking trade. Even more surprisingly, there is circumstantial evidence to suggest that three of the four women known to have breached the assize of bread on more than five occasions in the early fourteenth century were unwed. 'Amy the daughter of Roger de Checkelegh' (eventually referred to simply as 'Amy de Checkelegh') was amerced for breach of assize eight times over the sixty-six-month period from April 1330 to October 1335 and, although her father Roger last appeared in Ruthin's courts in July 1319, she was never identified with reference to any other man.[37] Likewise, neither Alice le Brounne, whose name is recorded in fourteen surviving assize lists from May 1321 to 1342, nor Hawysia le Rede, who breached the assize twelve times over a similar period, was ever identified as 'wife' or 'widow'.

Only the last of Ruthin's high-profile bakeresses, Olive, the wife of Adam *cirotecarius*, was working in the household of a spouse and was also amerced with frequency and consistency. Cited for breaching the assize of bread seven times between 1329 and 1342, she is the only female baker who appears, at least in the record, to have achieved anything like equality of status with her husband. In the same period, the extant court record indicates that Adam *cirotecarius* was also amerced for baking seven times, and that the size of the amercement typically paid by both he and his wife was the same at $3d.$ to $6d.$[38] Only the low value of these amercements casts a shadow of doubt over the material importance of Olive's equal commercial opportunities.

While in some ways the experience of Olive, who was still baking in the early 1340s, epitomizes a high point of recognition for the borough's female bakers, her longevity was atypical. For Ruthin's bakeresses, the post-famine years after 1330 were, as Goldberg's study of York suggests of the later

[37]   TNA, SC/216/2 session 9
[38]   For example, in October 1333 Adam was amerced $6d.$, in October 1335 Olive was amerced $3d.$, in October 1340 Adam was amerced $3d.$, in October 1341 Olive was excused because she broke the assize only once. *Dyffryn Clwyd Database*, GC1 #3451,3569; Roll1 #22, 100; SC2/216/14 m.22, SC/217/1 m.12, SC2/217/6 m.2, and SC2/217/7 m.3

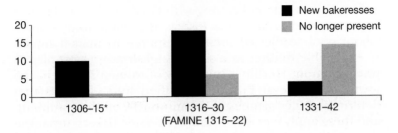

Figure 4.3. New and departing female bakers
Source: as for figure 4.1.
* The number of 'new bakeresses' in this period is misleadingly high, as no previous records survive. Therefore, all female bakers amerced in these years have been counted as new, though some are likely to have been previously active.

post-plague period, years during which, to use Leyser's words, any such 'halcyon days' for women had come to an end.[39] After a period of widening access in 1316–30, only four new women were amerced for breaching the assize of bread between 1331 and 1342, and none of them appeared for a period of more than three years (figure 4.3). Similarly, most of those women who were first amerced for breaching the assize during the famine period had stopped baking or were subject to diminished legal status by the 1330s and no longer featured in the assize lists.

As those women who had opportunistically entered the trade or gained market recognition during a famine-induced period of heightened demand either withdrew or were denied control of enough capital to justify further amercements, trade access became either too difficult to obtain or too unattractive to entice equal numbers of women to replace them. The sustained higher number of around ten bakers working in the borough at any one time in the late 1330s, as opposed to five between 1306 and 1308, testifies to the longevity of the increased market demand which had spurred trade entry in the famine years. Nevertheless, it was the unflagging trade activity of men like William de Wytemor and Roger Burgeys, combined with the participation of new bakers like Thomas *clericus* and John, the servant of William de Wytemor, which eventually squeezed out Ruthin's bakeresses.[40]

39 Leyser, *Medieval Women: A Social History*, p. 160.
40 Ibid.; William de Wytemor was active from October 1312 to April 1342, and

This shift, while in keeping with Goldberg's paradigm of opportunities gained and lost as the community's male labour pool readjusted itself in response to market forces, is explicable neither as a solely English nor a post-plague phenomenon. Herlihy's long view of women's work in the towns of medieval Europe identified four elements that determined the fortunes of urban women on the continent, and these apply equally to Ruthin's female bakers: urbanization, capitalization, market saturation and monopolization.[41] Herlihy observed that in growing settlements men needed to seek out an occupation and ply a trade in order to earn a living. Hence urbanization brought with it the professionalization and specialization of productive activities as markets became more competitive. Unlike male traders, women were never totally free to develop these specializations, as urban life and market participation did not release women from other time-consuming domestic obligations, such as childcare and food preparation.[42] The reality of this is reflected in the fact that, as previously discussed, three of Ruthin's four most active female bakers – Amy de Checkelegh, Hawysia le Rede and Alice le Brounne – were apparently unmarried.

Herlihy also maintained that to remain competitive in the long run required capital infusion. However, women who typically functioned as part-time workers in the urban setting neither accumulated, attracted nor controlled capital to the same extent as men.[43] As we have already seen, the court profiles of the borough's independent bakeresses, like Isolda de Stretton and Alice le Blake, were personified by credit- and trade-related litigation, and the average period of their market involvement was only around forty months.[44] This suggests that, while they were economically active, independent female bakers had difficulty in maintaining the capital necessary to sustain prolonged trade participation.

Roger Burgeys from November 1314 to April 1339, while Thomas *clericus* first appears in October 1335 and John, the servant William de Wytemore, in April 1338.

[41]　David Herlihy, *Women, Family and Society in Medieval Europe: Historical Essays, 1978–1991* (Oxford, 1991), pp. 91–5.

[42]　Ibid., p. 92.

[43]　Ibid., p. 93.

[44]　See table 4.1 above.

Alternatively, the disappearance of related bakeresses, such as Isabel le Chamberlain or Agnes the wife of William de Flitewyk, from assize lists in the 1330s, while their brothers or husbands continued to be amerced suggests that, though probably working at least part-time, they failed to maintain control of enough of the family enterprise's material capital to warrant continued curial recognition.

Even having overcome the obstacles of urban specialization and capitalization, Ruthin's female bakers may still have been faced by an increasingly saturated market as rural life returned to normal in the 1330s, and an attempted reassertion of male monopoly. As Herlihy explains, diminished opportunities pressed men into a defensive posture from which they sought to restrict market entry and thus limit competition.[45] Thereafter, the long-term consequence of restricted and specialized rivalry was a male monopoly that excluded women.[46] For related bakeresses this exclusion was probably more imaginary than real, as they are likely to have continued working as members of commercially productive households. But the disappearance of independent female bakers in the 1330s indicates a significant lost trade opportunity. Together, this curial and actual diminution struck a blow at the status of female bakers, relegating them from the prestige of skilled tradeswomen back to the obscurity of makeshift labourers from which they had come.

While Goldberg's and Herlihy's diverging opinions as to the nature of the progressive exclusion of women from the urban workplace in the later Middle Ages are reconcilable, they disagree as to when this decline in status began and why. In sum, Herlihy's thesis is that women's participation in urban economic enterprises declined dramatically during the later Middle Ages, beginning with a period of high visibility in the thirteenth century and ending in the sixteenth.[47] The Black Death of 1348–9, and the labour opportunities it created, he argues, delayed this development only for a time.[48] Goldberg, for his part, argues that it was not until the economic expan-

---

[45] Herlihy, *Women, Family and Society*, p. 93.
[46] Ibid., p. 94.
[47] Ibid., p. 91.
[48] Ibid., p. 93.

sion of the later fourteenth century, and under circumstances occasioned by the Black Death, that women moved beyond the most traditional of female tasks such as spinning and laundering.[49]

Yet perhaps these suggestions need not be seen as mutually exclusive patterns of development if female market access is viewed as cyclical and circumstantially based, rather than finite and chronologically bound, that is, limited to one specific chronography. The present study encompasses only the activities of women following one trade, in one location, at one point in time. But, by meeting the criteria laid out by Goldberg, in a different time frame, it illustrates the willingness of women to enter a skilled trade in a market at any point when labour shortages coincided with access to sufficient capital. When these criteria were met, the cycle of inclusion, decline and exclusion, as identified by Goldberg, was set in motion. Its duration and extent were regulated by the size and duration of the initial labour shortage, and the period of time the community required to readjust. This cycle could be set in motion by a small and specific labour shortage which lasted only a generation, as was the case with Ruthin's famine-induced need for greater food production. Alternatively, this cycle could be induced by a catastrophic and broad-ranging labour shortage such as that caused in York by the Black Death.[50]

RUTHIN'S SKILLED TRADESWOMEN IN PERSPECTIVE

The circumstances in which Ruthin's female bakers were working in the period 1312–21 may have been unique, or at least uniquely well documented due to the enforcement of the assize of bread. However, what this micro-study tells us

[49]   Goldberg, *Women, Work and Life Cycle*, pp. 86–7.
[50]   Another example might be the changing fortunes of London's women, as observed by Barron, who notes that while the later fourteenth century offered the same 'golden age' for women observed by Goldberg in York, as women's fortunes changed for the worse in the late fifteenth century, 'London was to some extent immune from this recession, since its economy was more diversified, but by the sixteenth century the demographic rise had wiped out a labour shortage and replaced it by a labour glut. For this reason women were pushed out of the skilled labour market ...' Barron, 'The "Golden Age"', 48.

about the nature of skilled female labour in the pre-plague borough almost certainly applies to other townswomen functioning as makeshift workers, or struggling to raise enough capital to enter a variety of trades independently. Doubtless these women too, if finding themselves presented with opportunities for market entry or formal recognition, should labour shortages and capital become available, would have responded as Ruthin's female bakers did.

In any trade, apart from the female-dominated work of brewing, the same internal division of craftswomen between those operating as part of a larger household unit and those working independently would have been present. Although lacking similar assize data for women other than bakeresses and brewsters, craft names and court roll appearances point towards similar circumstances in other trades. An analysis of some of Ruthin's charcoal burners/coal traders confirms this. Henry *carbonarius* was trading in the borough from at least 1315: acting as pledge, pursuing bad debtors and occasionally having altercations with his neighbours, until he was branded a fugitive in 1329 he promptly disappeared from the borough's records.[51] During this time he was married and maintained at least two female servants. The first of these maids, Diota, had left Henry's service by April 1317 when, as his 'former servant', she brought a plaint of debt against Henry in the great court of Ruthin which she later dropped.[52] Diota then seems to have become an independent tradeswoman. She later appears in the borough court of Ruthin when sued by Robert Box for failure to deliver thirteen hopes of coal/charcoal in a timely fashion, and when complaining of the theft of some coal/charcoal by Agnes de Hengoed in 1321.[53] It is probable that she carried on trading until at least 1324 by which time she had

---

[51] For example, TNA, SC2/215/74 session 6 (1315 pledge); SC2/215/76 session 4 (debt); *Dyffryn Clwyd Database*, GC1 #1614, SC2/216/3 m.21 (assault); and GC1 #2798, SC2/216/10 m.27 (1329 fugitive).

[52] *Dyffryn Clwyd Database*, GC1 #1233, SC2/215/76 m.14. This was presumably a dispute over pay, as such complaints were not uncommon. In the borough court of July 1314, for example, two such cases appear in which Matilda, the daughter of Peter and Madog ap Ieuan, sued her former employers, William le Palfryman and Cadwgan ap Gwyn cuit ('cuyt'), for 10*d.* and 7*d.* respectively (TNA, SC2/215/73 session 8).

[53] TNA, SC2/216/3 sessions 5 and 6.

married, making a sketchy appearance in a damaged court roll entry of 1324 as 'Diota ... wife of Deyne le colier'.[54]

Meanwhile, by 1322 Henry had acquired a new servant, Agnes, who along with his wife continued to work as part of his household in the 1320s. In May 1321, for example, Henry's wife Matilda and maid Agnes appeared in the borough court of Ruthin accused of housebreaking, after an incident in which they had gone to the house of John Balle and his wife Eva to collect a debt of 21*d*. As an inquest later reports, Agnes and Matilda were there 'frequently verbally abused and maliciously insulted' while they measured out and took the owed monies, held by Eva.[55] While collecting the household's bad debts hardly indicates the work of skilled tradeswomen, taken together with our knowledge of Diota's market entry after leaving service, a larger picture comes into focus.

As was the case with Ruthin's female bakers, even when not explicitly engaged in trade activity the borough's middling women were involved in activities well outside the traditional household sphere. The family unit contributed to household prosperity by informally training its younger members and familiarizing wives and servants with various aspects of its business.[56] Like Matilda and Agnes, wives and servants (including children) had roles in the broader community which made them responsible for at least moderate amounts of household capital. Furthermore, as Diota illustrates, they would also inevitably have acquired the skills of the household's trade. In possession of both these trade skills and some experience of handling capital, it is not surprising that, given access to moderate amounts of familial or independently acquired resources, women may have taken advantage of every opportunity to better their status and prosperity whenever a gap in the market appeared. Such may very well have been the circumstances which motivated Diota to begin trading independently after leaving Henry's service, in similar fashion to

---

[54]   *Dyffryn Clwyd Database*, GC1 #2233, SC2/216/5 m.30. The rarity of the name Diota and its association with the trade of a collier makes this a reasonable connection though it cannot be confirmed.

[55]   TNA, SC2/216/3 session 7.

[56]   Jewell, *Women in Medieval England*, p. 94.

the way in which new women began to bake commercially when famine levels of demand cleared the way for their increased recognition and market participation.

Although it is only sporadically possible to track the activities of women labouring within households as makeshift or semi-professional workers, the trade names taken up or assigned by the court to many independent tradeswomen can be extracted from the borough's records. These too are somewhat problematic, if, as by the example of female bakers in table 4.1, independently active craftswomen were liable to enter and exit a trade within a window of only forty months. Such brevity of market participation would limit the probability of their appearance and trade identification in the court record, and this may by compounded by the occupational transience of some women possessing the skills to work in more than one trade.[57] Nevertheless, table 4.2, though drawing on only borough court and great court of Ruthin records from 1312–21, offers a good sample of the kinds of skilled trades in which Ruthin's independent craftswomen, or those engaged in work requiring access to at least moderate amounts of capital, were active.

If, in addition to these years, we survey women appearing at court in the decades immediately preceding and following 1312–21, we find not only more skilled women of the trades identified in table 4.2 but also independent women described as barber, board-hewer, gardener, soaper and tailoress.[58] Inevitably, many more women were involved in all of these and other activities in the borough during this study's focus period, but either escaped the notice of the court or were identified only with reference to a male relation. As Goldberg discovered of late fourteenth-century poll tax returns – documents which he believes to reflect women's post-plague prosperity – for most areas surviving records can only indicate

---

[57] This problem is complicated by reference to widows who were identified by their Christian name and their husband's trade, such as 'Felicity who was the wife of William *parcarius*'; she was sometimes referred to simply as Felicity *parcarius* after her husband's death (as in TNA, SC2/216/3 session 1).

[58] TNA, SC2/215/69 session 6; SC2/215/69 session 7; *Dyffryn Clwyd Database*, GC1 #216, SC2/215/70 m.5; GC1 #1851, SC2/216/4 m.2; GC1 #2230, SC2/216/5 m.30.

Table 4.2. Ruthin's independent / explicitly named skilled craftswomen, 1312–21

Trade	Number		
Brewsters, women with significant quantities of investment capital	→		See table 3.6
Mealmaker	2		
Fuller (walker)	2		
Coal / Charcoal trader	1		*Women with access to*
Drystere	1	Total: 10	*moderate levels of*
Dyer	1		*investment capital*
Fisherwoman	1		*(Independent)*
Weaveress	1		
Wheelwright	1		
Cloth workers, regrators, prostitutes and other women with little or no investment capital	→		See table 5.1

Source: TNA, SC2/215/71–SC2/216/3.

the range of trades open to single women.[59] Nevertheless, the identification of independent tradeswomen at least alerts us to the consistent presence of a relatively numerous, if poorly recorded, body of married and unmarried skilled female labourers. If, as a crude guide, we apply to the number of independent tradeswomen identified in table 4.2, the 2:1 ratio of related to independent bakeresses appearing in table 4.1, we may estimate that there were (including bakeresses) around thirty-six such middling women (related and independent) working in the borough at any one time, or about 12 per cent of the borough's female population.[60] These were women willing and sometimes able to access the moderate

[59] Goldberg, *Women, Work and Life Cycle*, p. 93.
[60] A 2:1 ratio of related to independent craftswomen (as in table 4.1) would suggest that at least thirty women worked in skilled trades requiring moderate amounts of capital in the borough during the decade, plus about six female bakers. If the borough had a population of around 300 men and 300 women, this would suggest that about 12 per cent of Ruthin's women were so employed.

amounts of capital necessary for market entry into skilled trades, should labour shortages, large or small, make their more formal participation possible. While the general under-representation of these women in the court record makes it hard to remark quantitatively on the ethnicity of these women as a group, they seem more commonly to have been English; eight of the ten women in table 4.2 have English names. However, as we shall see in greater detail in chapters V and VI, it was access to capital rather than ethnicity which directly or indirectly dictated the capacity of any part of Ruthin's community to access labour opportunities.

V

CLOTH WORKERS, FORESTALLERS, SERVICE WOMEN: WOMEN WITH LITTLE OR NO INVESTMENT CAPITAL

Chapters III and IV have focused on the manner in which women with access to large or moderate amounts of investment capital attempted to make the most of the market opportunities available to them. Both of these groups were composed primarily of married women, and are likely to have often enjoyed relative stability and prosperity.[1] It is probable, however, that these two groups of women together comprised only a minority of the borough's female workers.[2] This chapter details the diverse occupations and life circumstances of those women living in the borough but having access to little or no investment capital. Unlike brewsters and bakeresses, this body of female workers was largely composed of unmarried women, and was characterized by socio-economic instability and exploitation.

Although less well documented than brewsters and bakeresses, many of the women active in trades requiring little or no investment capital are more conspicuous in the court record than most of Ruthin's skilled craftswomen, as the town's poorest women regularly found themselves at odds with borough statutes. These female workers can be divided into, and discussed as, three general categories: those operating at

---

[1] See table 3.6 and table 4.1 with the ensuing discussion.

[2] Estimates are highly problematic and should not be taken as more than the roughest of guides. Nevertheless, if we attempt to deconstruct proportionally the workforce based on the assumption that during the famine period the borough contained around 300 men and 300 women, a rough estimate based on assize data would suggest that the borough's most active ale-wives (25 or 8 per cent; see table 3.6) and skilled tradeswomen (36 or 12 per cent; see table 4.2) together would have comprised only about sixty-one women, 20 per cent of the borough's female population. If we further employ Hilton's rough estimate that about one-third of a pre-plague population would typically have been below the age of fourteen, then these women may have comprised about 31 per cent (61 of 200) of the 'adult' female workforce (R. Hilton, 'Low-level urbanization: the seigniorial borough of Thornbury in the Middle Ages', in Z. Razi and R. Smith (eds), *Medieval Society and the Manor Court* (Oxford, 1996), p. 491).

Table 5.1. Ruthin's female victuallers, cloth workers and service women, 1312–21

Labour type	Occupation	Quantity	Totals
victualling	forestallers and regrators	33	33
cloth	Knitter	2	5
	Kembstere	1	
	Burler	1	
	Kellemakere	1	
service	Maid	12	18
	Nurse	3	
	Prostitute	3	

Source: TNA, SC2/215/71–SC2/216/3.

the lower end of the victualling trade, those involved in the early or more menial stages of cloth production and those working in service occupations. Women active in the last two of these categories, cloth production and service work, are principally identifiable in the court rolls through trade-name data and, as we shall see, probably endured a consistently low level of prosperity. Those women who acted as the borough's forestallers and regrators were a more mixed group, including simultaneously some of the borough's poorest women, with whom we are immediately concerned, and a smattering of wealthier women with moderate or even high levels of capital at their disposal.

VICTUALLERS: FORESTALLING AND SMALL-SCALE RETAIL

The premature purchase, withholding and resale of goods for profit, collectively referred to as 'forestalling' or 'regrating', were a potential avenue to quick profit for members of all social classes. As Diane Hutton observed of fourteenth-century Shrewsbury, women were much more likely to engage in retailing than their male counterparts, and especially so where foodstuffs were concerned.[3] Therefore, it is not

[3] D. Hutton, 'Women in fourteenth century Shrewsbury', in L. Charles and L. Duffin (eds), *Women and Work in Pre-Industrial England* (London, 1985), p. 94.

surprising that Ruthin's women were more frequently cited for forestalling and regrating offences than their male counterparts. Hutton found that, in March 1400, twenty-two of thirty-five regrators named to take the view of frankpledge in Shrewsbury, or about 63 per cent of regrators, were women.[4] In Ruthin regrators were even more likely to be women. Thirty-three of the thirty-five persons, or 94 per cent, amerced for forestalling and regrating from 1312 to 1321 were women.[5]

Hutton identified many of Shrewsbury's post-plague regrators as both unmarried and possessing unique surnames. This suggested to her that many regrators were migrants who had been unable to marry in their native village due to a lack of men or money, and had therefore come to the town to try their luck.[6] Given Ruthin's character as a settler community, the uniqueness of many surnames is not a strong indicator of whether an individual was a first- or second-generation settler, poor migrant, or marginal member of the community. Nevertheless, it has been possible to search the borough's early fourteenth-century court records and derive a fairly convincing and consistent picture of these women's backgrounds, as shown in figure 5.1.

Around 52 per cent of women amerced for forestalling and regrating were persons relatively new to, or unestablished in, the community, typically with few if any previous court appearances and at most with one similarly low-status relation within the borough. In contrast to Shrewsbury, however, eleven of these sixteen unestablished women, or almost three-quarters of them, were married. This is probably the result (as noted above in chapter III, with regard to the community's low number of widows) of a proportionately high number of immigrant male settlers who would have helped to counter any gender imbalance caused by female migration, and absorbed migrant women into marriage partnerships.[7] The

---

[4]   Ibid.
[5]   R. R. Davies and Ll. B. Smith (eds), *The Dyffryn Clwyd Court Roll Database, 1294–1422* (Aberystwyth, 1995); GC1 #481, 483, 729–30, 988–90, 1102–4, 1274–5, 1402–9, 1425, 1720–1, 173–8; TNA, SC2/215/72 m.2d, SC2/215/73 m.26d, SC/215/74 m.16 & 18, SC/215/76 m.14d, SC2/216/1 m.20, SC2/216/2 m.6, SC/216/3 m.22–3; TNA, SC2/216/1 session 1, SC2/216/3 session 5.
[6]   Hutton, 'Women in fourteenth century Shrewsbury', p. 94.
[7]   These women probably represent Ruthin's clearest exception to the trend

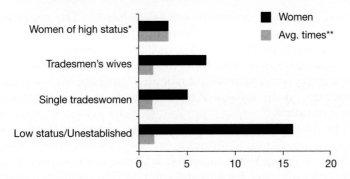

Figure 5.1. Ruthin's regrators and forestallers, 1312–21

Source: *Dyffryn Clwyd Database*, GC1 #481, 483, 729–30, 988–90, 1102–4, 1274–5, 1402–9, 1425, 1720–1, 173–8; SC2/215/72 m.2d, SC2/215/73 m.26d, SC/215/74 m.16 & 18, SC/215/76 m.14d, SC2/216/1 m.20, SC2/216/2 m.6, SC/216/3 m.22–3; TNA, SC2/216/1 session 1, SC2/216/3 session 5.

* The label 'high status' designates those women whose husbands meet at least one of the status indicators in table 2.6, chapter II.

** Average number of times each woman was amerced.

marital status of Ruthin's recorded regrators may also be relevant to the pre-plague context of this early fourteenth-century sample, as opposed to Hutton's post-plague source material from early fifteenth-century Shrewsbury.[8] Taking this period as a whole, Jeremy Goldberg has suggested both an increased female-to-male gender ratio in towns following the plague and an increase in the margin by which the number of urban retailers exceeded the number of producers.[9]

Even if married, however, the low-status or unestablished majority of these petty traders would only have possessed the bare minimum of working capital. The language with which their transgression was described hints at this, as they were regularly accused of the regrating of 'small' or 'petty foods'

noted by Llinos Smith, and evident among Ruthin's brewsters and bakeresses, namely, that marriage was often one of a woman's 'passports' to work and prosperity. Ll. B. Smith, 'Towards a history of women in late medieval Wales', in S. Clarke and M. Roberts (eds), *Women and Gender in Early Modern Wales* (Cardiff, 2000), p. 38.

[8]   It is unfortunate that the fragmentary late fourteenth-century court rolls of Caernarfon, the only parallel body of court rolls for a medieval Welsh town, do not contain similar systematic amercements of forestallers and regrators.

[9]   P. J. P. Goldberg, *Women, Work and Life Cycle in a Medieval Economy: Women in York and Yorkshire, c.1300–1520* (Oxford, 1992), p. 115.

(*rerum minutarum* or *minutarum victualium*).[10] The regrated items most commonly mentioned by name in amercements were butter, eggs, cheese and corn.[11] Notable is the lack of any finished, more expensive foodstuffs known to have been sold in the town, such as bread, pies, or ale. These are likely to have been beyond the means of most of the borough's regrators and forestallers.[12]

A problem for these women would have been the persistent competition of their wealthier neighbours (see figure 5.1). For independent tradeswomen such as Almarie *textrix* (weaver), amerced only once for forestalling in 1316, additional petty trading may have comprised a small but necessary supplement to their craftwork income.[13] For the wives of active borough tradesmen such as Felicity, the wife of David *pastillarius* (pie maker), amerced three times between 1318 and 1321, court censure may have come only in response to the selling of their husband's wares outside the market, or market hours.[14] Both these phenomena, however, which are also observed in Shrewsbury, would undoubtedly have impinged on the professional regrator's commercial activity.[15]

Most challenging to the ability of poor regrators to sustain themselves were undoubtedly the wealthy wives of craftsmen from outside the victualling trades who chose to deal in foodstuffs. Women ranging from the once-amerced Angharad, the wife of David *rotarius* (wheelwright), to Agnes, the wife of Robert Box, who was amerced five times (more than any other woman in the decade 1312–21), would have been competing directly with the borough's professional petty traders.[16] In the case of Agnes, whose husband was the borough's sixth most prolific creditor, the amount of capital available to her with

[10]   *Dyffryn Clwyd Database*, GC1 #729, 730, 1721, and 1737; SC2/215/73 m.26d and SC2/216/3 m.22–3.

[11]   For example: GC1 # 1737 and 998; SC2/215/74 m.16 and SC2/216/3 m.22.

[12]   This is different from the pre-plague situation in York, where some women described as regrators were in fact ale sellers; Ruthin's records more closely resemble those of early fourteenth-century Oxford, where a distinction is drawn between regrators and ale sellers. Goldberg, *Women, Work and Life Cycle*, pp. 115–17.

[13]   *Dyffryn Clwyd Database*, GC1 #1103; SC2/215/74 m.18.

[14]   Ibid., GC1 #254, 1318, and 1721; SC2/216/1 m.20 and SC2/216/3 m.22–3.

[15]   Hutton, 'Women in fourteenth century Shrewsbury', p. 95.

[16]   *Dyffryn Clwyd Database*, GC1 #483, 1403, 1425, 1721, 1738; SC2/215/72 m.2d, SC2/216/1 m.20, SC2/216/2 m.6, and SC2/216/3 m.22–23.

which to buy in bulk outside the market and resell for profit must have surpassed that of ordinary regrators. By comparison with poor traders like Emma de Lancaster, who appeared in the borough no earlier than 1319, had no identifiable property or relations, and was amerced in October 1320 for regrating, only to be imprisoned in December of the same year for stealing from one of the borough elite, Bleddyn ap Heilyn, Agnes must have had a relatively unattainable high level of prosperity.[17]

The borough's wealthiest, or highest status, regrators were also those most frequently amerced, typically at least three times in the decade. This is about twice as often as poorer women whose presence was probably largely ignored by market officials and the court which may actually have offered some minimal level of market protection to the borough's petty traders. Often referred to more generally as 'hucksters', regrators and forestallers were continuously present in Ruthin, as in other market towns, but appear only to have been amerced when flagrantly violating attempts at trade regulation. Retailing victuals in the streets of fourteenth-century Shrewsbury, for example, their trade may have been frowned upon by authorities, but was one which officials found hard to stamp out.[18] In Norwich even the city authorities occasionally traded with at least one huckster, and officials of post-plague York went so far as to admit women to the franchise of the city under the pretence of trading as 'hucksters'.[19] In this context of uneasy tolerance, the more frequent singling out and amercement of those women with the means to violate market regulations most flagrantly, through the purchase and resale of larger quantities of goods, was the easiest way for civic authorities sharply to curb illegal trading.[20] As a by-product of this

---

[17]   Ibid., GC1 #1721; TNA, SC2/216/2 session 11, SC2/216/3 session 3, and SC2/216/3 m.32; Bleddyn ap Heilyn was the borough's third most frequent pledge, as in table 2.6.

[18]   Hutton, 'Women in fourteenth century Shrewsbury', pp. 94–5.

[19]   Goldberg, *Women, Work and Life Cycle*, pp. 117–18.

[20]   Ruthin's three high-status women who were engaged in forestalling were Agnes, the wife of Robert Box, Angharad, the wife of Dafydd *saer*, and the wife of Llywelyn Llwyd. Although only three of the borough's thirty-one regrators, together they were responsible for one-third of all instances in which an individual huckster was singled out for amercement (see figure 5.1).

control, those struggling for survival with little or no working capital may have been saved from being undercut by higher-volume regrators. In contrast to the more frequent amercement of high-status regrators, it is notable that a woman known in Ruthin during the first decade of the 1300s simply as 'Nest *regratiatrix*' was herself amerced for regrating on only two occasions.[21]

Even working under these conditions of questionable legality, Ruthin's regrators and forestallers, who were dependent on their petty trading for survival, would probably have been in possession of more capital than either cloth or service workers. But much of what they possessed was unavoidably working capital into which they could not afford to delve. Their solvency and commercial viability were subject to the whim of regulatory enforcement and market participation by wealthier members of society, while any stoppage of trade lengthy enough to occasion the literal consumption of their working capital would have spelled disaster. For these reasons Ruthin's hucksters, despite possessing more capital than cloth or service workers, are likely to have endured a lower level of security.

Cloth workers: piecework and supplementary income

The borough's female cloth workers are a more difficult group than the victuallers to trace in the court record. The numerous processes involved in the town's medieval cloth industry undoubtedly absorbed a lot of female labour, but the lack of any consistent account of who participated makes estimating the number of these female workers, and their standard of living, difficult. Some indication of the importance of the cloth industry is evident by the 1330 introduction of an assize of weaving in Dyffryn Clwyd, but residents of the borough were exempt from its application.

When, in April 1330, presentments were made of those who had contravened the assize of weaving in rural localities, all save two of the 138 persons amerced were women.[22] Unless female

---

[21] *Dyffryn Clwyd Database*, GC1 #98, 122; SC2/215/69 m.3, SC2/215/69 m.4.
[22] Smith, 'Towards a history of women', p. 34. This assize excluded the borough.

weavers were being especially targeted, this suggests a highly feminized industry. But, as Smith has pointed out, the strong impression conveyed by the court record is that weaving was, for women, an activity ancillary to that of their husbands if they were weavers, or it was a seasonal by-employment in an agricultural household.[23] Jack agrees that of the four main stages of cloth production (carding/combing, spinning, weaving and fulling), the first three were feminine handcrafts in the countryside, but he also says that, like fulling, weaving was a masculine and professionalized trade in towns.[24] He further suggests that whereas weaving in the countryside took place on a small scale for domestic use, cloth making in towns was focused on a few professional weavers and fullers producing cloth for regional and long-distance trade.[25]

With around half a dozen such professional weavers working in the borough at any one time in the pre-plague period, Ruthin town may already have been a significant centre of cloth production during the reign of Edward II.[26] More importantly, in support of these urban tradesmen there must have been a body of women several times their number who worked at carding and spinning wool in preparation for the loom. Power has asserted that the number of spinners alone required to supply just one weaver for regular production was five.[27]

One indication of the presence of these preparatory workers is the appearance of unmarried women such as 'Agnes le Kembstere' or 'Margery le Kemster' who probably sustained themselves primarily by this work.[28] More explicitly indicative

---

[23]   Ibid., p. 35.
[24]   R. I. Jack, 'The cloth industry in medieval Ruthin', *DHST*, 12 (1963), 11.
[25]   Ibid. By 1447 Ruthin's weavers and fullers had formed a guild and enrolled its ordinances in the lordship's court roll, TNA, SC2/222/3 m.51d. These ordinances have been published as an appendix to Jack's article, 'The cloth industry in medieval Ruthin', 10–25.
[26]   Most of Ruthin's weavers were Welsh and appear under the trade name *weeth*, or 'whyth', 'wyth'. An example is Madog ap Dafydd wyth, whose house was broken into on 23 April 1323, when Madog de Whitford (presumably Flintshire; 'Wytford') robbed him of three ells of woolen cloth and one piece of linen cloth valued at 2s. 6d.
[27]   E. Power, *Medieval Women* (Cambridge, 1975), p. 67.
[28]   TNA, SC2/216/3 sessions 1 & 3; *Dyffryn Clwyd Database*, GC1 #1923, SC2/216/4 m.29. In this latter case Margery was robbed of two sets of combs; this

of the importance and ubiquity of cloth industry employment is that wool and yarn were the most common household items to be stolen in the lordship, and to be stolen by women. Ruthin court roll entries such as that of 1322, in which Angharad, the daughter of Ieuan ap Tudur, was found guilty of stealing one distaff and yarn from the house of Dafydd ap Tegwared, are common (this particular example implying perhaps that Dafydd's spouse or daughter was spinning as a source of additional income).[29] Taken together, the frequency and nature of these thefts reinforce the view that preparing wool, linen or even hemp for weaving was a common 'piecework' industry engaged in by the borough's women.[30]

In Ruthin, as Hutton found in Shrewsbury, women were chiefly employed in the preparation of raw wool in their own homes, spinning and sometimes weaving materials provided by wealthy merchant entrepreneurs.[31] For those with little or no access to capital, this type of piecework would have provided the means to generate some small income with little material investment. A few tantalizing cases, like that which brought Robert Fuller to the great court of Ruthin in 1307 to make his law, hint at what was probably a common type of relationship. In what appears to have been the last chapter of a long-running dispute, Robert was

> at law against Isabel de Alston that he did not receive from Isabel or from Roger the husband of Isabel de Alston nor from anyone else on behalf of Roger and Isabel warp and spindle to weave [*stamen et fusum ad texendum*] nor any money by that weaving nor any other goods before or after the war of Madog ap Llywelyn [1294–5] as Isabel imputed against him, nor does he owe Roger and Isabel anything.[32]

At first glance, it would appear that Robert Fuller had been accused of receiving goods from Isabel for which he did not

---

case appears only in the great court of Dyffryn Clwyd and so Margery does not feature in table 5.1.

[29] *Dyffryn Clwyd Database*, GC1 #2041, SC2/216/4 m.33. The gender bias of the court roll is very prominent here as no married woman could legally own property in her own right, and all entries of this sort state from whose household property was stolen. See above, chapter III.

[30] Wool – ibid., GC1 # 1924, SC2/216/4 m.29: hemp – GC1# 1829, SC2/216/4 m.2: linen – GC1 #2041, SC2/216/4 m.33.

[31] Hutton, 'Women in fourteenth century Shrewsbury', p. 93.

[32] *Dyffryn Clwyd Database*, GC1 #117, SC2/215/69 m.4.

pay. This reading is unlikely, however, given that Robert was a well-established borough property owner and tradesman (a fuller, as his name suggests), frequently acting in the role of personal pledge until his death (between August and October 1312). By contrast, the Alstons were relatively poor and without property. Isabel and Roger Alston appear in the court record only on this occasion, and their daughter Alice just once, ten years later, for possessing stolen wool in 1317.[33]

Although it risks character assignation on scant proof, given the circumstantial evidence and peculiar presentation of the Alston versus Fuller court roll entry, it may be fruitful to consider an alternative reading in which the Alstons were the poorer party. It is more likely that Robert Fuller had provided Isabel with equipment, and presumably materials, for piece-work production of cloth which he might then finish or full. Robert's claim would then be that he had not received the warp and spindle back from her, had not made 'any money by that weaving [which she had done] nor any goods [produced]' and did not owe Isabel and her husband anything in return.[34]

More important than proving which reading is correct is the demonstration that the relationships formed between women and the wider community through such non-capital labour arrangements may have been much more common and complex than they appear in the court record.[35] Spinning was not specifically an indoor activity, and as was the case with women engaged in commercial labours requiring larger quantities of capital, there is no reason to believe that women working in the cloth industry lived totally in the private sphere.[36] Nevertheless, it cannot be stressed enough that from a curial perspective this is an all but invisible area of women's work. By nature, piecework almost always involved inexpensive materials and small quantities of money, neither likely to occasion court action or lead to detailed court roll entries.[37]

---

[33] Ibid., GC1 #1317, SC2/215/76 m.15d.

[34] Ibid., GC1 #117, SC2/215/69 m.4.

[35] Ibid., GC1 #117, SC2/215/69 m.4. A later marginal note, next to the same court roll entry, confirms that Robert was vindicated and excused, whatever the exact circumstances of the dispute may have been.

[36] P. J. P. Goldberg, 'The public and the private: women in the pre-plague economy', in *Thirteenth Century England III: Proceedings of the Newcastle Upon Tyne Conference* (Woodbridge, 1991), p. 82.

[37] It is noteworthy that in the borough court record of Ruthin alone, between

Lack of consistent court roll evidence regarding these women also makes it difficult to calculate their numbers, but a fair estimate based on the related evidence might be made as follows. If Power's ratio of five spinsters to every borough weaver is applied, it may be assumed that there would have been around thirty spinsters working in the town at any one time. If we then draw on the evidence of later poll tax returns, showing that there was typically not more than one comber per ten spinsters, a further three combers would make a total of around thirty-three preparatory cloth workers.[38] Lastly, if women with the bynames 'burler', 'kelemaker' (headdress maker) and 'knitter' are included, it is reasonable to estimate around forty female cloth workers from the court record.

These labourers comprised 7 to 8 per cent of the town's overall population of five to six hundred, and possibly as much as 16 per cent of Ruthin's female population. With such a large proportion of the borough's women so employed, Power's reminder may be applicable to Ruthin, namely, that descriptions such as 'spinster' and 'the distaff side of the family' arose from the sheer number of women traditionally engaged in these tasks.[39] However, it is doubtful whether the mass of the town's female cloth workers experienced anything like stability or security. Such a large body of women employed in crafts for which the skills required were, by comparison with many trades, 'common knowledge' would have ensured intense labour competition and kept an individual's earning potential to a minimum. With no financial or intellectual prerequisite for engagement in the early stages of cloth production, the number of women available to work would always have outstripped the quantity of work available.

Goldberg's view that the exigencies of their regular employment may have forced some cloth workers to resort to theft and prostitution is in keeping with the points made above. The most common household goods to be stolen within

1312 and 1321, no less than forty entries concerning broken contracts and licences to settle out of court appear in which at least one party is a woman, but for which no details of the dispute are given (excluding cases directed against women by means of suits against their fathers or husbands).

[38]　This is a rough estimate of the ratio of combers to spinsters drawn from poll tax returns in table 3.2 of Goldberg, *Women, Work and Life Cycle*, pp. 94–5.

[39]　Power, *Medieval Women*, p. 67.

Dyffryn Clwyd were wool and yarn, and they were most commonly stolen by women.[40] Another indication of the inadequate earning potential of cloth workers is an entry in the rolls of the borough court of Ruthin from 1320 in which a Welsh woman described as 'Morfudd whore burler' was amerced for forestalling.[41] Having accumulated enough wealth to attempt to access the lowest rung of the borough's independent trade network, Morfudd was caught and amerced by market officials, inevitably setting back her attempts at social mobility.

Before applying this rather negative view more broadly, a few general reservations on female cloth workers need to be made. Single women such as Morfudd, searching for a stable income, may represent only a minority of those who spun, combed or wove. Similar to other areas of women's work, the cloth industry undoubtedly employed many married as well as unmarried women. The quality of life experienced by wives or daughters in supplementing family incomes would have differed markedly from that of independent workers. Moreover, given the scarcity of evidence, it is impossible to know the ratio of wives and daughters to independent female labourers in the industry.[42]

What can be said with certainty is that, as a whole, Ruthin's female cloth workers were the second largest sector of female labour in the borough (after the large group of women who did at least some brewing) and among the most likely to suffer economically should a large influx of migrant workers enter the community. This latter factor is likely to have led to hardship during the famine years when the number of migrants to the borough probably rose substantially.[43] For those women with little or no capital, the cloth industry would have been a difficult but accessible means by which to attain independence. It is likely, however, that in Ruthin as elsewhere this independence was gained only by entry into what Jewell has

---

[40]   Goldberg, *Women, Work and Life Cycle*, pp. 119–20.

[41]   TNA, SC2/216/3 session 8.

[42]   It is tempting, though, to apply the 2:1 ratio of wives and daughters to independent female workers found among brewsters and bakeresses, as above, in table 3.6 and table 4.1.

[43]   See chapter IV for famine-period migration.

described as a 'poor and exploited class' of 'pieceworkers ... cheated by employers using false weights', and whose wages were so low as to place them in need of charitable support.[44]

The only positive aspect of this arrangement is that the steady availability of work in Ruthin's ever growing cloth industry during the fourteenth and fifteenth centuries (eventually culminating in the formalization, in 1447, of a guild of weavers and fullers unique in north Wales) may have provided an income with slightly greater regularity than that enjoyed by poor victuallers.[45] Nevertheless, even a constant supply of such poorly paid employment is unlikely to have led to the level of capital accumulation necessary to participate in higher levels of trade. As with other areas of women's work, non-access to capital is likely to have been the limiting factor dictating that many women worked in this industry rather than above it. For young female migrants especially, be they Welsh or English, the hand-to-mouth lifestyle provided by the cloth industry would have tied them to it indefinitely, unless considerations of service or marriage dictated otherwise.[46]

SERVICE WOMEN: FOSTER CHILDREN, SERVANTS, NURSES AND PROSTITUTES

'Service women' are those persons sharing two general characteristics. Primarily, they were women who as adolescents or adults were not only lacking working capital, but were generally unwilling, incapable, or without the opportunity to maintain themselves by other means. Secondly, they were women whose occupations dictated the loss of at least some personal liberties or social standing. Hence, included in the range of women who might qualify as 'service workers' are those women whose occupations were among the most secure (in terms of the regular food and shelter they offered) and the least desirable in medieval towns.

Illustrative of this are the opposite extremes of paid or unpaid domestic service and prostitution. In deciding or being compelled to take up service in a household, a woman

---

[44]   H. Jewell, *Women in Medieval England* (Manchester, 1996), 108–9.
[45]   Jack, 'The cloth Industry in medieval Ruthin', 19–20.
[46]   Goldberg, *Women, Work and Life Cycle*, 108.

was in many ways surrendering her right to run her own affairs. Typically, young unmarried women, female servants would also have undertaken this form of employment during that period of their lives when, as Bennett has explained, they would normally have experienced the closest thing to cross-gender social and legal equality that they would ever have known.[47] This equality is reflected in young unmarried women's independent possession of property and their use of the courts.[48] Alternatively, in the strained economic conditions of the early fourteenth century, attempts to become independently self-sustaining without either knowledge of a skilled craft or the possession of even small amounts of capital would have placed women on a slippery slope to prostitution or other socially marginal activities. One only has to recall Morfudd and her threefold role as huckster, burler and prostitute to imagine how women might have found themselves unwillingly at the less desirable end of the service industry.[49]

The context of service work in Wales
The study of these women in Ruthin's court record is complicated by difficult issues of under-representation, terminology and social context. Mentioned in Ruthin's court rolls of 1312–21 are at least eighteen service women (table 5.1): twelve maids, usually referred to as *ancilla*; three nurses, called *nutrix* or *medicatrix*; and three prostitutes, labelled *meratrix* or 'hoir'. Attempts to ascertain the quality of life of these women are generally problematic because, like poor cloth workers, servants and especially prostitutes are well-nigh invisible in Ruthin's court record. These women were usually mentioned only indirectly, having been witness to, or having played some secondary part in, the events occasioning the court roll entries in which they are noted. Further specific uncertainties stem principally from social factors which impact on the meaning of these service-work by-names. The Latin words *ancilla, nutrix/medicatrix* and *meratrix* are not unique to Wales, but in the context of a Welsh borough the use of each may have

[47]   J. Bennett, *Women in the Medieval English Countryside: Gender and Household in Brigstock Before the Plague* (Oxford, 1987), pp. 71–91.
[48]   Ibid.
[49]   TNA, SC2/216/3 session 8; see above, section 2.

carried a particular significance compared with what may be safely inferred from English manorial records. For this reason it is essential to discuss the social context in which each of these terms is used before presenting an account of what Ruthin's court rolls tell us about the service industry.

Concerning *ancille*, it is not possible to distinguish with certainty whether this term was used to refer to foster-children, as opposed to resident household servants of the variety we typically associate with the early modern period.[50] The concepts and institutions of fosterage and servanthood were intimately entwined in early fourteenth-century Dyffryn Clwyd, and in medieval Wales generally. In Ruthin's court rolls of 1312–21, nowhere is any woman referred to as 'foster-daughter' (*nutricia*), only two women are identified as 'servant' (*serviens*), and it seems almost certain that this is because the fluid relationship between fosterage and servant-hood was such as to render any distinction dubious.[51] In this context, the comparatively numerous eighteen references made to Ruthin's *ancille*, in a variety of circumstances, paint a convincing picture of life for this substantial segment of Ruthin's female service workers; for, almost certainly, many of the borough's maids were foster-daughters.

For the uppermost social strata of medieval England it was common for children to be fostered in another household, or taken on as part of an apprenticeship agreement after they reached the age of seven or eight.[52] In Wales, too, this type of fosterage was common, but traditionally had the added dimension of reinforcing ties of communication and coopera-tion between branches of a child's kindred.[53] Such family ties were essential prior to the abolition of *galanas* and *sarhaed*, Welsh compensation payments for homicide and injury. Until

[50]   It has been estimated by Kussmaul that in the early modern period around 60 per cent of England's young people (sixteen to twenty-four years old) were servants: A. Kussmaul, *Servants in Husbandry in Early Modern England* (Cambridge, 1981), pp. 11–12.

[51]   Women as '*serviens*': *Dyffryn Clwyd Database*, GC1 #1233, SC2/215/76 m.14; TNA, SC2/215/75 session 7.

[52]   B. Hanawalt, *The Ties That Bound: Peasant Families in Medieval England* (New York, 1986), p. 156.

[53]   Smith has discussed various aspects of these ties at length: Ll. B. Smith, 'Fosterage, adoption and God-parenthood: ritual and fictive kinship in medieval Wales', *WHR*, 16 (1992–3), 1–36.

1284 these institutions had made extended family members legally and financially responsible for the misbehaviour of their kin to the seventh degree (fifth cousins).[54] Likewise, though it did not apply to burgage property, the continued legal inability of Welshmen to alienate traditional Welsh lands outside the borough also worked to keep family ties alive. As late as Henry VIII's Act of Union of 1536, Welsh property was subject to partible inheritance among relations to the fourth degree (second cousins).[55] For these and similar reasons, fosterage is often cited as a significant feature of medieval Celtic society as distinct from that of medieval England, though fosterage has never been as clearly defined for Wales as for other Celtic regions, especially Ireland.[56]

Fosterage had a second dimension in Wales for, as in the case of Icelandic and Scandinavian practice, Welsh freemen of substance, or *uchelwyr*, followed the practice of fostering their children with bond families in the fourteenth century and possibly later.[57] Smith has argued that this practice, common (or profitable?) enough to warrant a regular licensing fine of 2*s*. in the neighbouring marcher lordship of Bromfield and Yale, reinforced ties of dependence or subordination between an *uchelwr* and his bondmen.[58] In Dyffryn Clwyd this type of fosterage was outlawed by proclamation sometime during the constableship of Alexander de Saunderton, which began in 1319, but was still occasioning amercements when discovered by court officials as late as the 1340s.[59] In this way the institution of fosterage could reinforce social ties and relationships vertically as well as horizontally. While it is unlikely that this latter

[54]   W. Rees, *South Wales and the March, 1284–1415: A Social and Agrarian Study* (Oxford, 1924), pp. 18–19. In an instance of homicide, for example, a compensation payment would be calculated in accordance with the victim's social status. The murderer and his immediate family were then responsible for one-third of this compensation, and the murderer's extended family to the seventh degree were responsible for the other two-thirds.

[55]   Ibid., p. 209. Smith's article on the use of *prid* (Welsh gage) discusses in detail the particular culture of land transactions which grew out of this system: Ll. B. Smith, 'The gage and the land market in late medieval Wales', *EconHR*, 29 (1976), 537–50.

[56]   Smith, 'Fosterage, adoption and God-parenthood', 3.

[57]   Ibid., 25. Smith has also argued that this practice ensured that the gulf which separated bond and free was never too great in Wales.

[58]   Ibid., 4, 25.

[59]   *Dyffryn Clwyd Database*, Roll3 #735, SC2/217/8, m.14.

relationship existed commonly in the borough of Ruthin, the influence of its continued presence in the countryside cannot be ignored in determining social norms in the town.

As Smith has noted, the merging of the institution of fosterage with the creation of a retinue was a common and well understood practice among the social elites of late medieval Wales.[60] Putting this in a positive light, the contemporary poet William Llŷn praised the making of foster kinsmen and servants into one's 'men'.[61] Less impressed, Sir Hugh Paulet in 1559 was so confounded by these complex personal alliances, which he saw as a root cause of the endemic disorder of the Elizabethan March, that he went as far as to formulate a memorandum stating that fosterage should be forbidden in Wales.[62] The opinions of both Llŷn and Paulet attest to the enduring character of a distinctly Welsh social practice in which foster-children and servants held virtually indistinguishable positions in the medieval household, where foster-children often acted as servants.

There is also no reason to assume that Ruthin's English settler families of the early fourteenth century would have been any less likely to have blurred the lines between fosterage and servanthood. Hanawalt has observed of English households, as Smith did of their Welsh counterparts, that servants were not the equals of their employer's children and could not inherit family land. However, they were often treated through bequests in a manner typically reserved for godchildren, grandchildren, nieces and nephews.[63]

We must also consider that, by the end of our focus period in 1321, English settlers had been migrating to the borough for over thirty years. By this date many English burgesses of Ruthin were second-generation Anglo-Welsh townsmen, and it is not hard to imagine the scope for shared values. These groups already had shared living circumstances and the same practical needs for service within household and borough economies. It is noteworthy that even in Caernarfon, a legally segregated borough where Welsh persons were prohibited

[60]   Smith, 'Fosterage, adoption, and God-parenthood', 28.
[61]   Ibid.
[62]   Ibid., p. 28.
[63]   Ibid., 19; Hanawalt, *The Ties That Bound*, p. 167.

from becoming burgesses, the majority of those servants of English men and women who came before the borough court were Welsh.[64] Hence our ability to make an informed assessment of the common employment and mixed nature of *ancille* in the borough is an important component in understanding the shared interests of women from one particular socio-economic stratum and those of similarly wealthy persons in both ethnic groups.

Second, for nurses it is quite probable that the by-name *nutrix* in a Welsh context implied a wet nurse, as opposed to a *medicatrix*, or sick nurse.[65] Furthermore, in Wales *nutrix* also indicated a more intimate family–servant connection than in English society. Smith has emphasized the tendency for the relationship between a child's nurse and natural father to be 'quasi-tenurial' in nature, the father potentially providing food and housing to the wet nurse.[66] The nursing and fostering roles might then 'merge into each other' as the nurse's charge moved progressively into the role of foster-child, and perhaps eventually servant.[67]

Arrangements obviously being contingent on the standing and marital status of the service worker, it is more likely that single or widowed women entering into a nursing relationship would also have moved into the care of their employer. Married nurses would more commonly have accepted the infant into their own household. In the former instance the relationship would have ended with the weaning of the child, while in the latter it may have become more lasting.

Although the task undertaken by nurses from either background was initially the same, the socio-economic conditions of each were noticeably different. The single or widowed

[64]   From 1361 to 1402, in the borough's earliest surviving court rolls, 13 of 22 servants identified with English masters or mistresses were Welsh: G. Jones and H. Owen (eds), *Caernarvon Court Rolls, 1361–1402* (Caernarvon, 1951), pp. 15–177.

[65]   Smith makes no mention of the possibility that *nutrix* may have sometimes indicated a sick nurse in Welsh sources, perhaps in light of the use of *medicatrix*. On the other hand, Goldberg says that sick nurses are 'regularly found in the records' as opposed to wet nurses who 'may sometimes have been employed' (Goldberg, *Women, Work and Life Cycle*, pp. 134–5). The alternate frequencies of wet nurse and sick nurse are reconciled by acknowledging the difference between the records of the major urban centre of York, upon which Goldberg focused, and those of rural and small-town Wales which Smith used.

[66]   Smith, 'Fosterage, adoption and God-parenthood', 11–19.

[67]   Ibid.

woman moving into, and becoming a dependent of, the household of her charge was essentially selling her body (or the use thereof) in exchange for maintenance and income. Presumably she lacked the capital or skills necessary to sustain herself through other means, and so was engaged in this work. Alternatively the married nurse, even if her husband or household should be receiving partial payment in lands or discounted rents on a quasi-tenurial basis (as Smith has demonstrated was quite common in the early fourteenth century), was still more economically self-sufficient.[68] Moreover, the married nurse who took in a child who might eventually be her foster-child and servant was gaining a valuable future contributor to the domestic economy. As Hanawalt has observed, from ages six to twelve children were already aiding parents in their work and supplementing the income of the household.[69]

For the *medicatrix*, circumstances are likely to have been similar to those of the unwed *nutrix*. Essentially a specialized servant, she would have become a dependent member of her host household for the duration of care given to her sick or elderly patient. After her period of care provision, it is likely that the *medicatrix* would also have been in much the same position as a discharged (unmarried) *nutrix* or general servant, though specialization may have helped in finding subsequent work. Payments and bequests to sick nurses which would have helped to ease the transition from one period of employment to another are commonly found in medieval wills.[70] Furthermore, it has been estimated that, even in the post-plague period, around 10 per cent of the population was over the age of fifty.[71] This undoubtedly afforded regular employment opportunities to at least a few of those women with neither alternative means of making a living, fear of illness, nor compunction about the sacrifice of personal liberties involved in joining someone else's household.[72]

---

[68]   Smith, 'Fosterage, adoption and God-parenthood', 11
[69]   Hanawalt, *The Ties That Bound*, pp. 158–9.
[70]   Goldberg, *Women, Work and Life Cycle*, p. 134.
[71]   Hanawalt, *The Ties That Bound*, p. 229.
[72]   While we know medieval sick nurses to have tended persons of all ages, the greater susceptibility to illness which comes with age is a human constant which would almost certainly have done much to dictate their clientele.

Thirdly, it is possible that those identified as *meratrix* or 'hoir' in the court record were women who had been publicly proclaimed prostitutes by themselves or their families to avoid the repeated enforcement of the *amobr* fine, or Welsh virginity tax, rather than persons engaged primarily in prostitution.[73] Under Welsh law a woman could be held liable for *amobr* only once, upon marriage or on the occasion of her first illicit sexual relationship. Yet under post-conquest lordship, its repeated enforcement at marriage, remarriage and every instance of proven illegal intercourse became such a valuable pretext for increasing the lord's revenue that only publicly recognized prostitutes were excused.[74]

It must be stressed that there is no evidence that the *amobr* fine was enforced within the town of Ruthin during the pre-plague period. The borough charter's clause that burgesses 'may marry their daughters freely and without challenge', and its universal grant of liberties regardless of Englishness or Welshness, can probably be taken to have assured urban exemption.[75] However, amobrers' enforcement of the tax in rural Dyffryn Clwyd throughout the fourteenth century is well attested in the court rolls, the office having been routinely farmed out and women pursued vigorously.

In 1334 it was calculated in the neighbouring lordship of Denbigh that *amobr* generated a substantial £41 annually. If, as is probable, farms were granted independently for each of

---

[73]   R. R. Davies, *Lordship and Society in the March of Wales, 1282–1400* (Oxford, 1978), pp. 137–8.

[74]   In a strict sense *amobr* applied only to Welsh women, but many English women also found themselves subject to taxation if they chose to marry a Welshman. It was held within the lordship that a woman assumed an ethnic 'condition' from her husband at marriage, which was permanent until changed by the lord or a subsequent marriage. Hence in an example of 1358, Gwerful, who had held lands by English tenure and had been of English condition prior to her first marriage, to a Welshman, found herself forced to pay *amobr* at her second marriage (we do not know the ethnicity of Gwerful's parents, though her Christian name suggests they were Welsh). This was because upon embarking on her first marriage she had assumed the Welsh condition of her husband, and was thus technically Welsh when she married again (*Dyffryn Clwyd Database*, Llann3 #765, SC2/218/7 m.17).

[75]   Jack, 'The medieval charters of Ruthin borough', *DHST*, 18 (1969), 18. There appear in the borough court pleas of *amobr* for the first time in the 1390s, and it is likely that this was the product of an administrative change linked to the growing ethnic tensions which preceded the Glyn Dŵr rebellion.

Dyffryn Clwyd's commotes, total revenues of as much as £30 per annum may have been extracted from the countryside. A court roll entry from a 1346 commotal court of Llannerch states that the office was there to be farmed by two men for a twelve-year term, beginning that year, at £10 in silver per annnum.[76] From the early fourteenth century, pleas of *amobr* often appear in court records as unjust detentions in which a woman's *amobr* was withheld from the amobrer personally (a sort of common plea).[77] Each of these men was assisted by several 'servants of the amobrer', who could be charged to distrain or 'place the lord's prohibition on' goods of such a value as to cover an *amobr* fine in kind, apparently the usual manner of payment.[78] Moreover, a badly damaged court roll entry from Llannerch in 1358 suggests that they had the power to pursue cases throughout the whole of the lordship.[79]

The result was that freedom, for rural women, from the hefty 10*s.* tax, which would inevitably have been levied from them for *amobr* on one or more occasions, may have made the town a welcome refuge.[80] Likewise, those women already driven to public self-identification as prostitutes would perhaps have found it a sanctuary from the stigma they undoubtedly experienced in their home villages. In the neighbouring lordship of Bromfield and Yale this stigma, in combination with the practical need to avoid being repeatedly subjected to the *amobr* tax, led some women to be given white rods to carry in recognition of their status as common prostitutes 'so that their kinfolk would not henceforth be troubled for *amobr*'.[81]

The social significance of this tax and the strain it must have placed on the poorest of rural women can hardly be

---

[76] *Dyffryn Clwyd Database*, Llann2 #1406, SC2/217/12 m.15d.

[77] For example, in Llannerch in 1322: Ibid., Llan1 #1236, SC2/216/14 m.19.

[78] For example, Roll1 #624, SC2/217/6 m.16.

[79] Llann3 #789, SC2/218/7 m.17.

[80] Examples of the 10*s.* amercement for *amobr* are common (for example, Llann3 #765, 843, and 2218; SC2/218/7 m.17 and SC2/218/11 m.20), but in rare instances smaller amounts such as 5*s.* were negotiated as a result of poverty (Llann2 #2220, SC2/218/1 m.19). Alternatively, the court was often unyielding, such as in Llannerch in 1342 when, after Gwenllian, the daughter of Dafydd, claimed that she had nothing with which to pay, the court banned anyone within the lordship from receiving or feeding her until she had paid the farmers of *amobr* under a penalty of 15*s.*

[81] Davies, *Lordship and Society*, p. 137.

overstated, and hence it is with strong reservations that we must consider the place in borough society occupied by anyone described as *meretrix* or 'hoir' in the court record. This occupational by-name may indeed have been applied to those compelled to engage in prostitution as a supplementary source of income, but it may also be seen as an indication of unwed rural women moving into the lowest sector of the borough's service industry. Moreover, the potential impact on the psychology and status of those unfortunate women who may have been compelled to enter prostitution in a society conditioned by this tax would have been significant, though impossible to gauge precisely.

Service work in Ruthin

Evidence of the experience of those persons described by the terms *ancilla, nutrix/medicatrix* and *meretrix* in Ruthin in 1312–21 may be interpreted in the following manner. First, in relation to those foster-daughters and servants identified as *ancille*, the unique hardships created by the agricultural and economic conditions of the early fourteenth century exerted a powerful influence on the institutions of fosterage and servanthood in Ruthin. As Hanawalt has pointed out, in the early 1300s an increasing population and surplus of labour would have made the position of servant a very attractive one, for it often guaranteed meals, wages and a roof over one's head.[82] Razi found that in pre-plague Halesowen around 49 per cent of households employed servants at least occasionally.[83] If, as a rough gauge, we were to assume that Ruthin contained one household per each of the 100 or so burgage plots listed in the borough's 1324 rental (almost certainly an underestimate, given that the most common share of property was only half a burgage) and divided that figure by the number of male and female servants named in the borough's court

---

[82]   Hanawalt, *The Ties That Bound*, p. 165.

[83]   In the post-plague period, after labour costs had risen, only around 20 per cent did so. Zvi Razi, 'Family land and the village community in later medieval England', *PP*, 93 (1981), 31. Richard Smith has challenged this pattern of employment: R. Smith, 'Some issues concerning families and their property in rural England, 1250–1800', in R. Smith (ed.), *Land, Kinship and Life-Cycle* (Cambridge, 1984), pp. 22–38.

record (1312–21), the result would suggest that approximately 40 per cent of the town's households employed servants.[84]

It is likely that maturing girls who had grown up in a relatively secure environment as foster-daughters, when looking out from their foster-family's front door between 1315 and 1322 would have been faced with a difficult choice. On reaching the end of their fosterage, girls could step into a town swollen with a saturated labour market of paupers who had been compelled to enter the borough by the subsistence 'push factor' of countryside famine.[85] Alternately, they could choose to seek the shelter of adult service with their foster-family or other domestic employer.

Considering these options in the light of deep-rooted Welsh customs, our view that those older girls routinely referred to in the borough's records as *ancille* would on many occasions have been foster-daughters may be circumstantially reinforced. In addition, it is this familiarity which helps to explain the striking pattern of loyalty and close cooperation between master or mistress and maid in Ruthin's court record. On several occasions between 1312 and 1321 maids came into harm's way defending their employer. For example, when in April 1315 John 'carter of chapel works' (*carectarius operis capelle*) assaulted Almarica la Consteresse he had also to contend with (and 'beat') Alice her maid in the fray, before both women raised hue and cry against him.[86] More dramatically, in May 1313, Alice, the wife of Iorwerth ap Bleddyn, was set upon and assaulted by Angharad, the wife of Tudur ap Bleddyn, who shed Alice's blood. Meanwhile, Paula, Alice's maid, ran for help and was chased (*in felonia*) by Tudur

---

[84] Reasonable adjustments, up (+) or down (–), might be made to this percentage with respect to the number of households occupying less than a full burgage (– per cent), a likely influx of cheap labour in the famine period (+ per cent), the mixed nature of fosterage and servanthood (+ per cent), and the under-recording of servants by occupation on the court roll (+ per cent); unfortunately, the evidence needed to make such adjustments does not survive, making '40 per cent of households' the best guess.

[85] R. Smith, 'Demographic developments in rural England, 1300–48: a survey', in B. Campbell (ed.), *Before the Black Death: Studies in the 'Crisis' of the Early Fourteenth Century* (Manchester, 1991), for a discussion of the causes of 'push factors' (in particular pp. 74–7).

[86] *Dyffryn Clwyd Database*, GC1 #1041; SC2/215/74 m.17.

ap Bleddyn all the way to Alice's home where Paula finally managed to raise hue and cry against Tudur.[87]

Maids also accompanied their employers on dangerous or even illegal tasks. It is worth noting again the detailed entry of May 1321, in which Agnes, the maid of Matilda (wife of Henry *carbonarius*), accompanied her mistress to the house of Eva and John Balle to reclaim a bad debt, whereupon Agnes and Matilda were verbally and maliciously insulted while they counted out the monies owed.[88] Similarly, in July 1319 the bailiff of Ruthin was ordered to arrest Amilia, the maid of Jenkin Messor, along with Dafydd, Jenkin's son, for digging turf on the lord's land, the two having been jointly responsible.[89]

These court entries are suggestive of a situation in which female servants or foster-children were trusted and treated as near equals to the children of their host. More importantly, as shown in these examples, they are likely to have learned many of the monetary and trade skills necessary to make an attempt at economic self-sufficiency, or render themselves distinctly more nubile. Household servants, of whom about half were female and half male, frequently ended up marrying each other, and service did not always end with marriage.[90] Alternatively, we may here recall Diota, who first appeared in the rolls in 1317 as the 'former servant of Henry *carbonarius*', suing for back wages, then traded independently until the early 1320s and finally married Deyne le Colyer by 1324.[91] Some women, such as Isoud, the former maid of Richard *forestarius*, even made limited forays into brewing, the most prestigious of women's work in the borough.[92]

What is not evident among *ancille* is the freedom or capital necessary to accumulate property in the borough that Bennett has described for the young women of Brigstock.[93] Of the 140

---

87   Ibid., GC1 #469; SC2/215/72 m.2.
88   TNA, SC2/216/3 session 7.
89   TNA, SC2/216/2 sessions 9 & 10.
90   H. Leyser, *Medieval Women: A Social History of Women in England, 450–1500* (London, 1995), p. 156.
91   *Dyffryn Clwyd Database*, GC1 #1233, SC2/215/76 m.14; TNA, SC2/216/3 sessions 5 & 6; GC1 #2233, SC2/216/5 m.30.
92   Ibid., GC1 #1008, SC2/215/74 m.16d.
93   Bennett, *Women in the Medieval English Countryside*, pp. 78–81.

or so surviving sales of property in the borough of Ruthin between 1295 and 1318, in only one is an unmarried woman the purchaser, while on seventeen occasions (12 per cent of transactions) an unmarried woman or group of unmarried female co-heirs was the seller. Moreover, at the peak of the great famine, among transactions recorded between Easter 1316 and Michaelmas 1317, unmarried women were sellers of landed property in eleven of twenty-nine transactions (38 per cent). This is remarkable, considering the numerically small proportion of potential property owners they comprised, and goes far towards expressing how marginal the solvency of unmarried women in the borough truly was.[94]

Despite the atypical circumstances of the famine years, the long-term impression given by the property market in Ruthin is similar. Unmarried women seem most typically to have acquired property through inheritance, not purchase, and often to have sold it to alleviate poverty that labour could not dispel. While occasional demands for back wages in the court rolls attest that *ancille* were paid in at least some households, the sums involved are never large, and it is likely that the potential for destitution outside employment would have encouraged women to stay in service for little or nothing beyond room and board. Not unusual is the case of Matilda, the daughter of Peter, who in 1314, prior to the famine, successfully sued William le Palfryman for the small sum of 10*d.* in back wages and received 2*d.* in damages.[95]

Hence, the situation in Ruthin, where young women were not in a position to acquire property or become independent, contrasted sharply with that in pre-plague Brigstock, where young women did accumulate property and exercise their independence.[96] In Ruthin, as in Brigstock, a period of economic difficulty such as that of the famine years naturally curtailed the independence of those adolescents who were most often servants.[97] Bennett has argued that during times of prolonged hardship, parents would retain influence over

---

[94]   Most of the buyers in this crisis market were the same town notables identified above in table 2.6.

[95]   TNA, SC2/215/73 session 8.

[96]   Bennett, *Women in the Medieval English Countryside*, pp. 78–81

[97]   Ibid., p. 89.

their children by controlling the distribution of land and employment.[98] Yet, this runs counter to the findings of Razi, and as reflected in Ruthin, that the level of employment among young men and women of servant age was high in the pre-plague period.[99] Hence, the principal factors which may have curtailed the independence of these women would not have been dictated by family, but by the poor terms of service and low wages given by employers. At a time when labour was plentiful and wages low, employment would have been encouraged, not limited, especially by poor parents who could ill afford to support their children. Such conditions would have favoured the controlling influence of employers over that of parents.

For young women, low wages were coupled with the double-edged problem of being in many ways bound to an employer's household. Even apart from actually being the foster-child of an employer, in the larger sense of the word *familia* employed in the Middle Ages children and servants were dependents of the householder and his wife.[100] This created certain legal obligations whereby the householder was responsible for the actions of the servant, as he was those of his own children, and the servant had the curtailed freedoms implied by the householder's need to police the actions of his dependents.

This complexity is brought to light in a May 1317 presentment from the vill of Nantclwyd, in which it is recorded that Lleucu, keeper of the animals of Gwion ap 'Pilewerni' and Gronw ap Gwion, had burnt an oak tree (presumably by accident).[101] In response, Gwion and his son Gronw came forward and put themselves in mercy on behalf of their servant (*pro manupasto suo*), allowing Lleucu to escape amercement but undoubtedly leaving her in an unenviable position at home. Taking such responsibility was not voluntary, as Cynwrig Goch de Maesmaencymro discovered in 1314 when, 'without his knowledge', members of his household seized his horse from the small park of Ruthin, where it had been impounded.[102]

---

[98] Ibid.
[99] Razi, 'Family, land and the village', 31.
[100] Hanawalt, *The Ties That Bound*, p. 156.
[101] *Dyffryn Clwyd Database*, Llann1 # 749 SC/215/76 m.10.
[102] TNA, SC/215/73 session 5.

Despite his protestations of non-responsibility through ignorance, as head of the household Cynwrig was nevertheless amerced. Whether or not he was telling the truth is impossible to know, but his responsibility was seen by the court as real and could even impugn the householder as a third party.[103] As a result, we need to give close consideration to the restrictive social aspect of servanthood which undoubtedly accompanied the minimal capital gains made by *ancille*.

One final negative note needs to be sounded regarding what happened to female servants at the end of their household tenure. It would be wrong to deny the impression that service provided craft and money handling skills invaluable for facilitating opportunities for betterment through trade and marriage. Nevertheless, on leaving service women were confronted with low wages, high prices and a glut of migrant labour affecting the borough throughout the famine period. Hence, inevitably, some women did not prosper after service. In addition to the gross sale of property by unwed women in 1316–17 already mentioned, there appear in Ruthin's courts numerous cases of theft by female servants or ex-servants.

Some cases reflect the poverty of servanthood, such as that of Angharad, the maid of Bleddyn ap Heilyn, who was caught stealing one-third of a hoop or bushel of grain from her master's barn; or Isoud, the former maid of Richard Leg, who was amerced for accepting a small quantity of stolen malt from Alice le Blowestere.[104] Others illustrate ex-servants' attempts, born of desperation or malice, to attain some of their former masters' wealth. A good example occurred in 1324 when Agnes, 'lately the maid of Richard de Whytel', and her male accomplice broke into Richard's house and stole a tablecloth, a towel, six silver spoons, silver coins, brooches, rings and a ham to the total value of 60*s.*, before fleeing 'the country' or lordship.[105]

The fortunes of Ruthin's *ancille* on leaving service were mixed. These women almost certainly began life with little or

---

[103] This legal responsibility for household members also encompassed male servants, as in 1306 when Robert Box was amerced 3*d.* for not producing his 'lad' (*garcio*) to reply to William le Marchal in a plea of trespass (*Dyffryn Clwyd Database*, GC1 #76 SC2/215/69 m.3).

[104] Ibid., GC1 #1079, 1725; SC2/215/74 m.18, SC2/216/3 m.22.

[105] Ibid., GC1 #2082, 2083; SC2/216/5 m.10.

no personal capital. In the early fourteenth century at least, they laboured in relative poverty under the close scrutiny of their masters or mistresses. And it is probable that they left service with no more material wealth than that with which they began. It is also highly likely that most women working in those other parts of the service industry discussed here had a background which had begun in household service or even fosterage, implying that the tribulations of servanthood personified most women's first foray into the borough's labour market.

For the borough's women termed *nutrix* or *medicatrix*, the cycle of employment and dependency, followed by the struggle to survive after being discharged from service, was like that experienced by Ruthin's *ancille*. The only exception was the married *nutrix*, or wet nurse, who accepted a child into her own household in exchange for property or goods. There is no sound evidence in the borough's records for describing these wet nurses; this may be largely because their existence tended to be a rural phenomenon. It was probably bound up with the practice of wealthy families' compelling poor or bond tenants to foster their children.

An informative series of related roll entries for 1343 survives from the commotal court of Dogfeiling. In these an inquest was held to determine how many customary tenants 'hold free lands for a term, or at *prid*, and whether customary tenants have the sons of free tenants to bring up'.[106] One of several fines arising from this inquest was one paid by Iorwerth Goch, *rhingyll* of Dogfeiling, who acknowledged that he had given his daughter to a bondman, Einion Llwyd de Llandyrnog, *ad nutriendum* some seven years before (in 1336). This was despite the lord's prohibition in the early 1320s against freemen burdening (*ne liberi onerarent*) bondmen with the feeding of their children, horses, or greyhounds.[107] In reply to the inquest, Iorwerth made amends for having initiated the arrangement, yet there is no indication that the child was actually brought home in 1343.

Iorwerth's daughter, Dyddgu, does not appear in the court rolls in her own right until 1348, when some goats she was

---

[106] Ibid., Roll3 #700, SC2/217/8 m.13.
[107] Ibid., Roll3 #733, 735; SC2/217/8 m.14.

tending strayed illegally into the forest.[108] If we use Dyddgu's first amercement of 1348 as an indication that she had recently reached her legal majority of twelve to fourteen years, we may also reason that, when placed in the care of Einion's household in 1336, Dyddgu is likely to have been an infant.[109] Hence, it is probable that Einion's wife Gwenllian was Dyddgu's wet nurse, as well as her foster-mother. It is almost certain that, by the time she left Einion's household, Dyddgu had been contributing to the familial economy for at least a few years. By the end of Dyddgu's fosterage, Gwenllian is likely to have seen some practical return on her years of child-rearing, in addition to any goods or monies the family had otherwise received in payment.[110] Moreover, whatever the economic advantages of nursing and fosterage to Gwenllian's and Einion's household, they came without the employer policing to which live-in, unwed nurses were subject. Married wet nurses would additionally have had a level of long-term security in contrast to the circumstances of their unwed counterparts.

Among single wet nurses the sharp distinction between those who succeeded after service and those who met with hard times is evident. Some unwed wet nurses, such as Tibote *nutrix*, appear in the courts of Ruthin for nothing more sinister than forestalling, which in itself indicates her ability to accumulate at least small quantities of capital.[111] Others, however, like Isabel the former nurse of William Serviens, spiralled into destitution and crime.[112] William came to maturity and prominence within the community during the famine

---

[108] *Dyffryn Clwyd Database*, Llan2 #1695, SC2/217/13 m.18. It is likely that although Iorwerth Goch made a fine for his illegal fosterage in 1343, Dyddgu would have continued to reside in Einion's household until a prearranged time, probably her majority. For example, Llywelyn Du, who was also identified by the inquest of 1343 as having illegally placed his daughter with Gronw Brych ('Bregh'), nevertheless continued the arrangement until 1345 (Ibid., Roll6 #1169, SC2/217/11 m.17).

[109] Bennett, *Women in the Medieval English Countryside*, 67.

[110] As for goods, in a case of 1343, Ieuan ap Tegwared de Henfron claimed to have been given a cow in return for the support of a 'certain boy' (*Dyffryn Clwyd Database*, Roll3 #756, SC2/217/8 m.14d).

[111] Ibid., GC1 #1275, SC2/215/76 m.14d.

[112] William appears often in the lordship's courts and unambiguously uses 'Serviens' as his surname, itself an interesting note as to his family's humble origins.

years (1315–22), appearing with other young men (*garciones*) in the court rolls as early as 1312 and acting as a great court of Ruthin juror by 1326.[113] Meanwhile, Isabel probably left service in William's household because of, or shortly after, a dispute with him over the detinue of some chattels about which they reached an accord in October 1313.[114] Immediately afterwards, she was indicted for burning hedges and stealing 10*s.* in cash, a cheese, some flax and other small things (*res minutae*) before fleeing the lordship.[115] Only three years later, at the height of the famine in 1316, did she pay the receiver of Dyffryn Clwyd 12*d.* to return to the lordship, after which she disappears from the court record.[116]

It is also likely that such hardship was not uncommon among Ruthin's sick nurses. As this occupation was probably more typically casual in nature than wet nursing, it is not surprising that disputes leading to records which refer to a *medicatrix* are few and far between. Only one woman is so named in the borough within our focus period of 1312–21, and her court history reveals simply that she was probably resident in her employer's house, a conclusion reinforced by the evidence of a similar, later court roll entry from Caernarfon.[117] Such resident service, especially during the famine period, implies the same combination of restricted personal liberties known to *ancille* and single wet nurses. Furthermore, as a temporary member of someone else's household, a sick nurse's payment was probably mainly in the form of maintenance. Sick nurses would also have shared other service workers' minimal scope for capital accumulation and potential for post-employment poverty.

It is from the least fortunate of these ex-household servants and nurses that many members of the lowest rung of the service industry were drawn. The evidence of prostitution

---

[113] *Dyffryn Clwyd Database*, GC1 #284, 2319; SC2/215/71 m.14, SC/216/6 m.1.

[114] Ibid., GC1 #695, SC2/215/73 m.26.

[115] Ibid., GC1 #725, 727; SC2/217/73 m.26d.

[116] Ibid., GC1 #1133, SC2/215/75 m.16.

[117] Ibid., GC1 #436, SC2/215/72 m.1d. Cecily *medicatrix* seems to have stayed in the house of Roger Kay for nights as well as days; during one night Roger beat and drew blood from her. Presumably not himself at the time, Roger later claimed that the incident was not his fault, before paying for a licence to agree with Cecily. The nurse of Simon le Flesshewer was similarly assaulted by her master at Caernarfon in 1367. Jones and Owen (eds), *Caernarvon Court Rolls*, p. 38.

offered by Ruthin's courts reveals casual as well as occupational exploitation, each of which needs to be dealt with in
turn. Those court appearances concerning women explicitly
identified as *meretrix* or 'hoir' during the period 1312–21 are
indicative of casual prostitution. Each *meretrix* named appears
exclusively in either isolated incidents of minor assault or in
trading offences.[118] None of these women can be shown to
have worked as a prostitute over a long period of time, nor
were they party to litigation showing the sort of ensnaring
debt often manipulated by the keepers of medieval brothels.[119]
However, some later pre-plague evidence from Ruthin, from
the 1340s especially, suggests the systematic exploitation of
women engaged in prostitution on a semi-permanent basis.

Ruthin's casual prostitutes were those women, such as
'Morfudd *meretrix extuberatrix*', amerced for forestalling in 1321,
who were attempting to make a living by one or several
means.[120] Furthermore, there is a possibility that some of
these women were, as previously discussed, publicly self-
acknowledged prostitutes primarily for the purpose of
escaping the impoverishment caused by the *amobr* tax. As the
tax did not apply to native townswomen, this would suggest that
some 'prostitutes' were in fact rural migrants, a profile consistent with their curial transience and the social dislocation
caused by the great famine.[121] Regardless of origin, however,
there is a single overwhelming message conveyed by these
women's presence in the rolls. For those unemployed in more
traditional service, it is likely that an informal borough network
of casual prostitution was the closest thing to a safety net
between themselves and starvation in the famine years.

In parallel with this casual prostitution of women engaged
primarily in other employments was the more sinister spectre
of occupational exploitation within the borough. The
evidence for this is mainly indirect, but observable when
viewed across the entirety of the lordship's pre- and immediately post-plague records. As a starting point, figure 5.2 shows

[118] *Dyffryn Clwyd Database*, GC1 #1708, SC/216/3 m.23; TNA, SC/216/1 session
4, SC/216/3 session 8.

[119] Leyser, *Medieval Women: A Social History*, 159

[120] TNA, SC2/216/3 session 8.

[121] Ibid.; concerning Morfudd in particular, previous public recognition as a
prostitute would explain her unusual double-barrelled by-name.

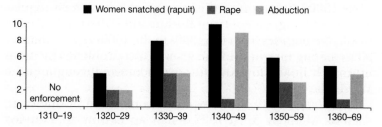

Figure 5.2. Rape and abduction in Dyffryn Clwyd, 1320–69 (attempted and successful)[122]
Source: TNA, SC2/215/71–SC2/219/6.

the dramatic increase in the number of women abducted in the run-up to and during the shift from an impoverished pre-plague economy of labour surplus to a more affluent post-plague economy of labour shortage; many of them were probably sold into prostitution.[123]

To some extent our knowledge of the general crime of 'snatching' women, cases of which can be separated into either rape or abduction, is coloured by the late incidence of its perpetrators' prosecution in Dyffryn Clwyd.[124] But from the

[122]   The values for 1320–29 and 1330–39 have been adjusted proportionately in relation to what percentage of the court record survives. For the decades 1310 to 1349 there were consistently held two sessions of the great court of Ruthin, two sessions of the great court of Dyffryn Clwyd and one session of goal delivery/fines to the lord. This means a maximum of 50 sets of records once existed on the court roll per annum, in which snatching cases seem to have been evenly scattered. For the years 1320–9 and 1330–9, 46 per cent (23 sets) of these sessions survive, 88 per cent (44 sets) exist from 1340–9, 66 per cent (33 sets) exist from 1350–9 and 80 per cent (40 sets) for the period 1360–9. Based on these percentages, the estimated total number of snatching cases per annum has been calculated.

[123]   Interesting parallels may be drawn between the increase in snatchings of women in pre-plague Ruthin and Razi's discovery of an increase in the number of leyrwyts (amercements for fornication) in pre-plague Halesowen. In each case, there is a decreased incidence of the transgression in the post-plague era. Unfortunately, directly comparable data to Ruthin's are not available and the similarities go no further than the generally decreased status of women suggested by an increase in either offence. Z. Razi, *Life, Marriage and Death in a Medieval Parish: Economy, Society and Demography in Halesowen, 1270–1400* (Cambridge, 1980), pp. 69–70.

[124]   The ambiguous nature of the Latin term *raptus*, meaning to abduct, ravage, or even rape, is a problem, and so the details of each case have been considered independently before categorization. Of cases that may accurately be termed rape or abduction, only abductions immediately resulting in a sexual assault have been counted as rape; this definition would include a case of 1352 in which Adam, the

early 1320s, litigation of this type quickly became a regular feature of the great courts of Ruthin and Dyffryn Clwyd. As a result, the decades from the 1330s to the 1360s especially offer a fascinating insight into the growth of a problem which was intimately linked to prostitution and known throughout the Welsh March.

While rape was a crime typically committed by one man, such as when in April 1323 Ieuan ap Gronw ap Ednyfed ('Edenwrith') alone 'snatched the virginity of Lleucu the daughter of Ednyfed Goch violently and in breach of the peace', abductions were usually carried out by groups of men not immediately bent on sexual assault.[125] Abductors were often armed, well organized and more inclined to target rural tenements. A typical case is that of October 1340, in which Madog ap 'Caranmen' and three armed accomplices went to the house of Madog le Tailor in the vill of Derwen (Llannerch) and attempted to abduct his *ancilla*, Lleucu.[126]

When abductors were successful, their victims seem to have been destined for sale in urban centres, either locally or in neighbouring lordships. Such was the implication of a case in November 1349, when Bleddyn ap 'Drew', a notoriously lawless and violent leader of certain local men, went to the house of Dafydd ap Gwion in the commote of Dogfeiling, intent on snatching his daughter Gwenllian. When Gwenllian could not be found, his gang instead abducted a woman tenant of the abbot of Valle Crucis who had the misfortune to be there at the time. They took her back to Bleddyn ap Drew's house in Llanfwrog (a patently rough neighbourhood of Ruthin), and sold her to Dafydd Brych ('Breth') for 10s.[127]

---

son of Nicholas de Llanfwrog, abducted Alice, the daughter of William Meurig, in Welsh Street, and took her to his home in Llanfwrog where he violated her against her wishes (*Dyffryn Clwyd Database*, Roll12 #146, SC2/218/3 m.5). For a general discussion of the term *raptus*, see H. Kelly, 'Statutes of rapes and alleged ravishers of wives: a context for the charges against Thomas Mallory, Knight', *Viator*, 28 (1997), 361–419.

[125] *Dyffryn Clwyd Database*, GC1 #1932, SC2/216/4 m.29.

[126] Ibid., Roll1 #50, SC2/217/6 m.4.

[127] Ibid., Roll10 #21, 27, 229, 264, 311, 358, 405, 1680; SC2/218/1 m. 1d, 5, 5d, 6, 6d, 7, 30. The character of Bleddyn ap 'Drew' is attested by his frequent appearance in the great courts of Ruthin and Dyffryn Clwyd throughout the 1340s, frequently involving sword-play and assault, and culminating in his being outlawed and having his various properties confiscated in 1350 and 1351 (Ibid., Roll1 #135, SC2/217/6

From outside the lordship, in September 1349 Ednyfed ap Iorwerth ap Llywelyn and three accomplices came to Dyffryn Clwyd, abducted Angharad, 'who was the wife' of William ap Madog ap Ednyfed, and took her back to the lordship of Denbigh ('Rhos and Rhufoniog') with them.[128] Similarly, in 1382 Gwyn ap Ieuan ap Cadwgan and three accomplices abducted Dyddgu, the daughter of Iorwerth ap Madog, out of the country.[129]

Yet, gauging the frequency with which women were brought into the lordship is particularly difficult, given the autonomous nature of marcher rule and jurisdiction. The writ of any one marcher lord did not run in the lands of his neighbours. Hence, even when an abductor from Dyffryn Clwyd was identified in a neighbouring lordship before returning home, no more comprehensive sanction could be placed on him than outlawry in the neighbouring lordship. For this reason, no record exists from which to deduce how many women were brought into the lordship, as the importers of abductees were not committing crime against the peace of the lord of Dyffryn Clwyd.

Although penalties for those found guilty of offences within the lordship could include heavy fines and even hanging, it was very hard to prosecute successfully any perpetrator of such a serious crime. In instances where known punishments included mortal sanction, or a fine greater than the value of the criminal's chattels, the offender would simply find it in his best interest to flee to the sanctuary of a neighbouring lordship. Probably less than half of all persons (identified by name) to have been charged with committing, or even acting as an accomplice to, a rape or abduction between 1320 and 1369 made recompense to the lord. Of those named as the principal rapist or abduction ringleader in a case, only a tiny proportion remained to receive the lord's justice.

m.3; Roll2 # 1501, SC2/217/7 m.35; Roll3 #1474, SC2/217/8 m.32; Roll5 #41, SC2/217/10 m.1d; Roll9 #49, SC2/217/14 m.1d; Roll10 #17, 605, 1483, 1679 SC2/218/1 m.1, 11, 25, 30; Roll11 #1148, SC/218/2 m.20d).

[128]   Ibid., Roll10 #9, 1577; SC/218/1 m.1, 28. It is unlikely that Ednyfed's objective was to enter Angharad's holding through marriage under duress, since as an outsider to the lordship he would still have had to pay a weighty entry fine to take up residence in Dyffryn Clwyd.

[129]   Ibid., GC5 #955, SC2/220/4 m.27.

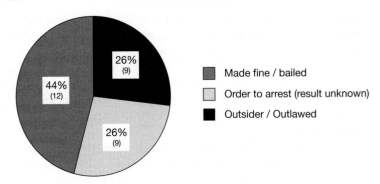

Figure 5.3. Men charged in connection with rape or abduction, 1320–69
Source: TNA, SC2/216/3–SC2/219/6

It must be said that a woman's abduction cannot always be taken as an indication that she was sold into prostitution. However, it is difficult to explain otherwise the bulk of this human traffic in predominantly young, single women at a time when the labour market was saturated with persons liable to be found working willingly for food and shelter. It is perhaps most useful to model our understanding of the social context which gave rise to this problem in the pre-plague decades on parallels with the late fifteenth century. High levels of poverty and exploitation were experienced by women towards the end of the fifteenth century when, 'in recessionary times', increased levels of casual prostitution 'sharpened up' concern in boroughs across England.[130] According to Leyser, in the medieval view 'just as towns needed sewers ... they needed brothels' and 'some female servants were undoubtedly sold into prostitution'.[131] At the bishop of Winchester's brothels in late fifteenth-century Southwark, in accordance with the bishop's own ordinances, his officials were expected to check regularly that no woman was being kept in prostitution against her will, indicating that such circumstances were not uncommon.[132] A similar statutory point of reference, to allow insight into the extent of

---

[130] Jewell, *Women in Medieval England*, pp. 110–11.
[131] Leyser, *Medieval Women: A Social History*, p. 159.
[132] Ibid.

occupational exploitation in Wales, is lacking for the early fourteenth century. Nevertheless, it requires little imagination to suggest that the complete disregard for human liberties shown by the captors of the abbot of Valle Crucis's female tenant (who was abducted in Dogfeiling and later sold in Ruthin for 10s.) represents a comparable state of affairs.[133]

Such conclusions are supplemented by direct evidence of some of Ruthin's prostitutes having fallen prey to 'ensnaring debt', another form of exploitation which the bishop of Winchester's officials were later to guard against.[134] Generys de Ruthin *meretrix* appears frequently in the borough's courts during the 1340s, by all accounts in a constant state of debt and poverty. Between March 1345 and July 1347 alone, her name appears on the roll of the borough court of Ruthin ten times, in conjunction with three different debt pleas, each of which was delayed and for which she was essoined repeatedly in a manner consistent with chronic avoidance of payment.[135] Her occupation as a prostitute was also likely to be semi-permanent. In 1341 her son Hywel, identified as *filius Kineris* (Generys) *meretricis*, was amerced for removing green wood from the lord's park and was excused because of poverty.[136] In the consciously patrilineal society of north Wales, where illegitimate children were normally recognized by their fathers, Hywel's specific identification as the son of a *meretrix* is a strong indication that Generys was already working as a prostitute at the time of the child's conception at least twelve years earlier.[137]

While we do not know the specific causes of Generys's debts, her situation calls to mind the late fifteenth-century story of a London woman, Ellen Butler. Apparently a certain Thomas Bowde offered Ellen what he claimed was good employment, in Southwark; it turned out to be prostitution. When Ellen refused to do 'such service as his other servants',

[133] *Dyffryn Clwyd Database*, Roll10 #27, SC2/218/1 m.1d.

[134] Leyser, *Medieval Women: A Social History*, p. 159.

[135] *Dyffryn Clwyd Database*, Roll5 #261, 305; Roll7 #1532, 1586, 1631, 1680, 1870, 1923, 1976, 2024; SC2/217/10 m.4d and 5; SC/217/12 m.23, 24, 24d,25, 27, 27d, 28.

[136] Ibid., Roll1 #1253, SC2/217/6 m.32.

[137] Hywel's amercement suggests that by 1341 he had reached his majority, generally at least twelve years.

he contrived to have her imprisoned for alleged debt.[138]
Leyser comments on this case: 'on the face of it the only sure
way she could have paid off the debt would have been by
accepting her job as a prostitute'.[139] Likewise, at Ruthin
during 1320–69, the majority of cases relating to women who
seem to have been involved in occupational prostitution were
debt cases.

This range of indirect and circumstantial evidence suggests
that below the ranks of those women who simply did not have
access to the capital or skills necessary to sustain themselves
adequately without sometimes engaging in casual prostitution
was one further sub-class. This comprised those who, through
abduction/captivity or manipulation, financial or otherwise,
were denied even the opportunity to attempt to accumulate
the wealth or skills necessary to change their condition. Of
prostitution in general, whether casual or occupational, the
pathway to employment in this lowest echelon of Ruthin's
service industry was broadened by the strained economic
conditions of the early fourteenth century. The reality was
that whereas the real value of female labour was declining, the
relative value of working on the margins of society had
become great enough to draw in women without capital and
attract those willing to exploit them systematically.

It may be concluded of all Ruthin's service workers that they
experienced a common inability to accumulate significant
amounts of capital. Most service workers were faced with the
same sort of 'sink or swim' scenario when finishing any particular period of service. They either buoyantly prospered by
utilizing skills learned, re-entered service, married, or started
on the downward spiral of negative social mobility toward
prostitution, debt or criminality. It is not possible to gauge
with certainty which was the more likely, but continued service
or marriage loomed largest. Furthermore, the commonness
of prostitution, cumbersome debt and crime among women
suggests that unfortunate endings were at least as common as
independent prosperity.

---

[138] R. Karras, 'The regulation of brothels in later medieval England', in J. Bennett
(ed.), *Sisters and Workers in the Middle Ages* (London, 1989), p. 119, cited in Leyser,
Medieval Women: A Social History, p. 159.
[139] Leyser, *Medieval Women: A Social History*, p. 159

CONCLUSION

Part 2 has certainly not exhausted the particular occupations in which women worked, but it has examined the range of socio-economic circumstances in which Ruthin's female labourers found themselves. This allows us to see the extent to which access to capital dictated the level of labour status – as high-profile brewer, middling tradeswoman, or low-status service worker – achieved by female workers in relation to their environment. It also gives us the wherewithal to offer some judgements as to the ability of women to take advantage of that environment.

The more capital available to an individual, the higher the level of trade in which they could engage, and the greater the flexibility they had to manipulate their environment to their own advantage. These realities are clear when set against the backdrop of the great famine and the economic crisis it created. The wives of Ruthin's wealthiest office holders and creditors comprised the majority of the town's most active brewsters (table 3.6). During the famine years, when the cost of brewing materials became great enough to exclude many women from the market, it was this same group of wealthy wives that colluded to fix prices and increase profits. Likewise, they had the resources necessary to participate in the borough's diverse commercial activities requiring smaller levels of capital, such as forestalling and regrating.

For tradeswomen with access to moderate levels of capital, their experience of the great famine was mixed. Those lucky enough to be working in profitable crafts, such as the baker-esses, were able to enjoy greater recognition during a period in which their skills were in high demand. Women working in crafts which, unlike food production, were inessential during times of hardship, probably experienced difficulties during the famine. Tradeswomen in general, even independent tradeswomen, were unlikely to have had the capital necessary to manipulate the market to their advantage. For the majority, the capital with which they worked was rarely their own. Unlike brewsters, married tradeswomen most commonly worked in their husband's or father's trade rather than as a parallel enterprise, and so the need for familial agree-ment would often have limited their capital flexibility. An advantage, however, was that tradeswomen, especially the producers of staple goods, are likely to have enjoyed relative stability even during the famine, while in better times they may often have accessed moderate amounts of capital and made limited ventures into the more profitable work of brewing and the marginal activity of forestalling.

Women with little or no capital formed by far the most varied group of labourers. The categories which this study has used to subdivide them into victuallers, cloth workers and members of the service industry are themselves problematic. These women, with minimal resources, were the most ubiquitous in relation to which tasks they carried out in order to survive. Virtually none of their various employments, however, offered great potential for the accumulation of adequate quantities of capital to enable them to move independently into higher levels of trade. In the case of prostitutes, they may even have been denied the opportunity to strive for the accumulation of wealth because of ensnaring debt or captivity. Service women were also those whose ability to survive was most impaired by the great famine. With a famine-induced increase in the borough's labour supply, it is highly likely that competition compressed victuallers, cloth workers and service women into one indistinguishable group of paupers. The forestaller, spinner and prostitute were undoubtedly one and the same at the worst of times. They were those who, having no material resources, had little control over their own destiny. Simply put, working capital meant prosperity and the flexibility to weather economic hardship. This is similar to the context in which Howell maintains that contemporary women's work on the continent must be understood. She has argued that, in the market economies of late medieval urban Europe, without the advantages of talent, training and access to capital, producers fell to the bottom of an increasingly hierarchical economic order.[140] In Ruthin, when a woman reached the bottom of the borough's economic hierarchy, her scant avenues of improvement lay primarily in the charity of a third party or, more frequently, in marriage.

[140] M. Howell, *Women Production and Patriarchy in Late Medieval Cities* (London, 1986), p. 24.

It must be said that the possibility of marriage was in many ways a 'wild card'. Smith's observation that wedlock and widowhood were a woman's 'essential passports to work opportunities' can not be ignored.[141] Common among domestic servants especially, marriage was not so much a passport to employment as a means by which the combination of two persons' resources might transcend the economic barriers to market access created by insufficient investment capital.[142] Likewise, for most married tradeswomen widowhood may have removed the constraints of patriarchal control, allowing them to access and manipulate household capital in a manner that wealthy brewsters might.[143]

Capital resources were also a more potent factor in determining a woman's labour status than was ethnicity. The reality of capital's primacy in determining a woman's occupation and her potential for mobility transcended ethnicity. The proportion of Welsh as opposed to English women engaged in different areas of the borough's workforce, as displayed in figure 5.4, is very much a reflection of the distribution of landed wealth as derived from the rental of 1324 and shown in table 1.1. Based on by-name and assize data, female Welsh workers, like Welsh property owners in table 1.1, are generally represented in every area of the labour market (except baking), but as a whole tend to gravitate towards less affluent sectors of the labour market. Although representing a significant number of the borough's wealthiest brewsters, they are absent from the ranks of bakers and other skilled tradeswomen in occupations requiring moderate levels of capital. In contrast to their place in skilled craftwork, Welsh women represented a more significant proportion of the borough's

---

[141] Smith, 'Towards a history of women', p. 38.

[142] Goldberg has gone so far as to introduce his chapter on servants in *Women, Work and Life Cycle in a Medieval Economy* with the statement that 'it is unhelpful' to discuss servanthood outside 'lifecycle terms' (Goldberg, *Women, Work and Life Cycle*, p. 158). This contrasts with the way in which it has been dealt with here as an aspect of the broader service industry, from all corners of which women may have found escape through marriage.

[143] While there were women working independently in Ruthin, the formalized institution of the *femme sole*, or woman whose business assets were legally separate from her husband's, or any other man's, does not appear to have existed in the borough.

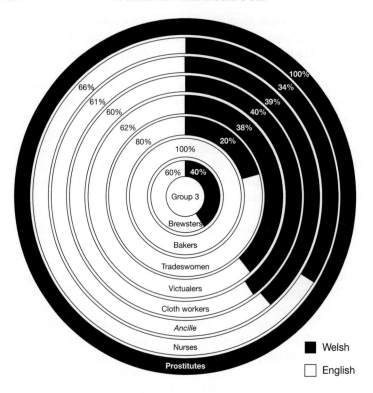

Figure 5.4. Welsh and English women in borough occupations, relative quantities
Source: as for table 3.6, figure 4.1, table 4.2, table 5.1, figure 5.1 and figure 5.2.

victuallers, cloth workers and *ancille*, occupations requiring little or no capital; but they dominated no occupation except that of prostitution. Just as a woman's place in the workforce was heavily influenced by her ability to access the capital necessary to engage in the most profitable of trades, so too was the overall character of Welsh women's work influenced by the same factor. Neither figure 5.4 nor court roll evidence speaks of any conscious exclusion of Welsh women from certain areas of work, only a lower overall level of prosperity. Welsh women able to access the capital necessary to engage in large-scale brewing, for example, were just as likely to prosper as their English counterparts. The overall distribution of wealth in the community simply made English women more likely to have larger quantities of capital to hand with which to prosper.

With the notable exceptions of baking and prostitution, the shared experiences of Welsh and English women with similar resource levels are the dominant themes in the story of the borough's female workforce and stand in sharp contrast to the ethnic dichotomy which Davies has ascribed to rural Dyffryn Clwyd.[144] As with the activities of the borough's masculine elite, it was the range of shared hopes and fears, of prosperity and hardship, which shaped women's lives. In this way, access to equal amounts of capital dictated an equal position within the borough's economy, society and court record.

[144]   Davies, *Lordship and Society*, p. 349.

Part 3

MEN AS WORKERS: OCCUPATION AND MOBILITY

Part 3 returns to the borough's men and surveys Ruthin's male occupation structure among high-, medium- and low-status working men in order to explain the dominance of one ethnic group over the other in certain areas of the economy. Part 1 of this book explored links between the distribution of wealth and male status with respect to ethnicity. It concluded that shared levels of prosperity, largely dependent on access to similar levels of investment capital, were a more significant determinant of an individual's socio-economic priorities than being English or Welsh. Part 2 demonstrated the similar experiences of Welsh and English working women with access to high, medium and low levels of capital. In part 3 male occupation is deconstructed with respect to social status and the potential for capital accumulation offered by different male occupations, highlighting why certain occupations were favoured by either Welshmen or Englishmen.

VI
MALE OCCUPATION AND MOBILITY

Just as the range of occupations of Ruthin's women stretched from commercial brewing to exploitative prostitution, so too did male occupations encompass service in seignorial offices and the menial toil of carting dung. For men, too, the more capital they possessed the more likely they were to increase their holdings and status. Tables 6.2–5 break down the trade and craft by-names by which many male borough court litigants were known between 1312 and 1321, subdividing them according to their status and potential to provide the investment capital necessary for social mobility. These offer a point of comparison with table 4.2, table 5.1 and figure 5.4, representing female skilled craftswomen and low-skill labourers. In discussing tables 6.2–5, this chapter returns to the line of inquiry in chapters I and II by addressing the three-way relationship between occupation, mobility and ethnicity. Table 6.1 is an overview of the data on which subsequent tables and discussions are based.

A central qualification of table 6.1 is that all occupational data presented are representative, not quantitative. This is inevitable, because only around 30 per cent of men appearing in the court identified themselves by occupation. Furthermore, the group of men who did identify themselves was comprised disproportionately of English litigants, owing to the primacy of patronymic naming practices among Welshmen, which poses a problem in interpreting local records in Wales. Lastly, those members of the community with moderate- to high-status occupations were markedly more likely to identify themselves by means of a trade-related title than by using a locational or descriptive by-name. This means that the occupations of both the poor and the Welsh of the borough, by no means coincident groupings, are less well known to us than those of their more prosperous and English counterparts.

Despite these limitations, what can be gleaned from tables 6.2–5 is a general sense of the industries on which male labour

Table 6.1. Male occupational by-names from the borough court of
Ruthin, 1312–21: overview of male occupation data

	Totals		English*	Welsh*
Men appearing in the borough court 1312–21	948		48%	52%
Men identified by occupation	282 (30%)	→	67%	33%
Men of unknown occupation	666 (70%)	→	37%	63%

Source: TNA, SC2/215/71–SC2/216/3.
*These percentages have a margin of error of approx. +/– 10 per cent, due to the
difficulty of establishing ethnicity based on naming practices and curial context
among infrequent litigators.

was focused, and the areas in which Welshmen or Englishmen
formed the dominant labour force. Where groups of five
or more persons have been identified as working at a particular occupation, the majority ethnicity of those tradesmen has
been specified in the table. In instances where the majority of
named tradesmen were Welsh, despite their marked under-
representation by occupational by-name, this has been taken
as an indication that they are likely to have dominated that
trade (as indicated in tables 6.2–5 by 'W'). Unfortunately,
given the over-representation of English tradesmen by occupational by-name, their numerical supremacy in a particular
area can often only be seen as inconclusive unless there is
supporting evidence in the court rolls (as indicated in tables
6.2–5: inconclusively English '(E)', conclusively English 'E').

ADMINISTRATION, ECCLESIASTICAL AND SECULAR

The most prestigious positions open to Ruthin's residents
were those occupied by the officers and administrators of the
borough, the lordship of Dyffryn Clwyd and the virtually con-
terminous rural deanery of the same name (part of the
bishopric of Bangor).[1] Appearing in tables 6.2 and 6.3 are
primarily those positions, ecclesiastical and secular, which are
likely to have represented an individual's chief office or occupation in the community. The office of borough juror, already

---

[1] A. Barrell, 'The clergy of a medieval lordship: the evidence of the Dyffryn
Clwyd court rolls', *DHST*, 44 (1995), 7.

discussed at length in chapter II, has been omitted from this table as it was a role ancillary to an individual's regular occupation. Similarly, many of the secular offices listed in table 6.3 have been introduced in part 1, and like 'borough juror' status, the distribution of these secular and clerical offices is almost certain to have reflected their occupants' social standing, wealth and, in some cases, personal loyalties. Hence, to know from which ethnic group these men came and which trade they left to take up an occupational office may indicate the nature of mobility in the borough at the highest level. By comparison, women were excluded from all clerical posts, and do not appear to have been allowed to hold any secular office in the lordship. But, as discussed in part 2, male office-holding was intimately linked to the mobility of those wives and daughters who utilized the substantial capital of related borough officials for their own ends. Again, these women were the brewsters and large-scale regrators who held disproportionate sway over the borough's ale and victuals market.

With these caveats in mind, the overall impression of high-level mobility in Ruthin suggests that English immigrants were most likely to be afforded opportunity to move into the highest-status positions. However, at this time mobility was not – or perhaps not yet – being purposely denied the Welsh community. The evidence is more suggestive of a phasing in of English officials at the highest level, creating previously non-existent opportunities for English social mobility, rather than a deliberate phasing out of Welsh administrators and clerics.

Ecclesiastical office holders
Already in the 1310s the borough's local clerics were being drawn, in large part, from the resident English population.[2] The bulk of *capellani*, or chaplains, appearing in the borough court, and especially those who appeared most regularly, were English clergy from the handful of benefices near or within Ruthin. Likewise, both the chaplain of Ruthin castle and those men named as prior of the borough's collegiate church of

---

[2] Spiritual 'clerics' are here taken to be men referred to as *capellanus*, as opposed to secular 'clerks' who are referred to as *clericus*. This distinction follows A. Barrell's reading of Dyffryn Clwyd's court roll evidence. Barrell, 'The clergy of a medieval lordship', 11.

Table 6.2. Male occupational by-names from the borough court of Ruthin, 1312–21: ecclesiastical workers (high status occupations, potentially offering social mobility)

Chaplain	(E)	11
*Cistercian	–	1
*'Crosier bearer'	–	1
Deacon	–	1
Parson	–	1
Prior (of St Peter's College, Ruthin)	–	1
Total churchmen		16

Source: TNA, SC2/215/71–SC2/216/3.
* Occupations which may not always have offered high status or mobility.
W: majority of persons were Welsh, probably Welsh occupational dominance.
E: majority of persons were English, probably English occupational dominance.
(E): majority of persons were English, but evidence is inconclusive.

St Peter were exclusively English during this period.[3] But the impression of ethnic dominance this may convey needs to be modified by the knowledge that these were newly created opportunities for advancement, almost certainly intended on some level to meet the needs of the English settler community. For example, Ruthin castle with its small chapel was a post-1282 construction, and was naturally serviced spiritually as well as militarily by Englishmen. Ruthin's collegiate church was a few years younger still, founded in 1310 and probably providing opportunities for six regulars in addition to the prior, again a niche to be occupied by promising sons of wealthy English burgesses.[4]

In stark contrast to the clerics who most frequently appeared in the borough court, those men who occupied the fourteen or so permanent benefices of rural Dyffryn Clwyd were almost exclusively Welsh.[5] From the 1290s Edward I had

[3] John de Tilton appears as 'prior of the college of Ruthin' in and around the years 1314–21 (*Dyffryn Clwyd Database*, GC1 #1731, SC2/216/3 m.22; TNA, SC2/217/76 session 1), and a William *capellanus castri* appears in 1314 (GC1 #750, SC2/215/73 m.27).
[4] Barrell, 'The clergy of a medieval lordship', 7.
[5] Of Dyffryn Clwyd's fourteen rural benefices in the years 1295–1329, we know ten occupants of eight posts, all of whom had ethnically Welsh names: Bodfari (much of this parish is in Flintshire) 1316–29, Madog (*Dyffryn Clwyd Database*, GC1 #1194, 2556; SC2/215/75 m.17d., SC2/216/9 m.11); Llanbedr 1313–18 and 1329,

established his supremacy over the marcher lords of Wales in matters ecclesiastical, but neither Edward I nor Edward II made any concerted attempt to anglicize the Welsh Church, continuing to appoint Welsh bishops in north Wales and men with strong local connections in south Wales.[6] Similarly, a recognized need for local clergy capable of communicating in Welsh ensured the appointment of Welsh clerics at the lowest level. While on his post-conquest visitations in north Wales in 1283 and 1284, the archbishop of Canterbury, John Pecham, ordered on at least one occasion that a Welsh-speaking suffragan be appointed to a border district where the needs of the Welsh-speaking community were inadequately provided for.[7] Hence, in the 1310s, opportunities for the Welshmen of Dyffryn Clwyd to achieve a degree of social mobility through the attainment of clerical office were still numerically much better than those of their English counterparts. But these opportunities were unlikely to be found within the borough, for the simple reason that the new posts created at Ruthin were intended for Englishmen.

The Welsh Church had long been the subject of harsh criticisms concerning the education and moral rectitude of its priests, criticisms voiced by men as diverse as Gerald of Wales in the late twelfth century and Archbishop Pecham in the late thirteenth.[8] The borough's new collegiate church was almost

---

Dafydd Du and Madog (Ibid., GC1 #2879, SC2/216/10 m.28d; TNA, SC2/215/72 session 2, SC2/216/1 session 7.); Llandyrnog 1313, Tudur (GC1 #537, SC2/215/72 m.13); Llanelidan 1315, Rhirid (Llan1 #617, SC2/215/74 m.11d.); Llanfair 1295 and 1312, Hywel and Dafydd Llwyd (Llan1 #24, 235; SC2/215/64 m.3, SC2/215/71 m.9d.); Llangwyfan 1320–31, Einion (GC1 #1602, 3072; SC2/216/3 m.21, SC2/216/12 m.15); Llangynhafal 1326, Cadwgan (GC1 #2388, SC2/216/6 m.3); Llanynys 1329, Madog (GC1 #2715, SC/216/10 m.25).

[6] D. Walker, 'The Welsh Church in the Middle Ages', in D. Walker (ed.), *A History of the Church in Wales* (Penarth, 1976), p. 43.

[7] Ibid., p. 44.

[8] In the late twelfth and early thirteenth centuries Gerald wrote several tracts which were generally critical of the Church in Wales, in particular his *Gemma Ecclesiastica* which 'affords a clear indication of what he believed to be the real weaknesses of the shortcomings of the (Welsh) clergy' (Walker, 'The Welsh Church', p. 37). Likewise, in his *Itinerarium Cambriae*, Gerald emphasized the 'lamentable use and custom by which the most powerful people in the parish have been appointed by the clergy as stewards ... (who) in the process of time their greed has grown greater and their greed has usurped full power' (Gerald of Wales, *The Journey Through Wales / The Description of Wales*, ed. L. Thorpe (London, 1978), p. 180). Archbishop Pecham's late thirteenth-century assessment of the Welsh Church was

certainly meant to bring about a perceived improvement of
clerical standards by English example, and so is likely to have
disrupted rather than reinforced any pre-existing pattern of
Welsh clerical patronage in the town. It is doubtful, however,
given the predominance of Welsh clergy outside the borough,
that any such patterns of patronage which had traditionally
offered Welshmen career mobility through the Church would
have been more than redirected, and then only for a matter of
decades. Comparisons may be drawn between, on the one
hand, the clergy appearing in the court rolls of the relatively
new borough of Ruthin and, on the other, those in older
mixed boroughs such as Knighton, where a Welsh chaplain
was named among the town's taxpayers as early as 1292–3.[9]

Secular office holders
The pattern of secular officials is much the same. Again there
were at least some prominent new positions created after 1282
which were dominated by Englishmen, in some cases for obvious reasons. Ruthin was a recently conquered district of Wales
in the 1320s, and the immediate core of men governing under
the lord, including the constable, chamberlain and receiver,
were English. Likewise, the office of *janitor* or porter/door-
keeper of Ruthin castle was filled by Englishmen, and they
were wealthy and socially significant figures throughout the
early fourteenth century.[10]

More revealing of mobility is the distribution of the larger
number of lesser offices, some of which were also English in
character, but many of which were held by Welshmen. The
parkers of Ruthin, for example, were usually English. A significant area of countryside surrounding the town was legally
designated part of the borough and contained at least two
parks, one large and one small. It is possible that these parks
had existed prior to the English conquest, but their formalization and inclusion as part of the new borough ensured that

no less scathing. After having visited Wales several times in the 1270s as royal
arbitrator with the Welsh princes, and having made a formal visitation of the four
dioceses of Wales in 1284, he 'declared that he could never remember having seen
such illiterate priests and clerics as he had found in Wales' (Walker, 'The Welsh
Church', pp. 44–5).
  [9] TNA, E179/242/57.
  [10] See Stephen *janitor*, table 2.6.

Table 6.3. Male occupational by-names from the borough court of Ruthin, 1312–21: officers and staff of governance (high-status and often highly profitable occupations, offering good opportunities for capital accumulation and social mobility)

Ale-taster	(E)	5
Assessor	–	1
Bailiff	–	3
Chamberlain	–	1
* Clerk / clerk of castle works	W/(E)	5 / 1
Constable	–	1
Forester / sub-forester	W	4 / 1
Granger	–	1
Hayward	(E)	5
Janitor, or door keeper, of Ruthin castle	E	3
Maer	W	1
Marshal	–	1
*Messenger	–	1
Parker	(E)	10
Rhaglaw	W	2
Receiver	–	1
Rhingyll	W	4
Serjeant	–	1
Warden	–	1
* Watchmen / cudgel-bearer	–	2
Total officers		55

Source: TNA, SC2/215/71–SC2/216/3.
* Occupations which may not always have offered high status or mobility
W: majority of persons were Welsh, probably Welsh occupational dominance.
E: majority of persons were English, probably English occupational dominance.
(E): majority of persons were English, but evidence is inconclusive.

many of those persons with whom the parkers would have to deal were anglophone immigrants. As a result, even in the earliest of Ruthin's court rolls (1296) there are citations referring to apparently English, and presumably English speaking, parkers of the borough.[11] By contrast, working in the lordship's commotes, where the bulk of the population was monolingual and Welsh speaking, the majority of commotal foresters and sub-foresters who came to the borough court to

[11]   The first borough parker to appear in Ruthin's court rolls is Martin *parcarius* in 1296: *Dyffryn Clwyd Database*, GC1 #14, SC/215/65, m.4.

pursue rural offenders were Welsh and presumably Welsh speaking.

The 'clerk of castle works' was an Englishman, though the majority of the lordship's other administrative clerks were Welsh.[12] A number of specifically Welsh manorial offices in the wider lordship, both fiscal and judicial, also seem to have remained in use throughout the period: the *rhaglaw*, a local Welsh judicial and administrative official; *rhingyll*, beadle or under-bailiff; and *maer*, a local collector of Welsh rents and dues. Again, as was the case with openings for rural chaplains and foresters, the number of opportunities for Welshmen to advance socially and economically by attaining these offices were probably numerically greater than those enjoyed by Englishmen (as per table 6.3). But the majority of openings most accessible to Welshmen were rural rather than urban.[13]

As with clerical advancement, it is unlikely that Welsh urban dwellers were denied access to many traditionally Welsh positions, but newly created offices such as that of borough parker or ale taster tended to be filled by Englishmen. Some Welsh burgesses, such as the ale tasters Dafydd Goch and Ieuan Potel, did secure these new urban offices, though they were in a minority.[14] We should also be hesitant about dismissing the possibility that Welsh burgesses, living at the administrative centre of government in Ruthin, saw and capitalized on opportunities in rural localities. As discussed in chapter 1, property investment by burgesses in the countryside and by rural folk in the town was not uncommon. While well-documented examples from Ruthin are scarce, burgesses could also invest in the farm of rural offices and wealthy rural landholders could be involved in borough administration. At Aberystwyth, for example, in the first decade of the fourteenth century a burgess,

---

[12]   Almary *clericus de opere castris* (1314–20): TNA, SC/215/73 session 10, SC/216/3 session 1.

[13]   The exact structure of rural administration in Dyffryn Clwyd is yet to be explored, but the wide range of officials needed for the parallel administration of each of Dyffryn Clwyd's three rural commotes is discussed at length in W. Rees, *South Wales and the March, 1284–1415: A Social and Agrarian Study* (Oxford, 1924), pp. 72–3, 92–128.

[14]   Ieuan Potel was named as ale taster in 1312: *Dyffryn Clwyd Database*, GC1 #391, SC/215/72 m.1. Dafydd Goch was named as ale taster in 1320 and 1321: Ibid., GC1 #1721 and #1741, SC/216/3 m.23d and SC/216/3 m.22.

William le Plumber, was also 'lead worker for the royal castles in west Wales', and his co-burgess, Ieuan Fychan ab Ieuan ap Rhys, had already been steward of Cardiganshire from 1299 to 1302.[15] Conversely, Geoffrey Clement, who had served as constable of Aberystwyth castle sometime prior to 1287, had a substantial north Cardiganshire estate from which his widow Margery fled to the borough during the Welsh rebellion of 1294–5.[16]

Skilled craftsmen and merchants

A survey of the borough's trade activities in the 1310s and 1320s also suggests the possibility that English immigrants were working to make a place for themselves, rather than usurping the prosperity of Welsh townsmen. Ruthin's relatively balanced ethnic composition reflected in the town's 1324 rental – half English and half Welsh – suggests that English immigration had probably doubled the town's size over the forty-two year period between 1282 and 1324. However, rather than creating a surplus of labourers in established industries, immigration doubled the number of the town's professionalized trades.

Those crafts clearly dominated by Welsh townsmen in 1324 are those which were presumably present prior to the 1282 formalization of the borough: carpentry, weaving, shoe making and milling (table 6.5 [D.]). These had arisen from local access to abundant quantities of certain raw materials, principally wool, leather and wood, and a need to process grains for domestic consumption. Those trades dominated by English burgesses in 1324 were generally out-growths of the community's urbanization, such as commercial food production (for example, baking and butchery), finishing crafts dependent on the availability of pre-processed raw materials (for example, tailoring and tanning) and processes more recently exploited, most particularly metalworking. That the position of Welsh

---

[15] I. J. Sanders, 'The boroughs of Aberystwyth and Cardigan in the early fourteenth century', *BBCS*, 15 (1954), 287, 289; R. A. Griffiths, 'Aberystwyth', in R. A. Griffiths (ed.), *Boroughs of Medieval Wales* (Cardiff, 1978), pp. 38–9.

[16] Sanders, 'The boroughs of Aberystwyth and Cardigan', 288–9; Griffiths, 'Aberystwyth', p. 30.

Table 6.4. Male occupational by-names from the borough court of Ruthin, 1312–21: skilled craftsmen and merchants (moderate- to high-status/earning occupations, often requiring significant investment capital, and offering some degree of social mobility)

Baker	E	6	Harper	–	1
Blanket maker	–	1	Mason	–	1
Brewer	–	1	Mercer	–	2
Butcher	(E)	11	Miller	W	13
Carpenter	W	6	Nailer	–	1
Cartwright	–	1	Painter 'ochere'	–	1
Caulker	–	2	Pie-maker	–	2
Chapmen	–	1	Plumber	–	1
Cobbler	W	16	Potter	–	1
Collier	–	1	Roofer	–	1
Cook	(E)	5	Salter	–	1
Cooper	–	3	Shearman	–	1
Doctor	–	3	Singer	–	1
Draper – clothier	–	1	Skinner	(E)	6
Dyer	–	1	Smith / Farrier	(E)	10 / 2
Engineer	–	1	Stall holder	–	2
Fisherman	–	1	Tailor	(E)	12
Fletcher	–	3	Tanner / Barker	(E)	4 / 3
'Flew'	–	1	Thatcher	–	1
Fuller	–	3	Tinker	–	2
Furbisher / armourer	–	3 / 1	Weaver	W	5
Gardener	–	2	Wheelwright	–	2
Glover	–	3	Wine merchant	–	1
Goldsmith	–	2			
Total craftsmen and merchants				156	

Source: TNA, SC2/215/71–SC2/216/3.
W: majority of persons were Welsh, probably Welsh occupational dominance.
E: majority of persons were English, probably English occupational dominance.
(E): majority of persons were English, but evidence is inconclusive.

carpenters, weavers, shoemakers and millers remained virtually unassailable in the 1320s, and that the prosperity and social mobility which these trades offered Welshmen continued, was a product of the way in which the skills of Ruthin's English immigrants were assimilated to the pre-existing craft network. A brief review of some of Ruthin's key industries illustrates the dominance of one ethnic group or the other in certain trades.

Carpentry

The importance of indigenous carpentry in north-east Wales grew out of the region's relative abundance of timber in the thirteenth and fourteenth centuries, and the local fashion in house building which that abundance inspired. While early fourteenth-century farmsteads in north-east Wales still maintained, in high pastures, the temporary turf-walled summer houses referred to by Gerald of Wales as 'wattled huts on the edges of the forest … strong enough to last a year or so', substantial lowland structures were also common in the post-conquest period.[17]

The medieval house in much of Wales was timber built, and the modern identification of slate as the quintessentially Welsh building material would have been 'unintelligible to a medieval audience who quickly came to associate stone with the castles of the Edwardian conquest'.[18] As opposed to south Wales, where houses were often walled with stone, in north-east Wales all parts of the dwelling as far as possible, including even walls of solid post-and-panel construction, were built of timber.[19] Moreover, the north-east was quite exceptional, both in Wales and by comparison with some parts of England, as an area where even middling men of what would come to be the region's yeomanry aspired to live in timber hall-houses from an early date.[20]

Gothic style and its more complex construction techniques had reached Wales by the mid-thirteenth century, and the use of pointed 'cruck' trusses are mentioned in records of the king's works in Wales from at least 1306 onwards.[21] Moreover, many of the English immigrants who came to north Wales from the midlands or Welsh border regions of England, where timber construction was also common, would no doubt have aspired to possess similar homes in Wales.[22] The

---

[17] Gerald of Wales, *The Journey Through / Description of Wales*, p. 525.
[18] R. Suggett, 'The interpretation of late medieval houses in Wales', in R. R. Davies and G. Jenkins (eds), *From Medieval to Modern Wales: Historical Essays in Honour of Kenneth O. Morgan and Ralph A. Griffiths* (Cardiff, 2004), p. 44.
[19] Ibid.
[20] P. Smith, 'Houses and building styles', in D. H. Owen (ed.), *Settlement and Society in Wales* (Cardiff, 1989), p. 101.
[21] Suggett, 'The interpretation of late medieval houses', p. 45.
[22] Smith, 'Houses and building styles', pp. 114–15.

continued survival of the well-preserved timber hall-house, Nantclwyd House on Castle Street, Ruthin, probably built by the weaver Gronw ap Madog and his wife Suzanna in the early 1430s, is testament to the craftsmanship of local carpenters whose forebears would have been crucial to the town's rapid development a century earlier.[23]

Weaving

The position of those Welshmen seeking to better themselves through participation in Ruthin's cloth industry was similarly secure during the first half of the fourteenth century. While it has long been argued that proximity to raw materials alone had little influence on the siting of centres of the medieval cloth industry, the 'simple minded conclusion', to quote Jack, that successful grazing encouraged industry should not be 'despised'.[24] Across fourteenth-century Dyffryn Clwyd extensive local flocks of sheep – the Grey lords' flock at Ruthin numbering between two and three thousand – combined with conscious capital investment, both seignorial and independent, to create a fast growing industry.[25]

The fact that Welshmen dominated the preliminary stages of the cloth industry, and weaving in particular, was again an out-growth of the environment in which the industry was encouraged. In England, wool often came from distant parts of the country to be turned into cloth in certain boroughs, themselves often located in areas of arable agriculture where cloth production was encouraged as a specialized trade in the economic interest of the lord. In north Wales it was already common for farmers to weave the wool of their own sheep as a cottage industry prior to the thirteenth-century foundation of the borough.[26] Hence, when the professionalization of Ruthin's

---

[23] TNA SC2/222/1 m.70.
[24] R. I. Jack, 'The cloth industry in medieval Wales', *WHR*, 10 (1980–1), 446, 459. For opinions arguing against the relevance of local raw materials, see A. Baker, 'Changes in the later Middle Ages', in H. C. Darby (ed.), *A New Historical Geography of England before 1800* (Cambridge, 1973); and J. Thirsk, 'Industries in the countryside', in F. J. Fisher (ed.), *Essays in the Economic and Social History of Tudor and Stuart England in Honour of R. H. Tawney* (Cambridge, 1961).
[25] Jack, 'The cloth industry in medieval Wales', 451, 457.
[26] E. A. Lewis, 'The development of industry and commerce in Wales during the Middle Ages', *TRHS*, n.s., 17 (1903), 155.

weaving was encouraged through borough privileges for urban traders and material investment in the form of at least two fulling mills constructed in Dyffryn Clwyd by the 1330s, there was already a skilled labour force present to capitalize on the industry's growth.[27]

Leather and shoemaking

Among the professionalized traders of Ruthin who tended to be predominantly Welsh were the borough's leather workers. The tanning of pre-modern leather required an abundant supply of three essential items: animal skins, water and oak bark.[28] All of these were widely available in and around Ruthin. Leather craft is evident in many of the borough's occupational by-names, such as tanner, barker, glover and, in particular, cobbler. By the 1320s, shoemaking occupied the single greatest concentration of Ruthin's craftsmen, English and Welsh, working in one specialization.

The combination of good grazing and oak trees which made Dyffryn Clwyd a favourable region for the production of leather products probably first emerged with the demands of Ruthin's pre-conquest inhabitants to provide a centre for leather crafts no later than the latter half of the thirteenth century. Before the Edwardian conquest Ruthin had been the administrative centre of the district, and the site of the *maer-dref*, where presumably Prince Llywelyn ap Gruffydd and his brother Dafydd held their courts.[29] The slaughter of animals to provision members of the ruling class, their retinues and other workers who settled around this administrative centre is likely to have provided the material catalyst that led to a trade later reflected in the large number of Welsh leather workers present in early fourteenth-century Ruthin. As Thorold Rodgers observed, some tanning or tawing was a by-product of

[27] Jack, 'The cloth industry in medieval Ruthin', 455, 457. It should also be noted that, on a regional level, between 1301 and 1349 at least eleven new fulling mills were constructed in the area of modern Denbighshire (ibid., 449), and in 1447 a guild of fullers and weavers was established at Ruthin, unique among the boroughs of north Wales. For a transcript of the guild ordinances, see ibid., 10–25.

[28] J. Cherry, 'Leather', in J. Blair and N. Ramsay (eds), *English Medieval Industries: Craftsmen, Techniques, Products* (London, 1991), p. 301.

[29] Jack, 'Welsh and English in the medieval lordship of Ruthin', *DHST*, 18 (1969), 37.

animal consumption in most rural villages and, as Ruthin
evolved from a small administrative outpost into a chartered
borough, its leather-craft industry grew accordingly.[30]

Where English market participation intersects with this
indigenous leather craft is a good starting point from which to
explain the way in which English immigrant labour found a
place for itself in the expanding borough. As evidence of this
process, table 6.4 contains what may at first appear to be an
anomaly, countering the argument that Welshmen were most
prevalent in trades which they had historically dominated.
The anomaly is that, while Welshmen comprised the majority
of shoemakers, by the 1320s they were supplied by an almost
exclusively English body of men styling themselves 'tanner' or
'barker'. The likely reason for this is that in small village tan-
neries there was little or no division between tanners and
leatherworkers.[31] By contrast, in more advanced urban communities, of the type into which Ruthin evolved as English
immigration doubled the borough's population in the 1280s
to 1320s, there was a much greater degree of specialization.

In medieval cities, such as London and York, the production of shoes might involve as many as three men: a tanner, a
currier (who readied leather for production through stretching, softening, etc.) and the shoemaker himself.[32] In Ruthin,
the town's growing population consumed an increasing quantity of meat, which in turn provided more hides for tanning,
and finally a larger and more specialized leather-craft industry.[33] A by-product of this specialization was that the production
of leather goods, principally shoes, was split between at least
two skilled workers, the tanner and the shoemaker.[34]

---

[30]   Thorold Rodgers, as cited in Cherry, 'Leather', p. 301.
[31]   Ibid., p. 308.
[32]   Ibid., pp. 298–9, 308. Until the mid-fourteenth century, shoemaking was in
many places subdivided into the work of cordwainers (who made high-quality or
high-value shoes), corvesers (who made new shoes of average quality) and cobblers
(who repaired or remade old shoes for sale). But in Ruthin only the blanket term of
cobbler, or *sutor*, appears.
[33]   The number of butchers typically amerced per session of the biannual great
court of Ruthin doubled in this period from about six in 1306–7, the date from
which the first records of the 'assize of meat' survive, to about twelve in the late
1320s. *Dyffryn Clwyd Database*, GC1 #97, 121, 2687, 2801; SC/215/69 m.3,
SC/215/69 m.4, SC/216/9 m.18, SC/216/10 m.27.
[34]   There is no documentary evidence suggesting that curriers worked in Ruthin
during this period, but their absence from the surviving court record need not

By the 1320s, Ruthin's Welsh leatherworkers came to focus primarily on the highly skilled craft of shoemaking, and the need this created for the dedicated production of leather seems to have been met by English immigrant tradesmen. Moreover, this particular division of the production processes may have fostered the creation of trade links, through Ruthin's immigrant tanners, for the export of leather to locations across England. The rise of towns like Ruthin gave new impulse to local traders, encouraged the development of better transport links and, in the period of relative stability experienced in north Wales in the early fourteenth century, established hides and skins as some of Wales's principal exports.[35]

In this way, English tanning would have provided an avenue to prosperity and potential social mobility parallel with, and complementary to, that available to Welsh leather workers, though not without significant cross-cultural and cross-occupational exchange. Richard *sutor* (cobbler), for example, was brought before the great court of Ruthin in October 1306 and fined 40*s.* for not paying tolls on goods which he had regularly exported from the lordship. The related court roll entry explains that Richard had come to the town seven years previously (in 1299), bought one burgage whereby he entered into the liberty of the borough and had since proceeded to trade (*fecit mercandisas suas*) in hides and other things 'bought in Ruthin and in the cantref of Dyffryn Clwyd and sold outside the lordship at Denbigh and elsewhere'.[36] While probably a shoemaker by trade when he immigrated to Ruthin, confronted with the competition of Welsh cobblers by 1306, Richard, like many English traders, had come to focus primarily on trading in unworked leather.

mean their absence from the borough. This is also the case with 'white tanners' who prepared thin and lightly tanned leather, principally for glove making; the presence of a few glovers in the borough attests to the presence of white tanners, as well as later borough regulations (see below, this chapter).

[35] Lewis, 'The development of industry and commerce', 166–8.

[36] As discussed in part 1, English settlers like Richard *sutor* seem regularly to have brought substantial amounts of start-up capital with them to the borough, allowing this kind of immediate trade participation. *Dyffryn Clwyd Database*, GC1 #73, SC2/215/69 m.3.

Tailoring

The process by which English immigrants adapted to the pre-
existing economy can also be seen in the emergence of
tailoring in the borough. The native cloth with which most
Welshmen would have been best acquainted prior to the conquest of 1282–4 was either *brychan*, a traditional rough cloth or
blanket produced in the home, or the improved *keyneth*,
known in Ruthin simply as 'Welsh cloth', which was being
produced and traded for general use in the 1290s.[37] Given the
low quality and limited production of these textiles, English
cloth was one of the necessities imported into Wales well into
the thirteenth century for refined use such as in the manufac-
ture of moderate- to high-value clothing.[38] But, by the end of
the fourteenth century, highly finished, domestically produced
cloth had become the most important of all Welsh trade
goods.

Not just in Dyffryn Clwyd, but more widely in what became
the county of Denbigh, at least eleven new fulling mills were
built for the finishing of cloth between 1301 and 1349, the
largest number in any of the counties which were later created
by the Act of Union.[39] As already discussed from a quantitative
standpoint, this rapid industrialization ensured the future of
Welsh weavers, but just as importantly from a qualitative standpoint this expansion reflected an abundant supply of
garment-quality cloth. This increase in the production of
more highly finished cloth likewise coincided with English
immigration to Ruthin, rapid growth and urbanization within
the borough and the emergence of a new and prosperous
social stratum which would have provided a buoyant market
for the work of English tailors. Additionally, while English
immigration and the granting of burghal privileges stimulated
urban growth across post-conquest north Wales in the early
fourteenth century, the only significant new markets to
emerge for Welsh cloth and locally produced clothes were

[37] 'Welsh cloth' may have been equated with 'burel', the cheapest and coarsest
of thirteenth-century English cloth; a presumably Welsh 'Morfudd bureler (*extuba-
trix*)' appears in Ruthin's courts as late as 1321 (TNA, SC2/16/3 session 8). Lewis,
'The development of industry and commerce', 155–6; *Dyffryn Clwyd Database*, GC1
#136, 2485; SC2/15/65 m.15, SC2/16/6 m.18d.

[38] Lewis, 'The development of industry and commerce', 155.

[39] Jack, 'The cloth industry in medieval Wales', 449.

Llanerchymedd in Anglesey and Ruthin in Dyffryn Clwyd.[40] Hence, for a considerable part of the region north and west of the cloth and clothing markets of Oswestry and Shrewsbury, Ruthin would have been a focal point for the procurement of cloth and clothing.[41]

On the whole, the combination of new expertise, the new tastes of an immigrant population and the increasing prosperity of the borough itself contributed to the rise of a craft to which English tradesmen were attracted. As with tanning and shoemaking, the function of immigrant labour was complementary to native enterprise, though in this instance providing finished work rather than bulk supply. The greater the demand for finished cloth and clothing, the richer English tailors grew and the better the prospects enjoyed by Welsh weavers. However, it must be stressed that, while tailors tended to be English and weavers Welsh, there was a strong element of interchange. Cynwrig *cissor* (tailor), for example, the only tailor known to have been among those men chosen as borough jurors in 1312–21, or among Ruthin's most frequent sureties, was probably Welsh.[42]

Milling and commercial food production
The preponderance of English men and women among Ruthin's commercial bakers and bakeresses reflects the same variety of professionalization of labour as is seen in tailoring. It was already the practice in late thirteenth-century Wales for corn to be ground at seignorially owned or licensed mills. Court roll evidence suggests that there was probably one principal mill in each commote of the lordship operating under direct seignorial supervision, supplemented by around a dozen privately owned enterprises which farmed the right to the suit of tenants in certain areas.[43] As early as 1306, the great

---

[40]   Lewis, 'The development of industry and commerce', 159.
[41]   Ibid.
[42]   See table 2.6.
[43]   The principal mills seem to have been the mill of Aberchwiler, in Dogfeiling, the mill of Bodangharad, in Colion, and the 'mill of Garthgynan, in Llannerch', all of which are referred to with unusual frequency in the court record, with the plaintiff in most cases being the lord (as opposed to a private miller). Furthermore, a court roll entry of 1332, in which the bond community of Llannerch was collectively amerced for not doing 'the work of the mill' suggests that these principal mills were

court of Dyffryn Clwyd was actively enforcing the principle
that all land in the lordship owed suit to a particular mill, a
policy almost certainly carried through from the period of
native rule.[44] However, it was a privilege granted by the 1282
charter of the borough of Ruthin that if the lord's mill could
not grind the corn of burgesses in a timely fashion, then they
could take it elsewhere for grinding without censure.[45]

The fact that the majority of millers who appeared in the
borough court of Ruthin were Welsh is also a sign of historical
continuity in the lordship's system of mills. The right to build
and operate these constructions had been farmed principally
by wealthy, rural property owners since before the conquest,
and the dislocation of these native elites seems to have been in
many cases minimal. A good example from Dyffryn Clwyd is
Hywel ap Madog, among whose extensive holdings in Colion
were 24 acres and a one-third share in the mills of Bryncaredig
and Maesmaencymro for which he paid 58s.11d. annually, and
where he doubtless employed Welsh millers to grind corn on
his behalf.[46] Likewise, such regular employment of Welsh
millers was almost certainly common in many other parts of
Wales, for in neighbouring Flintshire officials' accounts show
Welshmen regularly enjoying the farm of mills.[47]

The social and practical importance of these mill owners
and farmers, and their workers, often brought them into the
town to conduct trade. For this reason they feature regularly
in the borough court rolls of Ruthin (table 6.4), although

those which bond tenants were required to use and maintain. *Dyffryn Clwyd
Database*, Llan1 #2193, SC2/16/12 m.26. The named corn mills (1294–1339)
include: in the commote of Dogfeiling, Llannerch-deuddwr, 'Melin-y-wern', 'de
Aberchwiler' and Penbedw (in Aberchwiler); in the commote of Llannerch, 'de
Llannerch', Garthgynan, Killaro, Llysfasi, Ceidio, Trewyn and 'Wood Mill'; in the
commote of Colion, 'Melin-y-wig', Trefor, Glynpolfa, Bodangharad, Bryncaredig
and Maesmaencymro; and in the borough of Ruthin, 'de Ruthin' and Llan-rhudd.
Ibid., GC1 #194, 195, 517, 581, 1304, 1340, 1886, 1903, 1909, 2023; Llan1 #212, 336,
2193, 2384; Rental #34, 635. SC2/15/70 m.4, SC2/15/71 m.9, SC2/15/72 m.10,
SC2/15/72 m.14, SC2/15/73 m.24, SC2/15/76 m.15d, SC2/15/76 m.16,
SC2/16/4 m.28 and m.33, SC2/16/12 m.26d, SC2/16/14 m.17, Rental m.1d.,
Rental m.7d.

44   Ibid., GC1 #154, SC2/15/69 m.15.
45   Jack, 'The medieval charters of Ruthin borough', *DHST*, 18 (1969), 18–19.
46   Rental #635, Rental m.1d.
47   A. Jones (ed.), *Flintshire Ministers' Accounts, 1301–1328* (Prestatyn, 1913),
p. xlv.

their occupation was not particularly urban in nature. In the 1324 rental of the borough, only one miller, the Welshman Heilyn *molendinarius* (miller), resided in the borough, maintaining one burgage on Mill Street (where the town's corn mill was located) and another in Llanfwrog.[48] Nevertheless, the town's millers were part of an important Welsh occupational network that spanned the lordship.

By contrast, butchery and baking were specifically urban trades which required a substantial, focused community to support a volume of traders. That the rapid growth of such an environment was taking place in the early fourteenth century is attested by a doubling of the number of licensed workers in both occupations. The number of butchers typically paying to trade in the town doubled from six in the pre-famine years (1306–7) to twelve in the post-famine years of the late 1320s.[49] Likewise, as has been discussed in part 2, the number of male and female bakers typically amerced for trading in the borough doubled over these same years. Crucially, the number of bakers and bakeresses working in the borough proved extremely sensitive to changes in market size and population during the famine period of 1315–22.[50]

As with tailoring, the growth in food production was dependent on numerically significant English and native immigration and migration. English settlers arriving in the borough with even moderate amounts of start-up capital would have been in the right place at the right time to establish themselves in the borough's food production industry. William de Wytemor, for example, is totally absent from Ruthin's court record prior to October 1312, at which point he was amerced 12*d.* for the baking and selling of bread.[51] Less than five years later, in June 1317, William is recorded as

---

[48] While we may reasonably infer that a man named 'Heilyn *molendinarius*' and possessing a burgage on 'Mill Street' in 1324 would have been the holder of the farm of the mill of Ruthin, this cannot be proven. In 1316 the farmer of Ruthin mill was Alexander de Suywell, but he seems to have sold his interests in the borough prior to the time of the rental. *Dyffryn Clwyd Database*, GC1 #1080, SC2/15/74 m.18, Rental #50, Rental m.7d.

[49] Ibid., GC1 #97, 121, 2687, 2801; SC2/215/69 m.3, SC2/215/69 m.4, SC2/216/9 m.18, SC2/216/10 m.27.

[50] See figure 4.1.

[51] *Dyffryn Clwyd Database*, GC1 #409, SC2/15/72 m.1.

having sold to Bleddyn ap Heilyn and his wife one burgage in the market place of Ruthin for which the annual rent was 5s., five times the usual rent of an inhabited plot.[52] By the spring of 1320 William had reached the rank of borough official, acting as ale taster in that year and periodically thereafter, eventually to disappear from the court record with the arrival of the Black Death in mid-1349, after some thirty further years of baking.[53] William had come to the borough as a young man, probably with significant start-up capital; he quickly prospered, acquired valuable property and achieved social mobility all within eight years of his arrival.

Metalworking

A survey of Ruthin in the early fourteenth century indicates that metalworking, more than other industries, generated such prosperity as to place its practitioners among the borough's social elite.[54] Like tailoring and baking, metalworking was a trade which expanded from small-scale and limited production for domestic use to the provisioning of both common and specialist goods for urban and military consumption. However, in this area of trade, Ruthin's native craftsmen tended to be pushed aside in favour of immigrant workers, as happened to Welsh metalworkers elsewhere.

In the Anglo-Welsh town of Knighton, Adam and Richard, the sons (and presumably the heirs) of the probable Englishman Philip *faber*, together paid more in tax on moveable goods in 1292–3 than anyone else in the town, while fellow townsman Roger *faber* paid the third highest level of tax recorded.[55] At Aberystwyth, in a rental dating to the first decade of the fourteenth century, the likely Englishman Robert *faber* was the town's only burgess to be described as a smith and was among the top third of property holders (that is, those who held in excess of one full burgage).[56] At the

---

[52] *Dyffryn Clwyd Database*, Reliefs #317, SC2/15/76 m.1d.

[53] Ibid., GC1 #1722, 1741; SC2/16/3 m.23d, SC2/16/3 m.22. The Black Death reached Ruthin in June 1349. W. Rees, 'The Black Death in Wales', *TRHS*, 4th series, 3 (1920), 120.

[54] Between 1312 and 1322 two of the borough's wealthiest burgesses and two of its largest creditors styled themselves *faber*. See table 2.4.

[55] TNA E179/242/57.

[56] Sanders, 'The boroughs of Aberystwyth and Cardigan', 287.

bishop of St David's chief Pembrokeshire town of Llawhaden, which contained a significant Welsh element, all five *fabri* recorded in a survey of 1326 were English by name, one of them among just five of the town's 126 burgesses to possess four or more burgage plots each.[57]

The smith was an indispensable member of medieval society, for virtually all other crafts and occupations depended on his work.[58] The Welsh smith in particular had traditionally enjoyed an honoured place in native society since the drafting of the laws of Hywel Dda, as a fashioner of the weapons of war and tools of husbandry.[59] In the thirteenth century especially, Welsh arrows and spears were reputed to be of good quality and formed part of Welsh external trade.[60] Hence one might reasonably expect that in early fourteenth-century Ruthin, a town which had acted essentially as a military outpost for both the Welsh princes and Edward I in the late thirteenth century, there would have been a concentration of resident Welsh metalworkers. However, this was not the case.

Iron had never been produced in Wales in sufficient quantity to meet native demand.[61] Moreover, while it has been convincingly argued by Geddes that the problems of transporting iron in the Middle Ages could be adequately overcome, metals were not cheap and the later Welsh princes were never in a position to spend freely. Contemporary descriptions of the Welsh in conflict generally relate that they were lightly armoured and armed.[62] With little metal to work with, it may indeed be the case that Welsh smiths produced these light arms (arrowheads and spearheads, in particular) and agricultural implements with great skill. However, it is unlikely that they had either the specialist expertise or the necessary desire to equip Ruthin's post-1282 garrison with the heavy arms associated with English warfare.[63]

---

[57] J. W. Willis-Bund (ed.), *The Black Book of St David's* (London, 1902), pp. xvii, 139–51.

[58] J. Geddes, 'Iron', in J. Blair and N. Ramsay (eds), *English Medieval Industries*, pp. 167–88.

[59] Lewis, 'The development of industry and commerce', 126.

[60] Ibid., 142.

[61] The nearest known contemporary source of Welsh iron to Ruthin was the ironworks of Ruddlan, first mentioned in Doomsday Book. Ibid., 147 (note 4), 166.

[62] R. R. Davies, *The Age of Conquest: Wales, 1063–1415* (Oxford, 1987), pp. 254–5.

[63] In this period 'the military scene was dominated by the heavily armed knight'

After the collapse of the north Welsh principality, this situation would have changed rapidly. In the wake of conquest there was an immediate need to consolidate and defend the new English holdings in north Wales, and this was reinforced by the rebellion of Madog ap Llywelyn and his capture of Ruthin castle in 1294–5.[64] Likewise, the abortive raid on the castle in 1321, though led by external forces and failing to attract support among the Welsh townsmen, must have kept defence at the top of the seignorial agenda.[65] As a result, the provisioning and servicing of the castle provided opportunities for many Welsh and English merchants.[66] Additionally, it almost certainly created an immediate demand for metal tools and fixtures to be used in the construction of the castle and housing, however rude at first, to accommodate the borough's rapidly growing population.

The conquest and its aftermath would also have facilitated much better access to the iron necessary to meet these demands. That Reginald de Grey, the first marcher lord of Dyffryn Clwyd, was better funded than his immediate predecessors is evident from his ability to afford the rapid construction of Ruthin castle, a sizeable structure which superseded whatever Welsh fortifications may previously have defended the site. The probability that he also generated more revenues from the lordship than had been raised under native rule is suggested by the complaints of 'new and oppressive customs' delivered to Archbishop Pecham on his post-conquest tour of Wales.[67] But more than simply better funded, the borough's new patron was also justiciar of Chester, a prime port of supply through which imports of Spanish and English iron entered north Wales.[68] Lord Grey would have been well positioned to encourage and facilitate the trade links necessary to meet both seignorial and entre-

---

or English man-at-arms on horseback (P. Contamine, *War in the Middle Ages* (Oxford, 1984)), which has led King to categorize the English forces present in north Wales at the end of the thirteenth century as 'iron men on iron horses' (D. Cathcart King, 'The defence of Wales, 1067–1283', *AC*, 126 (1977), 15).

[64]   Davies, *The Age of Conquest*, p. 383.
[65]   See above, pp. 158–9.
[66]   Lewis, 'The development of industry and commerce', 167.
[67]   R. Newcome, *An Account of the Town and Castle of Ruthin* (Ruthin, 1829), p. 6.
[68]   Lewis, 'The development of industry and commerce', 148.

preneurial requirements for the production of metal goods in his borough at Ruthin.

That this opening up of new markets for metals and metal-working was a significant element in the urbanization and economic development of Wales in the fourteenth century is illustrated by the extraordinary life of the Chester man William de Doncaster. William was a merchant and vendor of ironmongery to the Crown during Edward I's Welsh wars and a purchaser of lead from Flintshire mines. By 1300 he was buying property in Flintshire; he had become a burgess of Beaumaris by 1305 and by 1312 he was able to acquire the farm of the whole of the lead mines of Englefield. William also acted as mayor of Flint in 1312, bought a messuage in Rhuddlan in 1323 and became mayor of Chester on three occasions.[69]

Although seignorial accounts for Dyffryn Clwyd have unfortunately not survived from this period, the practical needs entailed in the construction and provisioning of Ruthin castle would have demanded the direct or indirect employment of at least one or more smiths. Furthermore, the building of the castle implies that large amounts of the new revenues generated in the lordship's rural commotes were reinvested in the borough economy.[70] It was probably this type of exploitation which may have been distasteful to native craftsmen faced with immigration that led to English domination of the trade by the 1320s. Not only were seven of the twelve smiths and farriers who appeared in the borough court during 1312–21 English, but so were two of the three 'forbysours', or armourers, who were occasionally present in the borough in the 1320s. Perhaps more telling, all three of the wealthy smith-burgesses who featured in the borough court and rental of 1324 as moneylenders or high rent payers seem to have been English: Hugh *faber*, Peter *faber* and Robert *faber*.[71]

---

[69]   A. Jones (ed.), *Flintshire Ministers' Accounts*, p. xliv.

[70]   Ruthin castle was a smaller construction, but to provide some frame of reference we may note that the contemporaneous building of Beaumaris castle and repairs to Caernarfon castle after the rebellion of Madog ap Llywelyn, which like Ruthin castle had been captured by rebels, totalled around £16,000 of royal expenditure. Davies, *The Age of Conquest*, p. 384.

[71]   See table 2.6.

As a result, Welsh smiths were never totally absent from the court record, but they were certainly not as prominent in the borough as Welsh weavers, carpenters, shoemakers or other native craftsmen who had retained control over their respective industries and had grown to prosperity as the borough had grown. Hence, it was in the field of metalworking, perhaps more than any other, that Welsh and English tradesmen came most directly into competition, and in which prosperous mobility may be associated with workers of one ethnic group more than the other.

WELSH AND ENGLISH: TRADESMEN
PROTECTING MARKET INTERESTS

On the whole, there is little evidence of a conscious attempt to limit prosperity or mobility on grounds of ethnicity. In most instances English workers simply organized themselves around pre-existing Welsh trade structures, engaging in either complementary or newly created trades. Nonetheless, these same English tradesmen and office holders mainly accounted for the imbalance of material wealth reflected in the borough's rental of 1324.[72]

There are two reasons for this. The first is relatively straight-forward and revolves around the occupations which each ethnic group tended to dominate. By design or chance, the occupations of English immigrants were the most profitable ones. A large proportion of English craftsmen who came to the borough had specialist skills like smiths and armourers, sometimes aided by seignorial patronage; or they entered fast-growing areas of the economy like commercial food production. Both avenues offered opportunities for prosperity and social mobility.

The second reason for the disproportionate affluence of English tradesmen lies with the more subtle values of social protectionism. As was stated in the court record of 1296 with reference to brewing controls and price fixing, borough trade regulation was dictated by 'the twelve (jurors) of Ruthin, with the consent of all and singular'.[73] And, as discussed above in

---

[72]   See table 1.1.
[73]   *Dyffryn Clwyd Database*, GC1 #24, SC2/215/66, m.1.

part 1, Ruthin's twelve jurors were almost invariably a group comprised of six Englishmen and six Welshmen. Yet, the first attempts at trade protection put in place by the burgesses were those related to English-dominated crafts. Of paramount interest are the institutional barriers erected in the late 1320s prohibiting new leatherworkers and other typically English tradesmen, or at least requiring then to pay a special fine. From 1330 onwards, regular notes appear at the head of each great court of Ruthin roll noting (or deleting when appropriate) 'No purprestures, thieves and receivers, tailors, tanners, whittawers, skinners, dyers, abductors of heirs, married widows, snatchers of women, or malefactors in the lord's parks and fishpond'.[74] Unfortunately, details of why 'tailors, tanners, whittawers, skinners, [and] dyers' in particular needed to be as closely regulated as 'thieves' or 'snatchers of women' are not given, but much of the impetus for this scrutiny must have been economic protectionism against skilled immigrants and aspiring native traders alike. The presence of practitioners of 'clean' crafts such as tailoring, and the absence from this list of detritus-producing crafts such as butchery, makes these regulations unlikely to have been related to public health concerns. Instead, the system of flat-rate fines put in place to regulate these workers' trade participation, typically a half-mark (6s. 8d.) per annum, would have functioned as a barrier to market entry and mobility, and one much more significant than that faced by practitioners of trades more commonly engaged in, such as brewing or baking (where the typical amercement amounted to only 6d. to 2s.).[75]

It is difficult to track with any precision the development of trade regulation. However, in the pre-plague period not all women or men amerced for brewing and butchering in Ruthin were property-owning burgesses or the wives of such burgesses, and yet these persons amerced for breaching assizes were not amerced for 'stallage and toll' as outsiders to the community. In the post-plague period, by the 1360s

[74] For example, ibid., GC1 #2815, 3787, 3874: SC2/16/10 m.26, SC2/17/4 m.16, SC2/17/3 m.11.
[75] Post-plague examples of trading amercements are common (for example, GC3 #1643, 1657, 2418, 2419; SC2/218/9 m.40d, SC2/219/1 m.32); but for the pre-plague period they are rare.

especially, amercements for trading by non-burgesses (still normally citing illegal tanning or tailoring as the principal transgression) were becoming increasingly common. It seems that by the 1360s the community had reached a point where new traders were not welcome, and it is likely that many of the non-burgesses amerced for trading were residents of the borough who simply did not own any property, and so were denied market access on technical grounds which had previously gone unenforced.

It is remarkable that these restrictions on persons who might interfere with aspects of the English-dominated tanning and tailoring industries would be agreed by the borough's six English *and* six Welsh jurors, 'all and singular'.[76] Yet, while the more regular and general enforcement of the burgesses' exclusive market rights increased in the later fourteenth century, no similar initiatives were taken to formalize the special status of Welsh weavers or shoemakers until the mid- to late fifteenth century.[77] Ruthin's guild of weavers and fullers did not appear until 1447, and Ruthin's 'Brotherhood of Corvesers and Shoemakers' did not receive the right to regulate market entry until it was granted by the lord in 1496.

It is this difference, and more importantly the underlying social values which it reflects, that contributed to the greater accumulation of wealth among English craftsmen. When examining the amassed personal holdings or fortunes of English master craftsmen, such as those of the borough's three prominent smiths, knowledge of this underlying ethos of trade monopolization among English craftsmen helps to explain how the English community prospered. If, by comparison, Welsh craftsmen allowed a lack of market protections to diminish their prospects for prosperity and mobility, the absence of those protections might indicate that the Welsh community was less versed in the 'culture of commerce' than its English counterpart.

[76]   See above, note 73.
[77]   Jack, 'The cloth industry of medieval Ruthin', 22.

A POINT OF COMPARISON: THE SHARED
EXPERIENCES OF THE WORKING POOR

Ethnic distinctions were perhaps least apparent among the
thinly documented poor male workers of the borough. In most
medieval towns there existed two basic groups of paupers:
those who embraced poverty as an expression of religious devo-
tion and those who experienced it involuntarily.[78] It is this latter
group with which we are immediately concerned (table 6.5):
those who endured the 'working-poverty' defined by Mollat as
'the condition of those whose toil and effort did not assure
them food, happiness, or independence'.[79] Appropriate to
Ruthin is his further comment that 'the working-poor knew
and perhaps even worked at a trade and sometimes owned a
small amount of property, but the scantiness of their resources
and their dependency on an employer left them vulnerable to
accidents and economic circumstances'.[80]

Many of the varieties of female worker already discussed in
part 2, such as regrators and cloth workers, closely match this
description, as is emphasized by the presence of women
among those occupational groups compelled, at least occasionally, to resort to prostitution. But, while the close regulation
of female regrators in particular has given us a limited insight
into the relative insignificance of ethnicity as a determinant
of working-poverty (see table 5.1 and figure 5.4), statistical
evidence for Ruthin's male working-poor is even less forthcoming. The number of men identified in the court rolls by
generally low-skill or low-status by-names is small. Furthermore,
the chronic under-representation of Welsh tradesmen in the
court record, based on their use of patronymic by-names as
opposed to occupational by-names (table 6.1), was most acute
among Welshmen labouring at low-status tasks. As a result, little can be said with confidence about much of this sector of
borough society, except to stress that many of these men
would have conformed to Mollat's description of the working-

---

[78] Wedemeyere Moore, 'Aspects of poverty in a small medieval town', in
E. DeWindt (ed.), *The Salt of Common Life: Individuality and Choice in Medieval Town,
Countryside and Church* (Kalamazoo, 1995), p. 117.

[79] M. Mollat, *The Poor in the Middle Ages: An Essay in Social History* (London,
1986), p. 162.

[80] Ibid.

Table 6.5. Male occupational by-names from the borough court of Ruthin, 1312–21: manual labourers and servants (poorly paid occupations, requiring little or no capital, and offering very limited social mobility)

Builder		1
*Carter	(E)	6
Ditcher or digger	(E)	8
Groom or bateman	–	4
'Gutter'	–	1
Harrower	–	1
Shepherd	–	4
Mower	–	1
* Servant or lad/groom (garcio)	W	25
Spinner	–	1
Swineherd	–	1
Thresher	–	1
'Worker'	–	1
Total labourers and servants		55

Source: TNA, SC2/215/71–SC2/216/3.
* Occupations potentially offering mobility
W: majority of persons were Welsh, probable Welsh occupational dominance.
E: majority of persons were English, probable English occupational dominance.
(E): majority of persons were English, but evidence is inconclusive.

poor, with access to little or no investment capital. They were unlikely ever to have access to enough cash, coin or credit to invest in the tools, livestock or land needed to become more prosperous and economically independent.

Agricultural labourers

Any distinction drawn between agricultural and non-agricultural labourers in small towns such as Ruthin, in which livestock-owning residents were often closely integrated in the surrounding countryside, is inevitably a theoretical one. But it is a useful analytical device in so far as it allows us to recognize that while agricultural and non-agricultural labourers were often the same persons, those men meeting unskilled labour needs in the town would have carried out different tasks from men working in the countryside on behalf of townsmen, and would have found employment in different circumstances. While the fortunes of agricultural labourers were tied to the arable harvest cycle and pastoral life cycle of livestock, labourers working in town would have found their employment dependent on the growth or decline of the town's economic fortunes, though these were intimately linked to the rural economy at large.

Agricultural labourers such as the harrower, mower, thresher, swineherd and shepherds noted in table 6.5 (E) were probably both semi-transients with few resources, appearing almost exclusively in isolated court entries, and those most vulnerable at times of harvest failure and cattle murrain. In a borough court entry of 1316, for example, the hired hand Adam *bercarius* (shepherd, *bercarius … per mercede*) was sued by William le Serjeant, a member of the borough elite, an office holder and a prominent creditor, for the bad keeping (*male custodiendo*) of William's livestock, whereby William had lost forty sheep (hoggasters) and two muttons to his combined loss of £4 6s. 8d.[81] In reality, these animals had almost certainly died as a result of the first of several severe cattle murrains, possibly anthrax, which devastated Wales between 1316 and 1322.[82]

Regardless of the cause of William's livestock losses, the outcome for Adam, who wilfully acknowledged the animals' deaths, would have been destitution. That William sought more than symbolic satisfaction for the full monetary compensation he was awarded by the court is evidenced by the six sureties of payment required to swear on Adam's behalf; Ruthin's legal custom allowed for the prosecution of a debtor's sureties should the debtor fail to discharge his obligations. It is illustrative of the creeping poverty which would have caused the movement of men such as Adam into the borough, in search of affordable food or even alms as the famine became protracted, that with the exception of one borough tailor his sureties were also poor agricultural labourers like 'Philip Harrower' and 'Adam le Man'. Set against Adam's crippling debt of £4 6s. 8d., the wage he or his fellow labourers may optimistically have hoped to receive was around 6d. per day, or annual earnings of around £3 10s.,

81 TNA, SC2/215/75 session 3.
82 Jordan, *The Great Famine: Northern Europe in the Early Fourteenth Century* (Princeton, NJ, 1996), pp. 38–9.

should they have enjoyed the luxury of wholly cash wages.[83] Furthermore, only after the vast majority of these monies were spent on food might whatever pittance remained have then been applied to the repayment of William le Serjeant.

As the focal point of the lordship's economy, the borough was no doubt at the centre of the lordship's labour market. Men such as Adam *bercarius* would have come to the borough and its market in search of employment. However, such employment was probably unlikely either to be permanent or remunerative at such a level as to allow the accumulation of the capital necessary for the purchase of land, livestock, or tools for aspiring urban craftsmen. It bears noting that, even for those with basic trade skills, little headway could have been made without a significant body of relevant equipment necessary for trade participation. The purchase of a carpenter's, mason's, or tailor's tools, for example, required a considerable capital outlay: a 1320 inventory of one felon's goods at Ruthin valued a single pair of tailor's scissors as 10*d.*, or around two days' wages.[84] Equally, poor town dwellers would no doubt have worked in the countryside at harvest time. Hence there may have been little to distinguish 'townsmen' from 'non-townsmen' among those poor men who identified themselves with menial agricultural occupations in the borough court, except perhaps personal affinities with either the town or the countryside.

Non-agricultural labourers

The experience of townsmen who identified themselves through by-names such as builder, worker or carter is not likely to have been preferable to that enjoyed by workers whose primary source of income was agricultural employment. While the market value of the services offered by a simple labourer or carter in 1300 would have been nominal, those same services in 1315–22, when the town's population was augmented by persons displaced by the famine and seeking work, may have been valued even less. Moreover, medieval urban work was, at the best of times, episodic and seasonal.[85]

---

[83]   C. Dyer, *Standards of Living in the Middle Ages: Social Change in England, c.1200–1520* (Cambridge, 1989), pp. 224–5

[84]   *Dyffryn Clwyd Database*, GC1 #1540; SC2/216/3 m.18d–19.

[85]   Dyer, *Standards of Living*, p. 223.

Should high prices and livestock losses by wealthy elites such
as William le Serjeant have encouraged them to spend less,
thereby limiting the availability of work at a time when food
prices rose dramatically, the effect on urban labourers may
have been disastrous. Take, for example, 'John the carter of
chapel works', who was mentioned in a 1315 session of the
great court of Ruthin.[86] We may reasonably ask, given the long
duration of the great famine, what level of economic dislocation would have been required to cause job losses by
alienating the benefactors of the project on which John
worked, and others like it.

Male servants

The close parallels between the experiences of female and
male servants in the small towns of Wales are manifest. As was
the case with young girls, discussed in chapter V, young boys
may have been given to host families to be raised as foster-
children from an early age. And, in the context of medieval
Wales, these same boys would have grown up to form part of
the borough's servant population. As with female servants,
young men often acted with or on behalf of their masters in
various activities, such as trade work or money handling,
which implied a certain degree of on-the-job training in man-
aging the household economy. Sometimes this even extended
as far as illegal activity, as when, in 1313, David, the servant of
Tudur *molendinarius,* and his master were together amerced
for stealing the lord's apples at night.[87] Moreover, like female
servants, male servants often demonstrated a high degree of
loyalty, as when, in 1323, Henry the servant of Amelina, the
widow of Robert *ferrator* (farrier), assisted his mistress in a
struggle with John de Schirland, going so far as to strike John
with a spade.[88]

Most importantly, male servants shared with their female
counterparts poor prospects for capital accumulation during
their service, which resulted in potentially limited social
mobility thereafter. Some young, male heirs may have passed
part of their youth as servants until such a time as they came

[86] *Dyffryn Clwyd Database,* GC1 #1041, SC2/215/74 m.17
[87] TNA, SC2/215/73 session 1.
[88] *Dyffryn Clwyd Database,* GC1 #2003, SC2/216/4 m.31.

into their patrimony and gained both independence and the means to marry. For these men, the accumulation of capital during their tenure as servants was not essential in securing future prosperity. However, for many other servants, an inability to acquire more than modest capital reserves during service meant an uncertain future. While some servants would have become the unskilled labourers who identified themselves by the agricultural or non-agricultural by-names listed in table 6.5, the recording of some men before Ruthin's borough court simply as 'X the former servant of Y' is one indication that service was not always followed by even regular unskilled work.[89] Another indication of the sometimes unfavourable outcome of male service is the number of court roll entries which record former servants stealing food or valuables from their ex-masters and fleeing.[90]

On the whole, male servants, like female servants, probably had limited freedom and poor remuneration during a period of urban expansion and labour over-supply, which left few good options following their service. Within this economic context, the slim majority of servants appearing in the borough court of Ruthin from 1312 to 1321 who were Welsh, 13 of 25 servants (table 6.5), is unlikely to represent a strong social preference for servants of one ethnicity as opposed to another. Instead, during a decade when the agricultural crisis of the great famine would have limited labour opportunities in a predominantly Welsh countryside, it may well represent no more than an indication of the ethnic composition of the body of young men sent to the town either as servants or in order to find service work.

This discussion of labourers and servants emphasizes that the economic conditions affecting those who might realistically have found themselves among Ruthin's working poor affected both English and Welsh. The economic protectionism employed by wealthy borough oligarchs such as William le

---

[89] For example, 'William who was the servant of Martin': TNA, SC2/215/71 session 5.

[90] For example, Hugh de Whytlowe, the former servant of Richard de Whytel, who in 1324 broke into Richard's house and stole jewellery, silver utensils, money and a ham before fleeing the country: *Dyffryn Clwyd Database*, GC1 #2082 and 2083, SC2/216/5 m.10.

Serjeant, who was capable of deflecting even the costs of his losses during cattle murrain onto the working poor, amounted to a form of exploitation unlikely to have been mitigated in favour of either English or Welsh. Hence, in this environment of poverty, and before the spectre of the 'beast' Hunger described by Langland as leaping upon the 'waster' and seizing him by the belly 'until water ran from his eyes', English and Welsh in this lower social stratum probably shared a common plight.[91]

---

[91]   William Langland, *Piers the Ploughman*, ed. J. Goodridge (London, 1966), p. 86.

CONCLUSION

The themes of this book revolve around one fundamental question: what was the driving force behind the 'cultural assimilation' of English and Welsh in an atmosphere of 'racial' inequality?[1] The answer lies in the shared socio-economic interests and experiences of men and women, English and Welsh, in several social strata. What complicates the response is the need to understand the complex relationship between access to capital, occupation and status which gave rise to these common experiences, and the way in which these factors dictated the circumstances of an individual's everyday life.

There can be no doubt that an atmosphere of ethnic inequality existed in Ruthin throughout the period 1312–21. In the lordship's 1324 rental the borough's Welsh community was firmly focused on 'Welsh Street', where the town's largest concentration of Welsh burgesses and their families lived in densely packed tenements of one-half burgage or less. Likewise, the borough's English community was focused on nearby 'Castle Street', which ran along the ridge of high ground from the marketplace to the thick stone walls of the lordship's fortified seat of English control, the castle. Furthermore, Welshmen were doubtless aware that the accumulated wealth and property of their English neighbours were greater than their own, and that even the right to free devise, by which they might themselves attempt to accumulate property for personal gain, was a novel extension of their status as Welsh urban dwellers and was denied to their rural kinsmen.[2]

These realities created an atmosphere of ethnic discrimination, yet long-standing inequalities of material wealth were offset by more equitable social norms. The majority of Welsh and English burgesses did not reside exclusively on Welsh

[1] Davies's terminology: R. Davies, *Lordship and Society in the March of Wales, 1282–1400* (Oxford, 1978), p. 446; *idem, The Age of Conquest: Wales, 1063–1415* (Oxford, 1987), p. 421.
[2] See table 1.1 and accompanying text.

Street or Castle Street respectively, but lived side by side in the rest of the town, including the districts of 'Mill Street', 'Llanfwrog', 'New Street' and 'Town End'. Likewise, were a property-holding Welshman to have brought a complaint before the great court of Ruthin, or to have paid for an inquest in the borough court of Ruthin, he would have found half of the jurors considering the case to be fellow Welsh burgesses.

While a few key officials, such as the castle porter (*janitor*) or the borough parkers (*parcarii*), tended to be exclusively English, many townspeople probably had at least as much contact with the borough's Welsh ale tasters or court bailiffs as with its English officials. Although fewer in number, Ruthin's Welsh office-holding and wealthy elites headed a range of Welshmen who enjoyed just as many diverse degrees of prosperity as their English neighbours. Welsh men and women did not need to look beyond their own ethnic group in order to see the rewards of high status and affluence, nor to look only within it to find the effects of poverty.

Even closer ties of common experience were grounded in the shared conditions of men and women who lived their lives in the same socio-economic strata, and often worked at the same occupations. As Davies has suggested, the pace of assimilation was most rapid where English and Welsh found themselves coexisting 'cheek by jowl', and nowhere was the nature of that coexistence more closely apparent than among Ruthin's mixed communities of wealthy elites, middling tradesmen/women and the working poor of all descriptions.[3] The high levels of capital available to borough elites allowed them and their wives to flourish as landlords, creditors and brewsters, even during those years of agricultural crisis when many of their less wealthy neighbours endured extreme hardship. Ruthin's middling men and women, with access to moderate amounts of capital, were probably more vulnerable to economic change, but nevertheless had the capacity to weather hardship. As a group primarily composed of skilled craftsmen and -women who provided essential goods to the community, such as bread, meat, shoes and clothes, the

---

[3]   Davies, *The Age of Conquest*, p. 421.

products of their labours would have been indispensable even
during the lean years of the great famine. Lastly, there were
the working poor, such as spinsters, servants, carters, regrators
and other persons with access to little or no capital. These
townspeople were most vulnerable to economic and agrarian
crises; and at times of famine-induced urban migration or
seignorial sponsored immigration, they would have been most
acutely subject to rising food costs and the devaluation of their
labour.

These loosely definable social strata were internally frag-
mented by background and ethnicity. Some of Ruthin's
powerful elites, such as the Englishman Almary de Marreys,
held most of their property in the lordship's surrounding
commotes. Others' holdings, like those of the Welshman
William *saer*, were entirely within the borough. At the middling level, the practitioners of certain trades, such as weaving
and carpentry, tended to be Welsh, while most of the borough's bakers and tailors were English. Nevertheless, these
differences were not accentuated by any discernible internal
strife.

At the least, these groups exercised toleration towards one
another, and in some instances demonstrated cooperation or
even collusion, irrespective of their ethnicity. Ruthin's jurors,
for example, Welsh and English, seem consciously to have
refrained from litigating against one another. Likewise, the
distribution of various productive processes among the
borough's Welsh and English tradesmen was more complementary than divisive, as illustrated by the relationship between
the borough's Welsh weavers and English tailors, or between
English tanners and Welsh cobblers.[4] At its most developed,
this tolerance may have evolved into the type of collusion
hinted at by the fixing of ale prices among the borough's dominant Welsh and English brewsters during the great famine.[5]

Thus, an analysis of Ruthin's socio-economic structure
demonstrates a community divided by the 'social closure' of
urban wealth and status groups, rather than by ethnicity.[6] In

---

[4] See table 6.3 and accompanying text.
[5] See above, chapter III.
[6] H. Rigby, *English Society in the Later Middle Ages: Class, Status and Gender*
(London, 1995), p. 176.

other words, borough society was most strongly characterized by the struggle of particular interest groups to make the most of the social and economic opportunities available to them, to the exclusion of their competitors.[7] Examples of this would include the monopolization of the ale trade by wealthy brewsters during the famine period; the way in which a small group of borough elites dominated the personal pledging or surety market; and even the way in which wealthy individuals like William le Serjeant endeavoured to oppress their social inferiors through curial coercion.[8] In contrast to the importance of shared status and wealth, the comparative insignificance of ethnicity is demonstrated by the lack of any clear pattern of partiality or discrimination linking either English or Welsh members of the same group of elite sureties with pledgees of either the same or alternative ethnicity.[9]

How conscious this kind of 'social closure' may have been in Ruthin, and whether it signifies a nascent sense of social solidarity or simply the expression of common concerns and desires, are impossible questions to answer. Nonetheless, these common concerns among persons within any particular social stratum, as reflected in their ability to access capital for reinvestment and personal gain, were the driving forces behind the 'cultural assimilation' of English and Welsh in early fourteenth-century Ruthin. This is also the context in which Welsh townsmen and -women were reluctant to take up arms against their English neighbours in 1321 during a rebel raid on the town and castle.[10] The shared aspirations of these two peoples for economic security and prosperity outweighed the continuing tensions caused by Welshmen's 'memories of recent conquest and the nervous arrogance of English settlers', and ensured their eventual integration.[11]

---

[7] Ibid., p. 9.
[8] See above, chapter V, for details of William's unfair dealings with Adam, his shepherd.
[9] See above, chapter II.
[10] See above, chapter II; *Dyffryn Clwyd Database*, GC1 #2014, SC2/216/4 m.32.
[11] Davies, *Age of Conquest*, p. 421.

BIBLIOGRAPHY

1. UNPUBLISHED SOURCES

Court rolls
Aberystwyth: TNA, SC2/215/20
Ruthin and Dyffryn Clwyd, 1294–1422: TNA, SC2/215/64–SC2/221/11
Radnor: NLW 'Miscellaneous Documents, co. Radnor'
Wrexham Bailiwick: TNA, SC2/226/17–18
— (extracts) NLW, Peniarth MS 404D

Lay Subsidy Rolls for Wales, 1292–3
Flintshire: TNA, E179/242/52
Powys: TNA, E179/242/54
Radnor: TNA, E179/242/57

Account rolls
Caerleon, 1303–1320: SC6/920/16–28

Surveys/rentals
Aberystwyth, 1301–2: SC2/215/20
Bromfield and Yale (including Wrexham), 1391: BL, Add MS 10013
Carmarthen, 1307–27: TNA, SC12/20/32
Ruthin and Dyffryn Clwyd, 1324: TNA, WALE 15/8/1

2. PUBLISHED ORIGINAL SOURCES

Administrative
Davies, R. R. and Smith, Ll. B. (eds), machine readable database, *The Dyffryn Clwyd Court Roll Database, 1294–1422* (Aberystwyth, 1995); available from the Economic and Social Research Council on request, award number R000232548.
Jack, R. I., 'Records of Denbighshire lordships II – The lordship of Dyffryn Clwyd in 1324', *Denbighshire Historical Society Transactions*, 17 (1968), 7–53.
—— 'The medieval charters of Ruthin borough', *Denbighshire Historical Society Transactions*, 18 (1969), 16–22.
Jenkins, D., *The Law of Hywel Dda: Law Texts from Medieval Wales Translated and Edited* (Llandysul, 1986).
Jones, A. (ed.), *Flintshire Ministers' Accounts, 1301–1328* (Prestatyn, 1913).
Jones, G. and Owen, H. (eds), *Caernarvon Court Rolls, 1361–1402* (Caernarvon, 1951).

Lister, J. (ed.), *Court Rolls of the Manor of Wakefield*, vol. IV, Yorkshire Archaeological Society Record Series, 78 (1930).

Sanders, I. J., 'The boroughs of Aberystwyth and Cardigan in the early fourteenth century', *Bulletin of the Board of Celtic Studies*, 15 (1954), 282–93.

Williams-Jones, K. (ed.), *The Merioneth Lay Subsidy Roll, 1292–3* (Cardiff, 1976).

Willis-Bund, J. W. (ed.), *The Black Book of St David's* (London, 1902).

Literary

Geoffrey Chaucer, *The Canterbury Tales: A Selection,* Penguin popular classics edn (London, 1969).

Gerald of Wales, *The Journey Through Wales / The Description of Wales*, ed. L. Thorpe (London, 1978).

Margery Kempe, *The Book of Margery Kempe*, ed. B. Windeatt (London, 1985).

William Langland, *Piers the Ploughman*, ed. J. Goodridge (London, 1966).

3. SECONDARY SOURCES

Baker, A., 'Changes in the later Middle Ages', in H. C. Darby (ed.), *A New Historical Geography of England before 1800* (Cambridge, 1973), pp. 187–95.

Baker, J., *An Introduction to English Legal History* (London, 1979).

Barrell, A., 'The clergy of a medieval lordship: the evidence of the Dyffryn Clwyd court rolls', *Denbighshire Historical Society Transactions*, 44 (1995), 5–23.

—— and Brown, M., 'A settler community in post-conquest rural Wales: the English of Dyffryn Clwyd, 1294–1399', *Welsh History Review*, 17 (1995), 332–55.

——, R. R. Davies, O. J. Padel and Ll. B. Smith, 'The Dyffryn Clwyd court roll project, 1340–1352 and 1389–1399: a methodology and some preliminary findings', in Z. Razi and R. Smith (eds), *Medieval Society and the Manor Court* (Oxford, 1996), pp. 260–98.

Barron, C., 'The "Golden Age" of women in medieval London', *Reading Medieval Studies*, 15 (1989), 35–58.

Beckerman, J., 'Procedural innovation and institutional change in medieval English manorial courts', *Law and History Review*, 10 (1992), 197–252.

Bennett, J., *Women in the Medieval English Countryside: Gender and Household in Brigstock Before the Plague* (Oxford, 1987).

——, *Ale, Beer and Brewsters in England: Women's Work in a Changing World, 1300–1600* (Oxford, 1996).

Beresford, M., *New Towns of the Middle Ages* (London, 1967).

Berry, A., 'The parks and forests of the lordship of Dyffryn Clwyd', *Denbighshire Historical Society Transactions*, 43 (1994), 7–25.

Brand, P., 'Aspects of the law of debt, 1189–1307', in P. R. Schofield and

N. Mayhew (eds), *Credit and Debt in Medieval England, c.1180–c.1350* (Oxford, 2002), pp. 19–41.

Briggs, C., 'Creditors and debtors and their relationships at Oakington, Cottenham and Dry Draton (Cambridgeshire), 1291–1350', in P. R. Schofield and N. Mayhew (eds), *Credit and Debt in Medieval England, c.1180–c.1350* (Oxford, 2002), pp. 127–48.

——, 'Empowered or marginalized? Rural women and credit in later thirteenth-and fourteenth-century England', *Continuity and Change*, 19 (2004), 13–43.

——, *Credit and Village Society in Fourteenth-Century England* (Oxford, 2009).

Britnell, R., *Growth and Decline in Colchester, 1300–1525* (Cambridge, 1986).

Brown, M., 'Kinship, land, and law in fourteenth century Wales: the kindred of Iorwerth ap Cadwgan', *Welsh History Review*, 17 (1995), 493–519.

Cherry, J., 'Leather', in J. Blair and N. Ramsay (eds), *English Medieval Industries: Craftsmen, Techniques, Products* (London, 1991), pp. 295–318.

Clark, E., 'Debt litigation in a late medieval vill', in J. Raftis (ed.), *Pathways to Medieval Peasants* (Toronto, 1981), pp. 247–79.

Contamine, P., *War in the Middle Ages* (Oxford, 1984).

Davies, R. R., 'Colonial Wales', *Past and Present*, 65 (1974), 3–23.

——, 'Race relations in post conquest Wales, confrontation and compromise', *Transactions of the Honourable Society of Cymmrodorion* (1974–5), 32–56.

——, *Lordship and Society in the March of Wales, 1282–1400* (Oxford, 1978).

——, *The Age of Conquest: Wales, 1063–1415* (Oxford, 1987).

DeWindt, E., *Land and People at Holywell-cum-Needingworth: Structures of Tenure and Patterns of Social Organisation in an East Midlands Village* (Toronto, 1972).

——, 'Introduction', in E. DeWindt (ed.), *The Salt of Common Life: Individuality and Choice in the Medieval Town, Countryside, and Church: Essays Presented to J. Ambrose Raftis* (Kalamazoo, 1995), pp. xi–xvii.

DeWolf Hemmon, M. *Burgage Tenure in Medieval England* (London, 1914).

Dyer, C., *Standards of Living in the Middle Ages: Social Change in England, c.1200–1520* (Cambridge, 1989).

——, 'The consumer and the market in the later Middle Ages', *The Economic History Review*, 42 (1989), 305–27.

Edwards, N., 'Landscape and settlement in medieval Wales: an introduction', in N. Edwards (ed.), *Landscape and Settlement in Medieval Wales* (Oxford, 1997), pp. 1–12.

Geddes, J., 'Iron', in J. Blair and N. Ramsay (eds), *English Medieval Industries: Craftsmen, Techniques, Products* (London, 1991), pp. 167–88.

Given, J., 'The economic consequences of the English conquest of Gwynedd', *Speculum*, 64 (1989), 11–45.

Goldberg, P. J. P., 'The public and the private: women in the pre-plague economy', in P. Cross and S. Lloyd (eds), *Thirteenth Century England III:*

Proceedings of the Newcastle Upon Tyne Conference (Woodbridge, 1991), pp. 78–89.

——, *Women, Work and Life Cycle in a Medieval Economy: Women in York and Yorkshire, c.1300–1520* (Oxford, 1992).

Griffiths, R. A. (ed.), *Boroughs of Medieval Wales* (Cardiff, 1978).

——, 'Aberystwyth', in R. A. Griffiths (ed.), *Boroughs of Medieval Wales* (Cardiff, 1978), pp. 19–46.

——, 'Carmarthen' in R. A. Griffiths (ed.), *Boroughs of Medieval Wales* (Cardiff, 1978), pp. 131–64.

——, *Conquerors and Conquered in Medieval Wales* (Stroud, 1994).

——, 'Wales and the Marches', in D. Palliser (ed.), *Cambridge Urban History of Britain*, vol. 1, *c.600–c.1540* (Cambridge 2000), pp. 681–714.

Hanawalt, B., *The Ties That Bound: Peasant Families in Medieval England* (New York, 1986).

Hechter, M., *Internal Colonialism: the Celtic Fringe in British National Development, 1536–1966* (London, 1975).

Herlihy, D., *Women, Family and Society in Medieval Europe: Historical Essays, 1978–1991* (Oxford, 1991).

Hilton, R., *Bond Men Made Free: Medieval Peasant Movements and the English Rising of 1381* (London, 1973).

——, *The English Peasantry in the Later Middle Ages* (Oxford, 1975).

——, 'Small town society in England before the Black Death', *Past and Present*, 105 (1984), 53–78.

——, *English and French Towns in Feudal Society* (Cambridge, 1992).

——, 'Low-level urbanization: the seigniorial borough of Thornbury in the Middle Ages', in Z. Razi and R. Smith (eds), *Medieval Society and the Manor Court* (Oxford, 1996), pp. 482–517.

Holt, R. and Rosser, G. (eds), *The English Town in the Middle Ages* (London, 1990).

Howell, M., *Women, Production and Patriarchy in Late Medieval Cities* (London, 1986).

Howells, B., T. A. James, D. Miles, J. Howells and R. F. Walker, 'The boroughs of medieval Pembrokeshire', in R. F. Walker (ed.), *Pembrokeshire County History*, vol. 2: *Medieval Pembrokeshire* (Haverfordwest, 2002), pp. 426–79.

Hutton, D., 'Women in fourteenth century Shrewsbury', in L. Charles and L. Duffin (eds), *Women and Work in Pre-Industrial England* (London, 1985), pp. 83–99.

Jack, R. I., 'The cloth industry in medieval Ruthin', *Denbighshire Historical Society Transactions*, 12 (1963), 10–25.

——, 'Welsh and English in the medieval lordship of Ruthin', *Denbighshire Historical Society Transactions*, 18 (1969), 23–49.

——, 'The cloth industry in medieval Wales', *Welsh History Review*, 10 (1980–1), 443–60.

Jewell, H., *Women in Medieval England* (Manchester, 1996).

Jones-Pierce, T., *Medieval Welsh Society: Selected Essays*, ed. J. B. Smith (Cardiff, 1972).

——, 'The growth of commutation in Gwynedd during the thirteenth century', in J. B. Smith (ed.), *Medieval Welsh Society: Selected Essays* (Cardiff, 1972), pp. 103–26.

Jones, R. 'Problems with medieval Welsh local administration – the case of the *Maenor* and the *Maenol*', *Journal of Historical Geography*, 24 (1998), 135–46.

——, 'Changing ideologies of medieval state formation: the growing exploitation of land in Gwynedd, *c.*1100–*c.*1400', *Journal of Historical Geography*, 26 (2000), 505–16.

Jordan, W., *The Great Famine: Northern Europe in the Early Fourteenth Century* (Princeton, NJ, 1996).

Karras, R., 'The regulation of brothels in later medieval England', in J. Bennett (ed.), *Sisters and Workers in the Middle Ages* (London, 1989), pp. 100–34.

Kelly, H., 'Statutes of rapes and alleged ravishers of wives: a context for the charges against Thomas Mallory, Knight', *Viator*, 28 (1997), 361–419.

Kerr, M., 'Husband and wife in criminal proceedings in medieval England', in C. Rousseau and J. Rosenthal (eds), *Women, Marriage, and Family in Medieval Christendom* (Kalamazoo, 1998), pp. 211–51.

Kershaw, I., 'The great famine and agrarian crisis in England, 1315–1322', *Past and Present*, 59 (1973), 3–50.

King, D. Cathcart, 'The defence of Wales, 1067–1283', *Archaeologica Cambrensis*, 126 (1977), 1–16.

Kowaleski, M., 'Women's work in a market town: Exeter in the late fourteenth century', in B. Hanawalt (ed.), *Women and Work in Pre-Industrial Europe* (Bloomington, 1986), pp. 145–64.

Krause, J., 'The medieval household: large or small?', *The Economic History Review*, 9 (1956–7), 420–32.

Kussmaul, A., *Servants in Husbandry in Early Modern England* (Cambridge, 1981).

Laslett, P., *Household and Family in Past Time* (Cambridge, 1972).

Lewis, E. A., 'The development of industry and commerce in Wales during the Middle Ages', *Transactions of the Royal Historical Society*, n.s.17 (1903), 121–73.

——, *The Medieval Boroughs of Snowdonia* (London, 1912).

Leyser, H., *Medieval Women: A Social History of Women in England, 450 – 1500* (London, 1995).

Lilley, K., '"Non urbe, non vico, non castris": territorial control and the colonization and urbanization of Wales and Ireland under Anglo-Norman lordship', *Journal of Historical Geography*, 26 (2000), 517–31.

Maitland, F. W., *Township and Borough* (Cambridge 1898).

May, A., 'An index of thirteenth-century peasant impoverishment? Manor court fines', *The Economic History Review*, 26 (1973), 389–402.

McIntosh, M., *Controlling Misbehaviour in England, 1370–1600* (Cambridge, 1998).

Mollat, M., *The Poor in the Middle Ages: An Essay in Social History* (London, 1986).

Moore, E. Wedemeyre, 'Aspects of poverty in a small medieval town', in E. DeWindt (ed.), *The Salt of Common Life: Individuality and Choice in Medieval Town, Countryside, and Church* (Kalamazoo, 1995), pp. 117–56

Morris, W., *Frankpledge System* (New York, 1910).

Muldrew, C., '"A mutual assent of her mind?" Women, debt, litigation and contract in early modern England', *History Workshop Journal*, 55 (2003), 47–71.

Mundill, R., 'Christian and Jewish lending patterns in financial dealings during the twelfth and thirteenth centuries', in P. R. Schofield and N. Mayhew (eds), *Credit and Debt in Medieval England, c.1180–c.1350* (Oxford, 2002), pp. 42–67.

Newcome, R., *An Account of the Town and Castle of Ruthin* (Ruthin, 1829).

Nightingale, P., 'Monetary contraction and mercantile credit in later medieval England', *The Economic History Review*, 43 (1990), 560–75.

Olson, S., 'Jurors of the village court: local leadership before and after the plague in Ellington, Huntingdonshire', *Journal of British Studies*, 30 (July 1991), 237–56.

Owen, D. H., 'Denbigh' in R. A. Griffiths (ed.), *Boroughs of Medieval Wales* (Cardiff, 1978), pp. 165–87.

——, 'The Middle Ages', in D. H. Owen (ed.), *Settlement and Society in Wales* (Cardiff, 1989), pp. 199–224.

Owen, L., 'The population of Wales in the sixteenth and seventeenth centuries', *Transactions of the Royal Historical Society* (1959), 99–113.

Palliser, D. (ed.), *Cambridge Urban History of Britain*, vol. 1, *c.600–c.1540* (Cambridge, 2000).

——, 'Introduction', in D. Palliser (ed.), *Cambridge Urban History of Britain*, vol. 1, *c.600–c.1540* (Cambridge, 2000), pp. 3–16.

Partner, N., 'Introduction', *Speculum*, 68 (1993), 305–8.

Pimsler, M., 'Solidarity in the medieval village? The evidence of personal pledging at Elton, Huntingdonshire', *Journal of British Studies*, 17 (1977), 1–11.

Pollock, F. and Maitland F. W., *The History of English Law before the Time of Edward I*, vol. 2, 2nd edn (Cambridge, 1968).

Poos, L., Razi, Z., and Smith R., 'The population history of medieval English villages: a debate on the use of manor court records', in Z. Razi and R. Smith (eds), *Medieval Society and the Manor Court* (Oxford, 1996), pp. 298–368.

Post, J. B., 'Manorial amercements and peasant poverty', *The Economic History Review*, 28 (1975), 304–11.

Postan, M. M., *The Medieval Economy and Society: An Economic History of Britain in the Middle Ages* (Harmondsworth, 1975).

Postles, D., 'Personal pledging: medieval "reciprocity" or symbolic capital', *Journal of Interdisciplinary History*, 26 (1996), 419–35.

Powell, N., 'Urban population in early modern Wales revisited', *Welsh History Review*, 23 (2007), 1–43.

Power, E., *Medieval Women* (Cambridge, 1975).

Pratt, D., 'Wrexham's medieval market', *Denbighshire Historical Society Transactions*, 15 (1966), 8–14.

——, 'Medieval Bromfield and Yale: the machinery of justice', *Denbighshire Historical Society Transactions*, 53 (2004), 19–78.

Raftis, J. A., 'Social structures in five East Midland villages: a study of possibilities in the use of court roll data', *The Economic History Review*, 18 (1965), 83–100.

—— (ed.), *Pathways to Medieval Peasants* (Toronto, 1981).

Razi, Z., 'The Toronto School's reconstruction of medieval peasant society: a critical view', *Past and Present*, 85 (1979), 141–57.

——, *Life, Marriage and Death in a Medieval Parish: Economy, Society and Demography in Halesowen, 1270–1400* (Cambridge, 1980).

——, 'Family land and the village community in later medieval England', *Past and Present*, 93 (1981), 3–36; reprinted in T. Aston (ed.), *Landlords, Peasants and Politics in Medieval England* (Cambridge, 1987), pp. 360–93.

—— and R. Smith (eds), *Medieval Society and the Manor Court* (Oxford, 1996).

Rees, W., 'The Black Death in Wales', *Transactions of the Royal Historical Society*, 4th series, 3 (1920), 115–35.

——, *South Wales and the March, 1284–1415: A Social and Agrarian Study* (Oxford, 1924).

Rigby, H., *English Society in the Later Middle Ages: Class, Status and Gender* (London, 1995).

Roberts, G., 'Wales and England, antipathy and sympathy, 1282–1485', *Welsh History Review*, 1 (1963), 375–96.

Roberts, S., 'The study of dispute: anthropological perspectives', in John Bossy (ed.), *Disputes and Settlements; Law and Human Relations in the West* (Cambridge, 1983), pp. 1–24.

Robinson, W. R. B., 'Swansea', in R. A. Griffiths (ed.), *Boroughs of Medieval Wales* (Cardiff, 1978), 263–88.

Russell, J., *British Medieval Population* (Albuquerque, 1948).

Rutledge, E., 'Immigration and population growth in early fourteenth-century Norwich: evidence from the Tithing Roll', *Urban History Yearbook* (1988), 15–30.

Schofield, P. R., 'The late medieval view of frankpledge and the tithing system: an Essex case study', in Z. Razi and R. Smith (eds), *Medieval Society and The Manor Court* (Oxford, 1996), pp. 408–49.

——, 'Dearth, debt, and the local land market in a late thirteenth-century village community', *Agricultural History Review*, 45 (1997), 1–17.

——, 'Peasants and the manor court: gossip and litigation in a Suffolk village at the close of the thirteenth century', *Past and Present*, 159 (1998), 3–42.

——, *Peasant and Community in Medieval England, 1200–1500* (Basingstoke, 2003).

Smith, J. B. (ed.), *Medieval Welsh Society: Selected Essays* (Cardiff, 1972).

Smith, J. B. and Ll. B. Smith (eds), *History of Merioneth*, vol. 2: *The Middle Ages* (Cardiff, 2001).

Smith, Ll. B., 'The gage and the land market in late medieval Wales', *The Economic History Review*, 29 (1976), 537–50.

——, 'The *Gravamina* of the community of Gwynedd against Llywelyn ap Gruffydd', *Bulletin of the Board of Celtic Studies*, 31 (1984), 158–76.

——, 'Seignorial income in the fourteenth century: the Arundels of Chirk', *Bulletin of the Board of Celtic Studies*, 28 (1978–80), 443–57.

——, 'The Statute of Wales, 1284', *Welsh History Review*, 10 (1980–1), 127–54.

——, 'Fosterage, adoption, and God-parenthood: ritual and fictive kinship in medieval Wales', *Welsh History Review*, 16 (1992–3), 1–35.

——, 'Towards a history of women in late medieval Wales', in S. Clarke and M. Roberts (eds), *Women and Gender in Early Modern Wales* (Cardiff, 2000), pp. 14–49.

——, 'Towns and trade', in J. B. Smith and Ll. B. Smith (eds), *History of Merioneth*, vol. 2: *The Middle Ages* (Cardiff, 2001), pp. 225–53.

Smith, P., 'Houses and building styles', in D. H. Owen (ed.), *Settlement and Society in Wales* (Cardiff, 1989).

Smith, R., 'Kin and neighbours in a thirteenth-century Suffolk community', *Journal of Family History*, 4 (1979), 219–56.

——, 'Some issues concerning families and their property in rural England, 1250–1800', in R. Smith (ed.), *Land, Kinship and Life-Cycle* (Cambridge, 1984), pp. 1–86.

——, 'Demographic developments in rural England, 1300–48: a survey', in B. Campbell (ed.), *Before the Black Death: Studies in the 'Crisis' of the Early Fourteenth Century* (Manchester, 1991), pp. 25–78.

Soulsby, I., *The Towns of Medieval Wales: A Study of Their History, Archaeology and Early Topography* (Chichester, 1983).

Stephenson, D., *The Governance of Gwynedd* (Cardiff, 1984).

Stevens, M., 'Wealth, status, and "race" in the Ruthin of Edward II', *Urban History*, 32 (2005), 17–32.

——, 'Woman brewers in fourteenth–century Ruthin', *Denbighshire Historical Society Transactions*, 54 (2005–6), 15–31.

Suggett, R., 'The interpretation of late medieval houses in Wales', in R. R. Davies and G. Jenkins (eds), *From Medieval to Modern Wales: Historical Essays in Honour of Kenneth O. Morgan and Ralph A. Griffiths* (Cardiff, 2004), pp. 81–103.

Taylor, A., *The King's Works in Wales, 1277–1330* (London, 1974).

Thirsk, J., 'Industries in the countryside', in F. J. Fisher (ed.), *Essays in the Economic and Social History of Tudor and Stuart England in Honour of R. H. Tawney* (Cambridge, 1961), pp. 70–88.

Thorold Rogers, J. E., *A History of Agriculture and Prices in England* (Oxford, 1866).

Titow, J., *English Rural Society, 1200–1350* (London, 1969).

Walker, D., 'The Welsh church in the Middle Ages', in D. Walker (ed.), *A History of the Church in Wales* (Penarth, 1976), pp. 24–53.

Williams-Jones, K., 'Caernarvon', in R. A. Griffiths (ed.), *Boroughs of Medieval Wales* (Cardiff, 1978), pp. 73–102.

4. UNPUBLISHED THESES

Howard, S., 'Crime communities and authority in early modern Wales: Denbighshire, c.1660–1730' (unpublished Ph.D. thesis, University of Wales, Aberystwyth, 2003).

Rees, E. H. B., 'A study of urban populations in fourteenth-century Wales: a case study of Ruthin' (unpublished MA thesis, University of Wales, Aberystwyth, 1999).

Stevens, M. F., 'Race, gender and wealth in a medieval Welsh borough: access to capital, market participation and status in Ruthin, 1312–22' (unpublished Ph.D. thesis, University of Wales, Aberystwyth, 2005).

INDEX